POWER PLAY

JAMES P. PFIFFNER

POWER PLAY

THE BUSH PRESIDENCY
AND THE CONSTITUTION

BROOKINGS INSTITUTION PRESS
Washington, D.C.

Copyright © 2008
THE BROOKINGS INSTITUTION
1775 Massachusetts Avenue, N.W., Washington, D.C. 20036
www.brookings.edu

Library of Congress Cataloging-in-Publication data
Pfiffner, James P.
Power play : the Bush presidency and the Constitution / James P. Pfiffner.
   p.   cm.
Summary: "Analyzes the Bush presidency's efforts to expand executive power, putting them into constitutional and historical perspective. Explores the evolution of Anglo-American thinking about executive power and individual rights. Documents how the current administration has undermined the separation of powers and shows how these practices have imperiled the rule of law"—Provided by publisher.
Includes bibliographical references and index.
ISBN 978-0-8157-7044-2 (cloth : alk. paper)
   1. Executive power—United States—History—21st century. 2. Presidents—United States—History—21st century. 3. Bush, George W. (George Walker), 1946–
4. United States Constitution. 5. United States—Politics and government—2001–
I. Title.
   JK516.P49 2008
   973.931—dc22   2008012077

2 4 6 8 9 7 5 3 1

Printed on acid-free paper.

Typeset in Sabon with Times Ten display

Composition by Cynthia Stock
Silver Spring, Maryland

Printed by R. R. Donnelley
Harrisonburg, Virginia

For my brothers

PATRICK MEEHAN PFIFFNER

PETER STURTEVANT PFIFFNER

CONTENTS

Preface *ix*

Acknowledgments *xiii*

ONE   A Government of Laws or Men? *1*

TWO   The Nature of Executive Power *13*

THREE   Creating Individual Rights
and an Independent Legislature *33*

FOUR   The American Constitution *56*

FIVE   The Power to Imprison:
Habeas Corpus *84*

SIX   The Power to Torture *128*

SEVEN   The Power to Surveil *168*

EIGHT   The Power to Ignore the Law:
Signing Statements *194*

NINE   Conclusion: Constitutionalism
and the Rule of Law *229*

Notes *247*

Index *289*

PREFACE

I first arrived in Washington, D.C., on the day that President Nixon resigned from office, August 9, 1974. A friend and I had driven from the University of Wisconsin at Madison because we had been awarded fellowships to write our doctoral dissertations at the Brookings Institution. President Nixon had been impounding funds, that is, refusing to spend money appropriated by Congress, and he asserted that he had the constitutional authority to do so. I intended to study these claims in my dissertation and examine the legitimate allocation of authority in our separation of powers system.

Impoundment was an engaging subject, because the issues raised were fundamental to the nature of governance and the Constitution. The framers had written the Constitution in order to create an authoritative national government, but in order to assure that the new government would not abuse its power, they limited it by designing a separation of powers system. President Nixon was challenging that constitutional allocation of powers. As it turned out, the Supreme Court rejected his claim.

After President Nixon, the balance among the branches seemed to reassert itself. To be sure, President Reagan was a more assertive executive than Presidents Ford or Carter had been, but aside from the Iran-Contra affair, his administration did not claim exceptional constitutional authority. President George H. W. Bush also vigorously protected presidential authority without provoking major constitutional confrontations with Congress. President Clinton acted unilaterally in some of his military deployments; his other actions, however, did not provoke fundamental challenges to congressional authority.

But when President George W. Bush took over the presidency in 2001, he and Vice President Cheney believed that the powers of the presidency had been illegitimately claimed by Congress in the 1970s when it passed laws intended to recapture its own institutional prerogatives. Members of the Bush administration set out systematically to reverse what they saw as congressional usurpation, and they carefully avoided accountability through the courts. They carried out these plans in several particularly important ways that are the subjects of this book.

The atrocities of 9/11 significantly increased the Bush administration's leeway to assert executive powers; Congress and the public were willing to cede to the executive much authority in the hope of protecting national security in a time of terror. But in doing what President Bush saw as necessary to protect the country, he asserted extraordinary prerogatives that challenged the roles of the other two branches of government. He used his authority as the commander-in-chief to deny the writ of habeas corpus to U.S. citizens as well as others in the war on terror. He argued that the United States had to resort to "harsh" and "robust" interrogation methods in order to acquire intelligence that might prevent future attacks. The techniques used by some U.S. personnel amounted to what most people in the world would consider torture, though Bush and his administration said that they did not torture (by their definition). President Bush ordered secret wiretapping that broke the law, and only by chance did his actions became public. Furthermore, he challenged the validity of hundreds of provisions of laws by issuing signing statements that implied that he might not implement the laws when he thought they impinged on his own powers as president.

As I watched President Bush make these assertions of power, I realized that the United States government had come full circle during the course of my career. I began my scholarship in the 1970s with President Nixon's fundamental challenges to the rule of law and the separation of powers. In the twenty-first century President Bush was making even more extreme claims and also justifying them in the name of national security. I decided that these issues were fundamental to the rule of law and the Constitution and that it was important to examine rigorously the claims of President Bush. If his claims were allowed to stand, all future presidents would be able to make the same claims to unilateral executive power. Thus through his actions, President Bush posed a fundamental threat to the Constitution. In this book, my purpose is to separate judgments about the wisdom of particular policies from constitutional issues, so my concern here is only with constitutional matters.

I undertook much of the research for this book while on a fellowship at the University of London. One day I walked into the British Library and through the doors to the "Treasures of the British Library"; I then entered a special, dimly lit room where an original copy of Magna Carta, sealed in 1215, was on permanent display. Though the letters in medieval Latin crowded on to the ancient parchment were clearly discernible, their meaning was opaque to my untutored eye. But the significance of Magna Carta registered clearly. I was looking at one of the few remaining copies of those famous agreements that have inspired centuries of fighters for individual liberties against the often despotic powers of kings. I understood that Magna Carta was intended as protection of the rights of barons rather than common people and that only a few clauses of the document pertained to the fundamental liberties that we often take for granted today. However, those few phrases symbolize the striving for liberty, and they inspired the actions of thousands of individuals who, over the past seven centuries, struggled to assert the rights that were articulated in that famous document.

As I stared at this symbol of limited government and thought of the development of its principles over seven centuries, I was struck by how directly these ancient, fundamental principles were being challenged by President Bush in the twenty-first century. Citizens of the United States tend to take for granted our Constitution and the rule of law. We assume that they are so firmly established that they will continue to exist indefinitely. Thus we are not sensitive to the erosion of the rule of law and the constitutional balance. But as the framers warned, our republic must always be vigilant in protecting the principles upon which the United States was founded. That is why I wrote this book.

ACKNOWLEDGMENTS

I am grateful to George Mason University, particularly Dean Kingley Haynes and Vice Dean James Finkelstein of the School of Public Policy, for creating an atmosphere conducive to scholarship. And I want to thank the School of Advanced Study at the University of London for affording me the opportunity to pursue my research in the heart of London and George Edwards for his encouragement and support. James Dunkerley, Dean of the Institute for the Study of the Americas, and Nicholas Mann, Dean of the School of Advanced Study, were central to the wonderful experience I had while in London. I also owe thanks to other colleagues in the United Kingdom who extended their hospitality and helped with my research during my six-month stay as S. T. Lee Professorial Fellow: Sharer Ali, Niels Bjerre-Poulson, Nigel Bowles, Steve Casey, Michael Cox, Philip Davies, John Dumbrell, Jose Harris, Jon Herbert, Timothy Lynch, Iwan Morgan, John Owens, Mark Phythian, Jon Roper, Richard Rose, and Colin Talbot.

Colleagues in the United States who helped me in my research and writing and to whom I extend my thanks include: Joel Aberbach, David Adler, Mary Anne Borelli, Brian Cook, Mary Lenn Dixon, Bob Dudley, George Edwards, Matthew Holden, Tom Langston, David Luban, Stuart Malawer, Jeremy Mayer, John Ritzert, David Rosenbloom, Ron Rotunda, and Joseph Zengerle. I also benefited greatly from friends and colleagues who went above and beyond the call of friendship in reading portions of my manuscript and giving me their wise counsel: Lara Brown, Hugh Heclo, Mark Kann, Don Kash, Nancy Kassop, Michael

Korzi, Char Miller, Dick Pious, Paul Quirk, Jim Riggle, Claire Snyder, Herman Schwartz, Jeffrey Weinberg, and Benjamin Wittes. Bob Spitzer read the whole manuscript carefully and provided very insightful and useful advice on how to improve it. I also owe thanks to an anonymous reviewer who disagreed sharply with much of what I argue in the book, but whose comments helped me to improve my analysis. My research assistant, Mary Boardman, tracked down many citations and read carefully the whole manuscript, and I thank her for her help. I would also like to thank Brian Cook for inviting me to present the Harrington Lecture in American Politics at Clark University, which was my first formulation of the ideas that went into this book. The director of Brookings Institution Press, Bob Faherty, provided good counsel and encouragement throughout the writing of this book for which I am grateful. Press staff with whom I worked, Chris Kelaher, Mary Kwak, Janet Walker, and Susan Woollen, were wonderful to work with.

Special thanks are due to Lou Fisher, whom I first met in 1974 while we were standing in line to hear oral arguments before the Supreme Court on President Nixon's impoundment of funds. Fisher was an expert on the subject, and after I had drafted my dissertation on impoundment, he generously read it carefully and gave me comments that saved me from many errors. Throughout my career he has provided wise counsel and scholarly advice on my research. In 2007 Lou read and annotated the full manuscript for this book. Lou is a recidivist, and I thank him for it. We in the scholarly community who care about the Constitution and separation of powers all owe our gratitude to Lou for his career of tremendously productive and careful scholarship on constitutional issues. We have all benefited from his scholarship.

Finally, I owe thanks to my wife, Deb, and our children, Megan, KC, and Morgan, each of whom helped me in different ways as I wrote this book.

POWER PLAY

CHAPTER ONE

A GOVERNMENT
OF LAWS OR MEN?

"Power tends to corrupt, and absolute power corrupts absolutely."
—Lord Acton

From 2002 to 2005 the Bush administration argued that it could imprison an American citizen (Jose Padilla) indefinitely, deny him access to a lawyer or his relatives, deny him the constitutional right to appeal for a writ of habeas corpus, and subject him to solitary confinement and extreme sensory deprivation. This claim was based on the president's authority alone.

From 2002 to 2004 hundreds of detainees in the war on terror were imprisoned at Guantánamo and Abu Ghraib; some were subjected to inhumane treatment, and some were even tortured. During the war on terror, more than forty persons detained by the United States died at the hands of U.S. personnel. Many of the incidents of torture and abuse grew out of President Bush's claim that he could suspend the Geneva Conventions and authorize the use of harsh interrogation techniques on those suspected of terrorism. The suspension of the Geneva Conventions was based on the president's authority alone.

From 2001 through 2006 President Bush ordered the National Security Agency (NSA), without the warrant required by law, to conduct surveillance on American citizens thought to be communicating with foreign suspects of terrorism. This order was based on the president's authority alone.

During his first six years in office, President Bush issued signing statements that challenged the constitutionality of more than 1,000 provisions of laws enacted by Congress. The signing statements intimated that the president had authority not to execute those challenged provisions of laws. These assertions were based on the president's authority alone.

The purpose of this book is to examine these actions by President Bush and to argue that his claims were extraordinary. He claimed powers once asserted by kings—but the Constitution deliberately divides those powers and ordains that they be shared among the three branches of government. The constraints that the framers placed on the executive branch were not arbitrary or whimsical decisions on their part; they were based on carefully considered judgments about human nature and political power. In designing an elaborate system of shared powers, the purpose of the framers was to create a government that had enough power to govern, but that power was limited in its scope, especially with regard to individual rights and liberties. The framers were particularly concerned to ensure that the government did not degenerate into a tyranny, and they carefully constrained executive power to prevent tyranny from occurring. President Bush fundamentally challenged the separation of powers framework established in the Constitution. This book is an attempt to analyze how this happened and explain why it is a threat to republican government.

The concern here will not be with the wisdom of President Bush's policies but rather with the constitutional issues they raise. Congress provided President Bush with the authority to conduct a "war on terror." Regardless of whether members of Congress were misled by his assertions about WMD, most of them did not examine the evidence themselves and took the president's words at face value. The war in Iraq may have been unwise, but it was constitutionally legitimate. This book instead will focus on President Bush's actions that raise serious constitutional issues; the argument will be that he has exceeded his constitutional authority as president by asserting unilateral authority over decisions that the Constitution requires to be shared with Congress and the judiciary.

In his actions as president, George W. Bush challenged the basis of the separation of powers system. He and Vice President Richard Cheney chafed under the constraints placed on the presidency by the Constitution.

They felt that the congressional reaction to the "imperial presidency" of Presidents Johnson and Nixon went too far in tilting the balance of policy-making power toward Congress. They particularly saw the presidency as being illegitimately constrained by laws that did not allow the president free enough rein to deal with the challenges of the post-9/11 world. The atrocities of 9/11 gave them the opportunity to shape the separation of powers system to fit their own vision of the rightful balance among the three branches—with the president clearly in charge, particularly in national security matters. The Bush administration worked consciously and systematically to make the executive more independent of the other two branches by asserting presidential prerogatives and by shielding its actions from scrutiny by the public or the other two branches.

As the framers of the Constitution expected, the other two branches resisted being marginalized—but not too much or too effectively. President Bush was able to get through Congress a number of laws that provided congressional sanction for the actions that he claimed were his own constitutional prerogatives—the Authorization to Use Military Force, the PATRIOT Act, the Military Commissions Act, and revisions of the Foreign Intelligence Surveillance Act. The American public had been traumatized by 9/11 and was willing to give broad discretion to a president who promised to protect them. The fear of another attack like 9/11 was probably the primary factor in President Bush's electoral victory in 2004. A brief look at television campaign ads will confirm the appeal to fear that was central to the campaign.

The broad fear in the American public about national security was reflected in congressional campaigns and in voting patterns in Congress. Republicans, with a narrow majority, felt that it was their duty to support President Bush by passing most of the legislation he sought. Most Democrats felt that they needed to support President Bush's claims to executive power in national security issues, either because they believed that his initiatives were necessary for national security or because they feared the political consequences of resisting him. Even though President Bush's overall legislative record was mixed, he was highly successful in legislation touching on national security issues. The Republican Congresses from 2001 through 2006 did not undertake any major investigations of the executive branch.

3

The war against al Qaeda in Afghanistan was seamlessly extended into a war to depose Saddam Hussein in Iraq, and President Bush convinced many Americans that Iraq was the central front in the global war on terrorism. Even when the Democrats took control of Congress in 2007, they were not able to impede President Bush's policies in Iraq. The Bush administration was able to resist the legislature's efforts to investigate its policy leadership with claims of executive privilege, and the courts were stymied by the "state secrets" privilege.

This book will argue that President Bush has undermined the constitutional balance among the branches in four policy areas:

—by denying the writ of habeas corpus to people deemed to be "enemy combatants";

—by suspending the Geneva Conventions and allowing and encouraging harsh interrogation methods that amounted to torture;

—by ordering surveillance of Americans without obtaining a warrant as required by law; and

—by issuing signing statements that declare that the president has the option not to enforce parts of laws that he believes interfere with his executive authority.

These actions threaten fundamental rights and the rule of law in the United States and call into question the meaning of the Constitution and its limits on executive power. The Constitution constrained executive power for very good reasons, and the Bush administration has ignored those constraints in extraordinary ways. This book will argue that President Bush's actions, if allowed to stand as precedents, will encourage future presidents to ignore the other two branches in important ways and that this aggrandizement of executive power threatens fundamental freedoms and dangerously concedes to the president powers that the framers did not intend the executive to have.

These rights and liberties have ancient roots in Anglo-American jurisprudence and history and should not be abandoned lightly. The framers embedded constraints on executive power in the Constitution because they understood that executives are ambitious and tend to aggrandize power. Abandoning the constitutional constraints on executive power has led to abuses of power in the Bush administration, and if allowed to stand, threatens to distort the Constitution in ways that will lead to unfettered power at the disposal of future presidents. As the framers foresaw, there is no guarantee that only good individuals will be elected president.

President Bush has argued that the United States faces a new kind of war since the attacks of 9/11, against an enemy that is not a nation-state but that is loosely organized in cells that have allegiance to al Qaeda. These cells, Bush has warned, are determined to use terrorism to attack the United States. The Bush administration argued that we are engaged in a new type of warfare that requires us to embrace the "dark side" in our battle, and enhanced presidential power is the only way to deal effectively with these new threats. The executive must have the flexibility to detain enemy fighters without interference by courts, use harsh interrogation methods to interrogate suspected terrorists, engage in electronic surveillance at its discretion, and ignore congressional constraints on its actions.

President Bush was right that al Qaeda presents a serious threat to the national security of the United States and that novel means must be used to counter that threat. He was also correct that the president has the duty to protect the security of Americans. Certainly the president has the authority to capture suspected terrorists and imprison them. Certainly the president has the authority to interrogate the suspected terrorists. Certainly the president has the authority to conduct surveillance on foreign suspects and, with warrants, surveil people in the United States who are suspected of terrorism. And certainly the president has the right to make reasonable judgments about the extent of executive authority within the Constitution. But the extent of his claims to presidential power exceeds the bounds of the Constitution. Congress as well as the president has the duty to "provide for the common defense."

In addition, in the months immediately after 9/11, the Bush administration had legitimate fears that there might be another attack, and the president felt he had to do everything he could do to protect the nation. Thus extra-constitutional actions at that time were understandable. But after several years, the need to continue to ignore the law regarding wiretaps disappeared (there was time to obtain warrants or amend the law). Holding detainees indefinitely without charge became less tenable, especially since there was no hope for any quick end to the war on terror. As the years passed, the need to use torture in order to discover a "ticking time bomb" was attenuated, particularly in Iraq, which had no connection to the 9/11 atrocities.

5

The problem, however, was that President Bush pushed these reasonable rights and duties of the executive beyond the bounds that the Constitution established. He imprisoned hundreds of suspected terrorists indefinitely without charging them and denied them the opportunity to argue their innocence before an independent judge. He allowed, and arguably encouraged, interrogating them with harsh techniques that many consider to be torture. He claimed the unilateral authority to conduct surveillance secretly on Americans without obtaining warrants required by law. And he asserted that he was not bound by provisions of laws that he himself deemed to impinge on his executive authority. In contrast, the argument of this book is that the Constitution placed constraints on executive authority for important reasons, and that although the framers understood that the executive would act quickly in emergencies, such as "sudden attacks," they did not intend that the Constitution be suspended during wartime. After tracing the heritage of Anglo-American individual rights and the hard-won rights of the legislature to constrain arbitrary executive actions, this book will examine each of these claims to extraordinary power by President Bush.

In order to understand the importance of the constitutional constraints on executive power, it is necessary to examine the origins and development of individual rights and shared constitutional power. Thus the second chapter of this book will provide a brief overview of how executive power can be legitimized and constrained. Ideas in political philosophy provide the justification for the legitimate exercise of governmental power and the reasoning behind constraining its exercise. Understanding the development of the major ideas about executive power in Anglo-American political thinking will illuminate why the framers wrote the Constitution the way they did and how President Bush's actions depart from constitutional limits.

Chapter 2 will examine some of the key ideas about political power that influenced the framers of the Constitution. Niccolò Machiavelli, Thomas Hobbes, John Locke, and Baron de Montesquieu were familiar to the framers, and their ideas provide key insights into how royal power came to be limited in England and how the framers used those ideas in writing the Constitution. Machiavelli and Hobbes justified granting absolute power to princes and kings—to executives. Locke fundamentally changed the direction of western thought by arguing that governments are legitimately based on the consent of the governed and that executives were bound by laws passed by legislatures. Montesquieu insightfully emphasized that freedom was only possible if governmental powers were separated and not united in one institution or person.

The third chapter will trace the English origins of individual rights back to Magna Carta, which declared the principle that the king was bound by law and could not imprison people without due process of law. It took centuries of struggle before that principle was guaranteed in practice. It also took centuries and a bloody civil war before Parliament gained enough power to pass laws that bound the king of England. Chapter 3 will examine the rise of Parliament from a council advisory to an absolute monarch to a legislature that could constrain royal power, to a legislature that could exert sovereign power. The right of the legislature to bind the executive was fundamentally challenged by President Bush in the twenty-first century.

Chapter 4 will explain how the framers of the U.S. Constitution adapted the ideas, traditions, and constitutional premises from England and made them distinctly American. The framers wrote many of the individual rights of Englishmen into the U.S. Constitution, but they rejected the British governmental structure and created a separation of powers system. In designing the balance among the three branches, the framers carefully limited executive power so that the United States would not suffer from executive domination as England had for centuries. In particular, the framers decided that the powers of war be shared between the legislature and the executive and that the presidential powers during wartime are constrained by the Constitution. President Bush upset this balance with his assertions of unilateral authority.

With this background about the origins and development of individual rights, legislative powers, and constraints on the executive, the book will shift to an examination of how George W. Bush challenged these principles of constitutionalism and the rule of law. One of the premises of the framers was that those in governmental office will seek to aggrandize their own power. They realized that times of war presented particular challenges to the rule of law and to limits on executive actions. During crises the people are often willing to sacrifice ancient freedoms in the hope of more security. Although trade-offs between security and freedom often have to be made during times of war, the Constitution provides that the balancing must be done with the participation of all three branches, not by the president alone.

Chapter 5 will review the ancient right of English citizens who were imprisoned by the executive to have that action reviewed by an independent judge to assure that the imprisonment was legal and based on reasonable evidence. It will examine the legal battles over the right to writs of habeas corpus by detainees held by the administration, particularly in Guantánamo. If this fundamental right is denied to those accused of terrorism, legal precedent will be established that will allow the executive to imprison those accused of other crimes and deny them the judicial protections that have been enjoyed by people in England and the United States for centuries. The chapter will illuminate the practical importance of this right by examining several cases of "the wrong man" problem—people imprisoned by the Bush administration who turned out to be demonstrably innocent of the crimes of which they were accused.

Chapter 6 will examine the Bush administration's assertion of the authority to subject suspects of terrorism to harsh interrogation techniques that most of the world considers torture. President Bush argued that the attacks of 9/11 brought to the United States a new kind of war in which the enemy, by attacking civilians, did not respect the traditional canons of warfare. The administration argued that since the terrorists did not abide by the traditional rules of warfare, the United States had the right to abandon the constraints of the Geneva Conventions, which, they argued, were relevant only to traditional conflicts between signatories of the Conventions.

This initial decision to abandon the Geneva constraints cascaded into a series of memoranda and policy directives that led to the torture and inhumane treatment of captives by U.S. personnel. With evidence of harsh treatment and torture mounting, the administration defended itself by arguing that these methods of interrogation were necessary to prevent future attacks and by declaring that the aggressive techniques did not amount to actual torture. Chapter 6 will examine the legal arguments the Bush administration used to justify its interrogation techniques and argue that torture is very difficult to control once the strictures of hard-and-fast rules against it have been eroded.

President Bush also argued that, because the nation was under attack, he had the constitutional right, as president, to ignore the law forbidding wiretapping without a warrant. The framers thought the danger of government intrusion into the privacy and personal effects of individuals was so important that they prohibited it in the Fourth Amendment to the Constitution, which provides that (with certain exceptions) the executive must obtain a warrant from a judge before it can search the home, papers, or communications of a suspect. The Foreign Intelligence Surveillance Act (FISA) of 1978 required that the president get a warrant from a special court before wiretapping in the United States for national security reasons.

Despite the Fourth Amendment and the FISA law, President Bush ordered the National Security Agency to listen in secretly on the conversations of persons in the United States whom it thought were communicating with possible terrorists abroad. Although the trade-off between privacy and security represented by his decision may have been reasonable, the threat to the constitutional balance came from President Bush's assertion that, as president, he had the authority to make the decision secretly by himself, despite the law requiring warrants. That the administration could have easily accomplished its goals within the law or asked Congress to amend the law, underscores President Bush's claim to extraordinary power under the Constitution to ignore the law and the other two branches. He felt that, as president, he had the authority to act on his own rather than asking Congress to change the law. Chapter 7 will conclude that this assertion of unilateral authority by President Bush presents a fundamental challenge to the rule of law.

The rule of law itself was directly challenged by President Bush's use of signing statements, which are analyzed in chapter 8. When a bill is signed into law, a president may issue a signing statement in which he comments on the significance or meaning of the statute. In many cases this practice presents no problem, but when a signing statement is used to declare that the president might not enforce parts of the law that he claims interfere with his own constitutional prerogatives as president, the rule of law is undermined.

Other presidents have issued signing statements, some that challenged the constitutionality of a law, but President Bush used them to an unprecedented extent to indicate that he might decide not to execute faithfully the law when he claimed that it conflicted with his own authority under the Constitution. While all previous presidents combined issued fewer than 600 challenges to laws in signing statements, President Bush issued more than 1,000 in his first six years in office. Chapter 8 argues that this assertion of executive prerogative threatens the very foundation of the rule of law and the balance of power among the three branches of government.

The other two branches have not been entirely passive during President Bush's aggrandizement of presidential power, but they have not been very effective in countering his actions. The Supreme Court, in particular, has thrown a few roadblocks in his way, but they may turn out to be merely speed bumps, if Congress and the Supreme Court do not follow up. The Supreme Court invalidated the military commissions President Bush established through executive discretion alone and not through law. Court decisions have also declared that the judiciary is entitled to play a role in the determination of fundamental rights, such as habeas corpus, under the Constitution. They have challenged President Bush's right to incarcerate detainees indefinitely without allowing them a writ of habeas corpus or charging them with a crime.

Congress, in contrast, has acted primarily as a facilitator for President Bush's aggrandizements. One important exception was passage of Senator John McCain's proposed Detainee Treatment Act (DTA), which outlawed torture by U.S. personnel anywhere in the world. But this apparent victory against President Bush's policy on interrogation was diluted by restrictions placed on habeas corpus petitions from Guantánamo inmates. Congress further ratified some of President Bush's questionable policy decisions by passing the Military Commissions Act (MCA). This law further undercut the habeas corpus privileges for imprisoned terrorist suspects, and it also allowed President Bush to define what interrogation techniques would be allowed under Common Article 3 of the Geneva Conventions. President Bush's executive order implementing the provision interpreted Common Article 3 so as to give the CIA permission to employ a range of harsh interrogation techniques that, though classified, would be considered torture by much of the world.

President Bush was also able to win a victory in 2007 when Congress passed a revision of the FISA law that governed the use of wiretapping without a warrant of people in the United States. The new legislative authority allowed President Bush to engage in many of the practices that he previously undertook against the law under his own claimed constitutional authority. The legislative sanction provided by these laws (DTA of 2005, MCA of 2006, and FISA amendments of 2007), though making President Bush's prior policies legal, did not eliminate the threat to the Constitution from unrestrained executive power. The fundamental Constitutional issue arose not as much from the actual policies that he undertook as from his claim that he had the constitutional authority to decide public policy himself and exclude participation or oversight by the other two branches.

The denial of habeas corpus deprived terrorist suspects of the opportunity to demonstrate that they were not guilty of crimes or that they had been seized mistakenly. But the broader threat came from President Bush's assertion that he could designate people to be enemy combatants and deny them the right to appeal to a court for a writ of habeas corpus. Congress can suspend habeas corpus during a rebellion or invasion, but President Bush claimed the constitutional authority to deny it to suspects unilaterally, at his own discretion.

The torture of detainees at the hands of U.S. personnel certainly deprived the victims of their human rights, but the broader, constitutional threat came from President Bush's assertion that he could set aside the Geneva Convention Treaty, ignore U.S. law, and subject people he declared to be enemy combatants to harsh interrogation techniques considered by many to be torture.

The threat to the civil liberties of those in the United States whose constitutional rights were violated by NSA wiretaps was probably minor. But the assertion by President Bush that he had the constitutional authority to ignore the law and secretly order the wiretaps threatened the constitutional balance and the rule of law.

Most of the signing statements issued by President Bush probably did not lead directly to his refusal to execute the laws. But his use of them asserted, in principle, that he could ignore any provision of law he deemed to impinge on his own constitutional authority. The long-term implications of signing statements constituted a claim that presidents cannot be bound by the law and can refuse to execute any law that limits executive power under their own interpretation of Article II.

Only a formal rejection of these claims by a coordinate branch of government will refute the extraordinary claims President Bush made. Such a rejection might come if the Supreme Court ruled that the limitations on habeas corpus by President Bush and Congress violate the Constitution. Or Congress might pass laws forbidding interrogation techniques that the Bush administration claimed were not torture, for instance by requiring the CIA to conduct its interrogations according to the Army field manual on interrogations. In 2008 Congress did pass such a law, and President Bush vetoed it. Or Congress might pass the FISA requirements again and insist that the president obtain the required warrants before wiretapping persons in the United States. Signing statements may be litigated, but a broad judicial or legislative remedy to the problem is difficult to envision.

One might conclude that the threat to the Constitution is no longer a problem and the cases have become moot, since Congress has effectively legalized in statute some of what President Bush had been doing. But this line of reasoning misses the constitutional point. The real problem was President Bush's assertion that, as president, he had the constitutional authority to do what he had been doing already. He did not relinquish or renounce his claims to constitutional authority in pushing for congressional approval of his actions; he merely bowed to the political necessity of seeking congressional approval. He went to Congress out of prudence, not principle. The precedents of his constitutional claims, unless effectively challenged, will remain "loaded weapons" that future presidents can use to justify their own unilateral assertions of executive power. The conclusion of the book will take up the issues of the rule of law and constitutionalism and argue that they have both been imperiled by President Bush's actions.

CHAPTER TWO

THE NATURE OF EXECUTIVE POWER

You are "in what we call the reality-based community," and you "believe that solutions emerge from your judicious study of discernible reality. That's not the way the world really works anymore. We're an empire now, and when we act, we create our own reality. And while you're studying that reality—judiciously, as you will—we'll act again, creating other new realities, which you can study too, and that's how things will sort out. We're history's actors . . . and you, all of you, will be left to just study what we do."
   —senior adviser to President Bush

The ideas of economists and political philosophers, both when they are right and when they are wrong, are more powerful than is commonly understood. Indeed the world is ruled by little else. Practical men, who believe themselves to be quite exempt from any intellectual influences, are usually the slaves of some defunct economist. Madmen in authority, who hear voices in the air, are distilling their frenzy from some academic scribbler of a few years back.
   —John Maynard Keynes

The framers of the Constitution were practical men, experienced in the art of governing, but they were also familiar with the ideas of political philosophers, especially John Locke and Charles-Louis de Secondat, baron de La Brède et de Montesquieu. They drew their practical approach from their study of history and their experience with the king and Parliament of England.

This experience was supplemented with their experience in the colonies before 1776 and in the states after the War of American Independence. The ideas of these political philosophers are relevant to the assertions of executive power by the Bush administration because the legal briefs and memoranda justifying the administration's extraordinary actions are based on constitutional interpretation, and academic defenders often refer to the thinking of some of these philosophers, particularly Locke, Blackstone, and Montesquieu.[1]

This chapter will trace some of the ideas that influenced the framers in their design of the Constitution. It will begin with an examination of several political philosophers: Machiavelli, Hobbes, Locke, and Montesquieu, all of whom were familiar to the framers. The following chapter will consider some of the major turning points in limiting the sovereign power in England, first the development of individual rights and then the rise of Parliament in its struggles with absolute monarchy. The fourth chapter will present an overview of how the framers of the Constitution adapted some ideas about limited government from England and how they rejected England's monarchical system.[2] The revolutions in individual rights and legislative power were accomplished through much struggle and bloodshed over many centuries. These individual rights and the balance of executive power by legislative power are the fundamental tenets of the Constitution that the Bush administration threatened. The conclusion of this book is that these hard-won restraints on executive power should not be surrendered easily.

Political Theory and the Framers

One might reasonably ask, Why this diversion into the history and development of ideas about government? If one wants to analyze President Bush's actions as chief executive and see how they square with the Constitution, why look at political philosophers such as Machiavelli, Hobbes, Locke, and Montesquieu? The answer is that the authority of governments is maintained on the basis of ideas about the legitimate use of power.

Common phrases such as "I know my rights," or "I can say what I want; we have freedom of speech here," or "There ought to be a law," or "I have a right to a lawyer," or "You can't come in here without a warrant," or "Sue the bastards" are all based on implicit principles about the legitimate use of governmental power. The people uttering such phrases may not be able to articulate and defend the fundamental principle upon which their sentiments are based, but the ideas are founded upon principles of government that are derived from the thinking of political philosophers. The framers of the Constitution were well read, and they derived many of their ideas about government from these political philosophers as well as their own experience and reading of history.

People accept the exercise of governmental power because they see it as legitimate, even if they often disagree with some of the policies that any particular government pursues. If a government is to be able to rule, most of the people, most of the time, must consider the exercise of power to be legitimate. If most of the people, most of the time, do not see that government as legitimate, it will not be able to sustain itself. Brute force can intimidate many people, but it cannot long sustain a government the people see as illegitimate.

The Constitution provides the basis for the legitimate use of governmental power in the United States. In using the power of the state, presidents of the United States derive their legitimacy from the Constitution. In order to understand how the Constitution justifies and constrains the use of presidential power, we must first have a sense of the how the Constitution was framed and what the intentions of the framers were. To understand why they formulated the Constitution the way they did, we should examine some of the sources of their ideas about government.

To be sure, the framers were not mere theoreticians, and they were in many ways practical politicians, sensitive to the range of the possible in the context of postcolonial America.[3] Their ideas were powerfully affected by their views of history, particularly of England, and, indeed, most of them considered themselves loyal Englishmen up until the final break with the mother country. This is not to argue that we must discover the original intent of the framers, but we can best understand the appropriate role of the president in the Constitutional system if we have some sense of the origins of the range of and limits to presidential power. One does not have to take a rigidly textual literalist or originalist approach in order to argue that the plain words of the Constitution should be our primary guide to its meaning. When there is any ambiguity, the deliberations of the framers provide useful indications of what they intended.[4]

Machiavelli and Executive Power

Niccolò Machiavelli was one of the first modern political thinkers to break with classical political thought as well as with medieval Christian political philosophy. His writings support the idea that the chief executive of a polity, the "prince," should exercise power ruthlessly and that whatever tactics the ruler deems necessary to maintain that power are therefore justified.[5] The framers clearly rejected this approach to executive power in favor of subsequent political theorists, primarily John Locke and Montesquieu. A brief look at Machiavelli's ideas about executive power can help explain why John Locke had such an important impact on the framers.

Machiavelli began modern political thought with the idea that power in the executive was necessary to bring order and control to the warring city-states of Renaissance Italy. His classic book, *The Prince* (1513), was written as a handbook to guide a ruler who would bring order and coherence to Italy. Machiavelli preferred that power be accumulated in honorable ways, but his basic premise was that in the pursuit of the power to establish political control, whatever means a ruler found necessary would be justified. Thus his book *The Prince* was a handbook for seizing and sustaining political power.[6]

His ideas about power were based not on religion but rather on the secular political realities of Medici Italy in the sixteenth century. One of Machiavelli's contributions to political thought was the modern idea of executive power, which entailed the usefulness of decisiveness, the importance of secrecy, and the advantages of having a single person to execute governmental policy.[7] Machiavelli conceived of his prince as a secular mortal, not a religious leader, and he was an executive who ruled rather than a monarch who reigned.[8]

Machiavelli saw himself as a realist who eschewed mere theoretical arguments about the legitimate means of gaining political power. Since he was writing for practical men who had to deal with the real world, "It seemed . . . more appropriate to go after the effectual truth of the thing than the imagination of it."[9] That is, he wanted to address the actual reality of political power, not theories of justice or legitimacy. Potential rulers must not be naïve: "A man who would wish to make a career of being good in every detail must come to ruin among so many who are not good."[10] And Machiavelli's prince must keep power by sometimes using arbitrary force to keep his enemies off balance.

He thought most men would act in their own self-interest and would be treacherous if it suited them. It was thus necessary for the prince to use whatever means were at his disposal to protect his power. "Hence it is necessary for a prince, if he wishes to maintain himself, to learn to be able to be not good, and to use this faculty and not to use it, according to necessity."[11] He argued that if a prince were gentle on miscreants "through too much compassion," it would "allow disorders to occur from which arise killings or robberies."[12] The resulting disorder would harm all of the people in the polity. So harming a single individual through the use of arbitrary force would be justified to preserve order, even if the person were not guilty of a crime. This injustice would help prevent the greater harm of chaos or general disorder. It would give the prince of a new state the reputation for cruelty, and this would shore up his power.[13]

Machiavelli argues that it would be best for a prince to be both loved and feared by his subjects. But since "men are wretched," the obligations engendered by love will easily be abandoned when they conflict with self-interest. He concludes that fear is a greater motivator than love: "It is much safer to be feared than loved."[14] Thus the prince must be ruthless in gaining and retaining his power. Appearing to be kind and generous to the masses was at times useful, but the threat of arbitrary power must always lie in the background and put to use if it becomes necessary. Humans "are ungrateful, changeable, pretenders and dissemblers, avoiders of dangers, and desirous of gain." So in order to maintain power, a prince "is often required to act against faith, against charity, against humaneness, and against religion."[15]

Machiavelli thus laid out a convincing argument for executive power that was justified by human nature and demonstrated throughout history. No argument is offered here that monarchs in Europe ever read Machiavelli, but he provided a secular analysis that justified the power that monarchs claimed was granted to them by God. The doctrine of absolute monarchy dominated Europe into the eighteenth century. Monarchs were believed to receive their right to rule directly from God and were often seen, along with the clergy, as representatives of God on earth. In reality, the effective power of kings and queens varied and depended on their ability to enforce their decisions with physical means as well as on their perceived legitimacy. As the eighteenth century approached, monarchs of the major nation-states of Europe consolidated their power, through the domination of the nobles and barons within their realms. The more effective the centralization of power, the more the reality of absolute power matched the theoretical principle of absolute monarchy asserted in the divine right of kings.

Thomas Hobbes and Absolute Monarchy

In the middle of the seventeenth century Thomas Hobbes made a fundamental contribution to western political thought by shifting the source of legitimacy of monarchical power from God to the people in a polity. Hobbes basically agreed with Machiavelli about human nature. Hobbes posited a state of nature, before any regular government was established, and argued that humans would (and should) be willing to surrender their individual rights to an absolute ruler so that basic safety and order could be enforced.

Hobbes was the first major thinker to propound "contract theory," the idea that polities are based upon a "contract" among the members of the polity to give up voluntarily some of their rights as free individuals in order to gain the benefits of an orderly society. In such a society they can engage in productive activities safely and not fear for the well-being of themselves or their families. There is no factual assertion that such an original contract historically occurred; Hobbes's point was that the existence of governmental power gains its legitimacy on the basis of the consent of the governed. He thus initiated a line of thinking that eventually led to republican government, though Hobbes himself was certainly no republican. He named his famous book *Leviathan* (1651), a name that denoted a large sea monster or whale, and argued that his ideal government would be so powerful as to be immune from challenge.[16]

Hobbes is correctly known as an advocate of absolute monarchy, so how can his ideas be seen as the glimmerings of republican government? Before governments, Hobbes posited, people lived in a "state of nature" in which everyone followed his own self-interest. In this state of nature humans had the liberty to do whatever they wanted or whatever they must in order to protect themselves and acquire property. "The Right Of Nature . . . is the Liberty each man hath, to use his own power, as he will himselfe, for the preservation of his own nature; that is to say, of his own Life; and consequently, of doing any thing, which in his own Judgement, and Reason, he shall conceive to be the aptest means thereunto."[17]

Hobbes and Machiavelli agreed that human beings without the constraining power of government would continually be at war with each other. This condition leads to chaos and anarchy. "Hereby it is manifest, that during the time men live without a common Power to keep them all in awe, they are in that condition which is called Warre; and such a warre, as is of every man, against every man." Thus the state of nature is one of continual warfare "where every man is Enemy to every man," and there is no possibility of economic development or social peace. In Hobbes's much-quoted phrase, people would live in "continuall feare, and danger of violent death; And the life of man, [would be] solitary, poore, nasty, brutish, and short."[18]

Hobbes, writing during the Civil War in England, saw his country descend into terrible fighting, which probably contributed to his conclusion that a peaceful order, even if imposed by an absolute monarch, was far superior to the chaos of civil war. In this state of nature, "Where there is no common Power, there is no Law: where no Law, no Injustice. Force, and Fraud, are in warre the two Cardinall vertues."[19] To prevent this state of warfare, according to Hobbes, humans establish a contract or agreement to surrender their natural rights to an absolute sovereign. "A Common-wealth is said to be *Instituted*, when a Multitude of men do Agree" to surrender their rights to the sovereign in order "to live peaceably amongst themselves, and be protected against other men."[20]

In giving up their individual right to do as they please and act as the enforcer of their own rights, people willingly surrender their own absolute rights to a strong ruler, the absolute monarch, who is the source of authority and order. Thus the king is the lawmaker and possesses absolute authority to rule the polity. The power to make law and the power to execute it are fused in the same institution, and in fact, the same person. This power of the monarch is necessarily absolute. "And because the End of this Institution is the Peace and Defence of them all; and whosoever has right to the End, has right to the Means," the monarch should be able "to do whatsoever he shall think necessary to be done."[21]

Thus Hobbes derived the absolute authority of the monarch from the need of humans to live in peace with each other. Since humans were so warlike in the state of nature, the monarch needed unquestioned power in order to establish and maintain domestic order. Furthermore, this surrendering of their rights is irrevocable: "And therefore, they that are subjects to a Monarch, cannot without his leave cast off Monarchy, and return to the confusion of a disunited Multitude."[22]

Hobbes's ideas, as expressed in *Leviathan,* justified the institution of absolute monarchy. But a critical turning point had been reached: Hobbes argued that the legitimate authority of the absolute monarchy derived not from God, but from the people who voluntarily sacrificed their right to do whatever suited them personally in order to live in peace under the laws and rule of the monarch. People would willingly sacrifice their liberty for the certainty of security under an absolute monarch.

According to Hobbes, the connection between the absolute power of the chief magistrate (executive or monarch) and republican government lies in this shift in the source of legitimacy of the state's power. The key change is Hobbes's break with previous political thinking in the West by his rejection of the traditional basis for absolute monarchy, the divine right of kings. For Hobbes, the king would still have absolute power, but the legitimacy of that power would be based on the willingness of the people to surrender their rights to the king, not on divine grace manifested through hereditary lines of succession. Even though Hobbes's prescription for the best form of government was absolute monarchy, the founding of that power in the rights of individuals and their willing sacrifice of freedom for safety was a revolutionary idea. The consequences of this revolutionary idea would be further developed by other political theorists, most important of whom was John Locke.

John Locke and Limited Government

In the intellectual development toward the idea of republican (representative) government, John Locke, in contrast to Hobbes, made the case that the authority of the monarch was not absolute. Although rejecting Hobbes's conclusions and prescriptions for the best polity—absolute monarchy—Locke built his argument on much the same premises. Locke called for a king, or chief executive, but would limit the power of the monarch by the nature of his rule. As long as the monarch protected the rights and safety of his citizens, he retained his legitimate authority. But Locke's revolutionary conclusion was that if the monarch failed to protect the rights of the individuals who had surrendered some of their authority to him, they could undertake to change the monarch.

THE PURPOSE OF GOVERNMENT

Locke's initial premises, like those of Hobbes, posited an initial "state of nature" that was marked by conflict because there was no final arbiter of disputes. However, while Hobbes focused on mere security and survival, Locke posited a broader set of values that individuals would pursue by leaving the state of nature. Thus he was more optimistic about human nature—humans had the capacity for cooperation and could enjoy rights to economic improvement and individual liberty by leaving the state of nature. For Locke the state of nature was "a state of perfect freedom" in which individuals could "order their actions, and dispose of their possessions and persons, as they think fit." It was as well "A *state* also of *equality* wherein all the power and jurisdiction is reciprocal, no one having more than another."[23] In this condition of equality, each person would be the judge of his own case. "*In the state of nature every one has the executive power* of the law of nature. . . . It is unreasonable for men to be judges in their own cases . . . [and] self-love will make men partial to themselves and their friends." Like Hobbes, Locke argued that the creation of government and its legitimacy are based upon the necessity of escaping the implied chaos of each being judge in his own case. "Civil government is the proper remedy for the inconveniencies of the state of nature."[24]

Unlike Hobbes, Locke saw a danger in allocating too much power to an absolute ruler. Locke reasoned that, just as all people are motivated by self-interest and thus need to be constrained in their actions, so also are monarchs guided by self-interest and in need of imposed constraint. Locke, like Hobbes, rejected the divine right of kings and held that "*absolute monarchs* are but men."[25] Locke saw in the absolute power of monarchs the danger that "he who attempts to get another man into his absolute power, does thereby put himself into a state of war with him." This is dangerous because "he who would get me into his power without my consent, would use me as he pleased when he had got me there, and destroy me too when he had a fancy to it."[26] The temptations of absolute power were dangerous to the liberty of all: "I have no reason to suppose that he, *who would take away my liberty,* would not, when he had me in his power, take away every thing else. And therefore it is lawful for me to treat him as one who has *put himself into a state of war with me,* i.e. [to] kill him if I can."[27]

In delegating power to the ruler, care must be taken not to delegate too much or the ruler might use that power to oppress the people, and they will have escaped the chaos of the state of nature only to find themselves oppressed by an absolute ruler. In contrast to Hobbes, Locke argues that after subjects cede the right to rule to a monarch, they still retain some rights themselves. Locke begins this line of thought by asking what creates value in a society or economy. He argues that the fundamental source of value is work, rather than raw materials or land. Land or raw materials only become of use or value if they are manipulated by people to create value, for example by growing crops, constructing buildings, or making roads. Thus Locke derives the right to property from the labor that puts value into property, "for it is *labour* indeed that *puts the difference of value* on every thing."[28]

This labor creates valuable property for those who apply work to basic materials, and individuals have the right to defend their property from others, including the monarch. "Man . . . hath by nature a power . . . to preserve his property, that is, his life, liberty and estate, against the injuries and attempts of other men."[29] And since the monarch is merely another man (not the representative of God on earth) who received his power from the consent of the governed (not from God), people can protect their lives and property from an unjust monarch. Note that Locke's conception of property is much broader than mere realty or possessions; it includes his life and liberty as well as his land and possessions.

The purpose of creating a state with its ruler is to protect the property of the citizens. "MEN being, as has been said, by nature, all free, equal, and independent, no one can be put out of this estate, and subjected to the political power of another, without his own consent." Consenting to be governed occurs when "one divests himself of his natural liberty, and puts on the *bonds of civil society.*" Thus the person agrees with others to "unite into a community for their comfortable, safe, and peaceable living one amongst another, in a secure enjoyment of their properties." Consequently the agreeing parties have created "one *body politic,* wherein the *majority* have a right to act and conclude the rest."[30]

Locke has moved from Hobbes's conceding absolute power to the monarch to the premise that people create governments in order to protect not only their mere safety, but also for "*the preservation of their property,*"[31] which includes their lives and liberty. Thus the legitimacy of the power of the monarch is limited to the extent that he in fact protects the lives, liberty, and property of the citizens of the polity. And who should make the fundamental decision about whether property is being adequately protected? The *"majority"* of citizens. While Hobbes's monarch merely provides safety to the people, Locke's monarch protects the safety, life, liberty, and property of the citizenry. Locke then makes the jump to the rule of the majority of the citizens in the polity. A chief magistrate, or executive, is clearly necessary for Locke, but the legitimacy of that executive derives from his protection of the liberties of the citizens.

The purpose of government for Locke necessarily implies that the rule of the monarch or executive should not be arbitrary, but rather bound by law. The rule of law is necessary for the legitimacy of the ruler. "And so whosoever has the legislative or supreme power of any commonwealth, is bound to govern by established standing laws, promulgated and known to the people, and not by extemporary decrees."[32] To preclude arbitrary rule by "extemporary decrees," the law-making power should be separated from the law-enforcing authority.

LEGISLATIVE SUPREMACY

Following from his conception of the rights of citizens and from his advocacy of majority rule, Locke argued that in a commonwealth the legislature is supreme: "The first and fundamental positive law of all commonwealths is the establishing of the legislative power; as the first and fundamental natural law, which is to govern even the legislative itself."[33] The legislature cannot be arbitrary and rule by ad hoc decisions or "extemporary arbitrary decrees." Rather, it *"is bound to dispense justice, and decide the rights of the subject by promulgated standing laws."*[34]

Included in the rights of citizenship is the right not to be deprived of property without consent or due process of law. "The supreme power cannot take from any man any part of his property without his own consent."[35] Locke did not mean that consent must be given in each instance, but rather the consent was to a set of general rules or laws that prescribe the ways in which a person's property can be taken legitimately by a government. The rule of law must prevail in a legitimate, republican polity.

Given Locke's argument for legislative supremacy, what is the appropriate role for the monarch or executive? Even though the legislative power is supreme, a real-world legislature cannot always be in session and actually apply its laws throughout the realm. For the application or administration of the laws on a continual basis, an executive is necessary. This single person "in a tolerable sense may also be called *supreme*: not that he has in himself all the supreme power, which is that of law making; but because he has in him the *supreme execution* [of the laws]."[36] In effect the rule of the executive is supreme, but only insofar as he is carrying out the rule of law established by the legislature.

Of course for practical purposes, the executive necessarily must have some discretion: "It is not necessary . . . that the legislative should be always in being; but absolutely necessary that the executive power should, because there is not always need of new laws to be made, but always need of execution of the laws that are made."[37] It also follows that if the executive breaks or ignores the law, he forfeits some of his legitimate claim to power. If the executive violates the law, "he has no right to obedience, nor can claim it otherwise than as the public person vested with the power of the law."[38]

The executive is bound by the law and may not rule on the basis of his own preferences: "Thus he has no will, no power, but that of the law. . . . The executive power . . . is visibly subordinate and accountable to it [the legislature]."[39] The executive thus gains his legitimacy from the delegation of power to him from the legislature, and the legislative authority can decide to revoke that power if it is not exercised responsibly. "When the legislative hath put the execution of the laws they make into other hands, they have a power still to resume it out of those hands."[40]

Obviously, Locke has come a long way from Hobbes's idea of the absolute power of the monarch. Beginning with the same premise of a state of nature and the delegation of some rights for the general good, Lock extends his analysis to the broad nature of property and concludes that the purpose of government is the protection of that property. He concludes that government is limited by law that is made by the legislative authority, which in turn delegates the execution of the laws to a chief executive. But that delegation is conditioned on the executive's carrying out the law in accord with the statutes created by the legislature.

The founders of the United States were influenced by Locke's ideas, and the influence of his ideas echoes throughout the Declaration of Independence and the Constitution. The Declaration of Independence posits that if the sovereign (the king and Parliament of England) "act contrary to their trust," and do not protect the rights of the citizens, the people have the right to dissolve their ties to that government. And "when the government is dissolved, the people are at liberty to provide for themselves, by erecting a new legislative."[41]

The Americans declared that "all Men are created equal, that they are endowed by their Creator with certain unalienable Rights, that among these are Life, Liberty, and the Pursuit of Happiness." The purpose of government is to secure these rights, and governments "derive their just Powers from the consent of the Governed." Since their current government (George III and Parliament) failed to secure their natural rights, the colonists had the right to abolish that government and create a new one. With this justification, the Americans fought the Revolutionary War to throw off British rule and establish their own government. The framers of the Constitution followed Locke's lead by separating executive from legislative power; Congress would make the laws, and the president would carry them out.

I do not assert here that most of the framers actually read Locke's *Second Treatise,* but Locke's thinking permeated their debates over the Constitution. According to historian Forrest McDonald, "Locke's version of the compact theory of the origin of legitimate government became a fundamental part of Americans' thinking about constitutional authority[;] everything Locke said about government was important to the founding."[42]

LOCKE'S PREROGATIVE POWER

In order to understand the intent of the framers with respect to executive power, an examination of John Locke's ideas about prerogative is useful. Prerogative, as Locke saw it, was not the same as the prerogative power of the crown before the Glorious Revolution of 1688. Before the English Civil War the prerogative power gave the monarch broad leeway to administer the kingdom as he chose and to suspend those laws that he found objectionable.

Locke in chapter 14 of his *Second Treatise* on government rejected the royal interpretation and substituted his republican version. For Locke, the prerogative power denoted the necessary discretion that any executive must have in order to execute the laws. The legislature cannot cover every possible contingency in making the law. So it is desirable and necessary for the executive to have a reasonable amount of discretion in order to apply the general law to specific situations.

Locke provided for the possibility that in certain circumstances the executive could act contrary to the law. "Many things there are, which the law by no means can provide for; and those must necessarily be left to the discretion of him that has the executive power in his hands, to be ordered by him as the public good and advantage shall require; nay, it is fit that the laws themselves should in some cases give way to the executive power."[43] But this seemingly broad grant of power to the executive is limited by the first part of this sentence: "For the legislators not being able to foresee, and provide by laws, for all that may be useful to the community, the executor of the laws, having the power in his hands, has by the common law of Nature a right to make use of it for the good of society, in many cases, where the municipal law has given no direction, till the legislative can conveniently be assembled to provide for it." Thus Locke gives the executive the prerogative to deal with circumstances or emergencies in which "many accidents may happen, wherein a strict and rigid observation of the laws may do harm."[44] But when the legislature "can conveniently be assembled to provide for it," it can make authoritative decisions.

Locke illustrated his meaning of "many accidents" with the example of a man who pulls down a person's house in order to stop the spread of a fire to the house next door. A person in such a situation would be justified in breaking the law. Locke's reasoning is that the fundamental purpose of government is the "preservation of all,"[45] and thus a rigid obedience to the law should not stop the executive from doing what is necessary to preserve the polity. This discretion of the executive to act outside the law, however, was not open-ended; it was limited to acting for the good of the polity and in situations comparable to stopping a raging fire. Locke continues:

> This power to act according to discretion, for the public good, without the prescription of the law, and sometimes even against it, is that which is called prerogative for since in some governments the lawmaking power is not always in being, and is usually too numerous, and so too slow, for the dispatch requisite to execution;

and because also it is impossible to foresee, and so by laws to provide for all accidents and necessities that may concern the public,
or to make such laws as will do no harm, if they are executed with
an inflexible rigor, on all occasions.[46]

Abraham Lincoln exercised this type of executive discretion, or prerogative, when he suspended the writ of habeas corpus and called out the
militia in the spring of 1861 in order to deal with the beginning of the
Civil War. But when Congress returned to Washington and came into
session in July of that year, Lincoln asked it for retrospective approval of
his actions. (This will be treated more fully in chapter 5.)

Those who want to increase executive discretion argue that Locke
maintained that the president has prerogative authority, inherent in the
office of the executive, which allows the president to override or ignore
the laws when he deems that national security demands it.[47] They argue
that the framers of the Constitution accepted that expansive interpretation of Locke's prerogative. But Locke's intent was that the prerogative
power could be legitimately exercised only "for the good of the people"
and not against it. In Locke's *Second Treatise* the necessary use of discretion is not a grant of authority to ignore the law; he merely argues that
in some exigencies, the executive must act in ways not in accord with the
law in order to deal with a crisis or emergency: "Prerogative being nothing but a power, in the hands of the prince, to provide for the public
good, in such cases, which depending upon unforeseen and uncertain
occurrences, certain and unalterable laws could not safely direct."[48] In a
Lockean republic the legislature is still supreme.

Locke referred to control over foreign and national security policy as
the "federative" power: "The power of war and peace, leagues and
alliances, and all the transactions, with all persons and communities
without the common-wealth . . . may be called federative."[49] He saw the
federative power as separate from the executive power, and, though it
was usually exercised by the executive, it was subject to legislative control: "The same holds also in regard to the *federative* power, that and
the *executive* being both *ministerial and subordinate to the legislative*,
which as has been shewed, in a constituted common-wealth is the
supreme."[50]

The practical exigencies of government often give the executive a wide range of latitude, particularly with respect to national defense. But admitting that the executive is usually better equipped to conduct a war does not entail agreeing in principle that the framers placed the decision to go to war and to control all of its incidents in the executive.[51] The framers of the American Constitution explicitly rejected the British model of royal power; they created a republic with legislative supremacy, despite the historical reality that presidents have often dominated national security policy. This issue will be examined more thoroughly in chapter 4.

According to Locke it is incorrect to say that the prerogative power has been "encroached upon" by the legislature when it legislates in the federative area, as the Bush administration has argued regarding the executive power. When the legislature passes laws, "they have not pulled from the prince any thing that of right belonged to him, but only declared, that that power which they indefinitely left in his or his ancestors' hands, to be exercised for their good, was not a thing which they intended him when he used it otherwise."[52] Thus in republics the executive does not have authority to ignore the law, and he is subject to legislative control, except in special circumstances.[53]

As the framers recognized, in case of an attack on the United States, the president could legitimately act militarily to repel the aggressors. In contemporary times the prerogative power might be legitimately exercised in the case of a terrorist attack similar to 9/11. For instance, the president could suspend habeas corpus when acting to deal with the emergency. But Locke's ideas cannot be legitimately used to justify ignoring the law once the emergency is over and courts are operating normally.[54] President Bush might claim that the threat of terrorism is a continuing reality and he thus has the authority to ignore habeas corpus and keep the courts from hearing any cases. But since the threat of terrorism will continue indefinitely into the future, such a claim would amount to the assertion that the president no longer has the duty to execute the laws faithfully as long as there is any threat of terrorism. The same argument holds true for breaking the law on surveillance of Americans without warrants. In Locke's metaphor, when the fire has been extinguished, the rule of law must be resumed. The threat of fire may still exist, but the executive may not ignore the law until the fire is again imminent, and then only if necessary to protect the nation.

Baron de Montesquieu and Separation of Powers

The idea of separation of powers developed from the Aristotelian idea of mixed government in which there would be representatives from several classes of society, for instance, royalty, aristocracy, and common people. This plan would assure that no one class dominated the others. Without this balance, the rule of one (monarchy) might degenerate into tyranny; the power of the few (aristocracy) might degenerate into plutocracy; and the rule of the many (democracy) might degenerate into mob rule. In England the idea of mixed government developed into the idea of a balanced constitution in which the king, House of Lords, and House of Commons operated in an equilibrium that assured each a voice in governing the country. This idea of balance later developed into the idea that the functions of government would be exercised by different and separate institutions of government, that is, the separation of powers.[55]

The idea of separation of powers in England began as a result of the English Civil War, in which the legitimacy of the absolute or divine origins of the authority of kings was, in theory and practice, demolished. After the restoration of the monarchy, the king still retained significant constitutional power (for example, an absolute veto, the naming of ministers, and the making of foreign policy). But the Civil War established Parliament as supreme in both theory and practice. Parliament, insisting that William and Mary sign the Declaration of Rights before they were crowned in 1689, confirmed the principle that Parliament played a legitimate role in governing England. Thus the English Constitution at that time confirmed that England had a "balanced constitution" in which the king-in-parliament was sovereign.[56] Montesquieu argued that the judicial power should be separate from the executive power, as it was in England. However it was the U.S. framers who elevated the judicial power to equal status as a separate branch of government.

Montesquieu drew some of his ideas about separation of powers from Locke, who argued that the legislative and judicial powers should be separated "because it may be too great a temptation to human frailty, apt to grasp at power, for the same persons, who have the power of making laws, to have also in their hands the power to execute them, whereby they may exempt themselves from obedience to the laws they make, and suit the law, both in its making, and execution, to their own private advantage."[57] Montesquieu used some of Locke's ideas as well as his own observations of the operation of the government of England in his treatment of separation of powers. Some scholars have pointed out that Montesquieu did not accurately characterize the actual operation of the English government in his writing.[58] But M. J. C. Vile argues that we should view Montesquieu's analysis of separation of powers as an ideal type rather than as an attempt to present a historically accurate account of the government of England.[59]

Montesquieu deals with his ideas on the separation of powers primarily in chapter 11 of *The Spirit of the Laws,* which was published in 1748. This chapter, "Of the Constitution of England," emphasizes the separation between legislative and executive powers, and introduces the idea of a separate judicial function. Montesquieu begins the chapter: "In every government there are three sorts of power: the legislative; the executive in respect to things dependent on the law of nations; and the executive in regard to matters that depend on the civil law."[60] Montesquieu calls the executive power dealing with the law of nations (foreign policy) what Locke calls the "federative power." In contrast to Locke and Montesquieu, the framers of the U.S. Constitution decided to split control of foreign policy and the war powers between the legislature and executive.

Montesquieu's most important contribution to the idea of separation of powers was to separate the "judiciary power" from the legislative and executive powers.[61] By judiciary power he means the "punish[ing] of criminals, or determin[ing] the disputes that arise between individuals."[62] He warns that the power of judging should not be vested in the aristocracy or nobles, but should be exercised by ordinary people: "The judiciary power ought not to be given to a standing senate; it should be exercised by persons taken from the body of the people."[63] He thus does not want the power of judging to be given to any one class, but rather he argues that it should be independent, that is—merely administrative or mechanical, rather than policymaking. In Montesquieu's formulation, the judicial power would not rival the legislative or executive powers of government: "Of the three powers above mentioned, the judiciary is in some measure next to nothing."[64] Thus, though he conceptually separates the judicial power from the executive and legislative functions of government, he does not see the judiciary as a separate branch, but merely a separate function to be isolated from the legislative and executive functions. It was the framers of the U.S. Constitution who placed the judiciary in a separate and equal branch of government.[65]

Part of Montesquieu's influence on the framers came from his sweeping historical analysis of government from classical times to the mid-eighteenth century, when he wrote *The Spirit of the Laws* (1748). The framers, in addition to following Montesquieu by separating the judiciary as an independent function of government, heeded his warning that all governmental powers should not be exercised by one person or institution. "When the legislative and executive powers are united in the same person, or in the same body of magistrates, there can be no liberty. . . . Again, there is no liberty, if the judiciary power be not separated from the legislative and executive."[66] Neither Montesquieu nor the framers prescribed a pure separation of powers in which each branch had no influence on the others, but rather both suggested a design in which the different functions were separated, but in which there was some overlap of function, such as the veto power of the executive or the war powers of Congress.

Conclusion

Some of the important ideas about government, traced briefly above, changed over time in ways that foreshadowed the development of Anglo-American governments. Machiavelli justified the exercise of absolute and arbitrary power by a ruler. Hobbes legitimated absolute monarchy based on a hypothetical contract with the subjects of a realm. Locke changed the terms of the contract between citizens and the government to include the protection of life, liberty, and property; he also posited a right to change the government if it did not meet its obligations. Montesquieu favored the separation of executive from legislative powers in order to prevent tyranny and saw the judicial function as separate from legislating or executing the law.

The development of these ideas about the purpose and legitimacy of limited and republican government has had a lasting impact on the United States through the embodiment of these ideas in the Constitution. The framers clearly rejected the absolute and arbitrary executive that Machiavelli prescribed. They accepted Hobbes's idea that governmental power should be based in the people through a symbolic contract, but they rejected the absolutism that he favored. Locke's extension of the nature of the contract to the protection of the life, liberty, and property of the citizenry was an important source of the Declaration of Independence. The framers derived their ideas about the separation of powers from Locke's prescription for legislative supremacy and Montesquieu's separation of the judicial power from the legislative and executive. The framers' great contribution to the nature of governance was the Constitution of the United States, which embodied an original blend of these ideas.

The next chapter will examine the historical development of individual rights and the rise of Parliament in England. Kings and queens had for centuries been able to treat subjects pretty much as they pleased and had absolute control of public policy. The struggle for individual rights went on sporadically and eventually resulted in imposing limitations on the power of the monarch and government in general. The development of Parliament proceeded in fits and starts, and finally resulted in parliamentary democracy, with the monarch playing only a symbolic role. The following chapter will show how the framers of the Constitution accepted British traditions about individual rights but rejected the structure of the British government in favor of a separation of powers system. In the twenty-first century, President George W. Bush presented fundamental challenges to both individual rights and the separation of powers. The remaining chapters of the book will examine his extraordinary claims to presidential power.

CHAPTER THREE

CREATING INDIVIDUAL RIGHTS AND AN INDEPENDENT LEGISLATURE

"No free man shall be seized or imprisoned, or stripped of his rights or possessions, or outlawed or exiled, or deprived of his standing in any other way, nor will we [the king] proceed with force against him, or send others to do so, except by the lawful judgment of his equals or by the law of the land."
—Magna Carta

"There is no expressed grant of habeas corpus in the Constitution."
—Alberto Gonzales

The English (and later British) Constitution developed over many centuries and influenced the framers of the United States Constitution in important ways. After all, most of the architects of the U.S. Constitution considered themselves to be loyal Englishmen virtually up until the War of Independence. In fact their reasons for rebellion revolved around the convictions that they were being denied their rights as Englishmen by an oppressive monarch and Parliament. This chapter will present an overview of some of the highlights of English constitutional development. In medieval England the monarchy reigned supreme, and held, more or less, arbitrary say over public policy in areas in which it chose to intervene. The practical exercise of power varied from time to time, but in principle monarchs considered their word to be law, and most of their subjects agreed with them. By the thirteenth century, however, common law had established some limits in principle to the monarch's right to raise taxes and imprison people without due process of law.

The principles of limited governmental power were gradually expanded over the centuries through (often bloody) struggles between monarchs and their subjects. The first part of this chapter traces some of those struggles and notes some of the highlights in the establishment of individual rights, as opposed to monarchical decree. The second part of the chapter traces the rise of Parliament as a limit to executive power. Again, the establishment of parliamentary rights, in principle, preceded the ability of Parliament to exercise its authority in practice. As with individual rights, the struggle for parliamentary supremacy took centuries to accomplish. It is these two principles—individual rights and legislative authority—that President Bush threatened in the first decade of the twenty-first century.

The Origins of Individual Rights

The early glimmerings of individual rights and their common law enforcement became more robust over the centuries after the decline of Roman rule of Britain. These traces embodied some of the customs of the Anglo-Saxon tribes that replaced Roman law. When William the Conqueror came to power after the Battle of Hastings in 1066, he brought with him the doctrine of the divine right of kings and absolute monarchism. He proceeded to centralize his control of England, despite the resistance of local lords who were accustomed to controlling their own shires. William ordered the compilation of the Doomsday Book, which was in effect, a census of England and its economic assets.

Despite the centralization of control by William, the seeds of limited government soon began to sprout again, and constitutional monarchy gradually developed over the next seven centuries, ebbing and flowing with the political circumstances of the times and the power of individual monarchs. The first part of this chapter will briefly outline how the English governmental system of a relatively strong monarchy was punctuated with assertions of the rights of the nobles (and later the people). The rise of Parliament will be considered in the second half of the chapter.

Not long after the death of William's first son, William II, his second son, Henry I, acceded to the throne in 1100. In order to maintain the loyalty, or at least acquiescence, of the lords, Henry formally agreed to a *Charter of Liberties,* which acknowledged some limits on his own authority in several ways. The *Charter* was published by sending copies to all of the shires of the kingdom. The first provision of the *Charter* began, "Know that by the mercy of God and the common counsel of the barons of the whole kingdom of England I have been crowned king of said kingdom."[1] This formal acknowledgment that his power derived not from God alone, but also from the barons of his kingdom was an important concession both to the reality of the barons' power and also to the principle that the king's legitimate authority was not absolute.

The *Charter* spelled out a number of rules by which King Henry would administer his kingdom; these included rules about inheritance, taxes, and the criminal law. He proclaimed that he would "restore to you the law of King Edward with those amendments introduced into it by my father with the advice of his barons." In effect, he was promising to be bound by the laws of the kingdom. Thus important precedents were set by acknowledging that the legitimacy of the king's rule was based in part on the agreement of his barons and that the king was bound by law. These concessions by Edward constituted important precedents that would eventually be embodied in the principle of the rule of law, despite the fact that later English monarchs would rule with virtually absolute power.

Magna Carta, 1215

The next century saw the issuing of Magna Carta, one of the world's most famous declarations of the principles of individual rights and limited government. Magna Carta (Great Charter) originated in the rule of King John (1199–1216), who pursued wars on the continent that were costly; the consequent taxes were burdensome to the lords of the shires of England. In order to raise money for his military campaigns, John increased traditional taxes and fees, but he also went beyond the traditional bounds of legitimate revenue raising. He seized land and imprisoned those who did not pay, holding them hostage in order to force payments.[2]

During this time, the barons' resentment was building, and by 1215 they demanded that John restore the principles of the *Charter of Liberties* of 1100. King John's rejection of their demands culminated in the barons' gathering military forces and confronting him at Runnymede on June 15 in 1215. Over the next few days, the articles of Magna Carta were drawn up, sealed by John, and promulgated throughout the Kingdom. (Magna Carta was not one particular document, but rather the list of articles to which King John agreed. Copies of the articles were transcribed [in Latin] and authenticated not with John's signature, but with the royal seal impressed in wax.)[3]

The provisions of Magna Carta were negotiated by the representatives of King John, and the barons intended to reassert baronial rights and limit the power of the crown. They were not originally intended to be a broad declaration of human rights or to protect the rights of the common people.[4] Many of the articles specified long-standing grievances of the barons and limited specific types of taxes that the king could collect. Nevertheless some of the 63 clauses of Magna Carta articulated more general limitations on the power of the king. From these statements some of the most important principles of limited government have been derived.

Among the most important of the articles of Magna Carta were provisions that

—The king could not arbitrarily seize property owned by his subjects without appropriate compensation. Section 28 states: "No constable or other royal official shall take corn or other movable goods from any man without immediate payment";

—Any charges against a person had to be supported by sufficient evidence. Section 38 states: "In [the] future no official shall place a man on trial upon his own unsupported statement, without producing credible witnesses to the truth of it";

—The king was limited by law. When imprisoning a person, the king had to follow due process of law and provide the principle of trial by jury. Section 39 states: "No free man shall be seized or imprisoned, or stripped of his rights or possessions, or outlawed or exiled, or deprived of his standing in any other way, nor will we [the king] proceed with force against him, or send others to do so, except by the lawful judgment of his equals or by the law of the land";

—Justice must not be subject to bribery, and it must not be unnecessarily delayed. Section 40 states: "To no one will we [the king] sell, to no one deny or delay right or justice."[5]

Magna Carta also authorized an assembly of twenty-five barons to ensure that the king and his ministers kept their part of the agreement. The final clause of the document states: "Witness the above-mentioned and many others. Given under our [King John's] hand in the meadow which is called Runnymede between Windsor and Staines."[6]

In anticipation of the possibility that King John might try to renege on his agreement, Section 61 of Magna Carta states: "We [King John] will not seek to procure from anyone, either by our own efforts or those of a third party, anything by which any part of these concessions or liberties might be revoked or diminished. Should such a thing be procured, it shall be null and void and we will at no time make use of it, either ourselves or through a third party."[7]

Nevertheless, after affixing his seal to the documents, King John immediately appealed to the pope to annul his concessions. As payment for granting John's request, Pope Innocent III demanded that John cede formal rule of England to the papacy. Once John agreed to the pope's demand, Innocent on August 24, 1215, issued a papal bull that declared that Magna Carta was "as unlawful and unjust as it is base and shameful."[8] In explaining his reasoning, the pope said in his bull, "King [John] at length returned to his senses" and "he yielded his kingdom and Ireland to St. Peter and the Roman church." The pope accepted John's kingdom "as fief" for the "annual payment [to John] of one thousand marks." Thus, concluded Pope Innocent III, "The charter . . . we declare to be null, and void of all validity forever."[9] John had sold his kingdom for 1,000 marks per year in exchange for the pope's nullification of Magna Carta.

Whether John could legally renege on his agreement not to try to annul Magna Carta or whether the pope had the authority to do so, are moot points. What is important about Magna Carta is not its specific legal standing in 1215 or how closely King John adhered to its provisions. Magna Carta's significance resides in the general principles of limited government that several of its provisions proclaimed.[10]

Despite its rejection by King John and some of his successors, Magna Carta (in addition to its many provisions specific to the king's policies in the thirteenth century) established several general principles of governance that have influenced centuries of English and American law as well as the Universal Declaration of Human Rights. These principles include prohibitions against the government's seizing property without due process of law, imposing punishment without credible evidence, imprisonment without the judgment of peers or due process, and selling of justice.

Edward Coke later argued that Magna Carta was not merely an ad hoc compilation of remedies of grievances of the barons, but a restatement of ancient law established in England in previous centuries.[11]

Whether Magna Carta reflected canons of ancient English law, it was an important statement of principles of individual liberty. Perhaps most important, Magna Carta established the general principle that the king (or government) is bound by the law. That is, the king (or chief executive) is not above the law. George W. Bush was to challenge this ancient principle in the twenty-first century by denying habeas corpus, suspending the Geneva Agreements, ordering secret surveillance without warrants, and also through some of his signing statements.

THE PETITION OF RIGHT, 1628

One of the recurring themes of English struggles to limit monarchical power was resistance to taxes imposed by the crown to support foreign wars. King Charles I (1600–1649) had been pursuing foreign wars that were unpopular and for which he was extracting excessive taxes, partly through forced loans to the crown. In addition, in order to save money, he insisted on quartering troops in the homes of the local people. These policies were greatly resented, and parliament was provoked to present the *Petition of Right* to King Charles in 1628. Since Charles needed the funds to fight his wars, he agreed to the provisions of the *Petition,* and Parliament granted him more revenues.

The *Petition* was initiated by Sir Edward Coke and was based on earlier understandings of common law rights of Englishmen established in part by "The Great Charter of the Liberties of England" (Magna Carta) and laws passed by Parliament. The petition was framed "humbly" as a request (petition) to King Charles, but the implied threat was that Parliament would not grant King Charles the taxes he sought for his wars unless he agreed to the terms of the *Petition.* Among other things, the petition reaffirmed some of the formerly established rights of Englishmen and echoed Magna Carta, including

—trial by jury and due process: "no freeman may be taken or imprisoned . . . but by the lawful judgment of his peers, or by the law of the land";

—the right of writs of habeas corpus so that subjects could not be imprisoned "without being charged" unless "cause was certified";

—the king could impose no taxes except "by authority of parliament";

—no quartering of troops would be undertaken against the consent of the people;

—martial law could not be declared in peacetime.[12]

As in the case of Magna Carta, the king agreed to the *Petition of Right* only because he needed revenues to conduct his wars. But after Charles got the funds he needed, he reneged, ignored his agreement, and dissolved Parliament.

Nonetheless Charles continued to need more money for his wars with Spain and France and was forced to call "the Long Parliament" in 1640 in order to raise tax revenues. Parliament, however, would not provide him with the money he needed unless he agreed to a number of conditions. Among many other things, the demands included:

—That Parliament would meet every three years, regardless of the king's consent;

—That the king could not dissolve Parliament without its own consent;

—That Charles would abolish the Court of Star Chamber, which was seen as a political tool that was used arbitrarily and imposed extreme punishments merely to enforce Charles's own personal wishes;

—That Charles would sign "the Grand Remonstrance," a compilation of his abrogations of the rights of the people.[13]

These demands led to the English Civil War, which pitted Charles I and his Royalists in the west and north of England against Oliver Cromwell and his Roundheads, who were determined to rid England of any remnants of Catholicism and royal oppression. In 1648 Cromwell's forces defeated Charles I, disbanded the House of Lords, abolished the monarchy, and beheaded Charles in January of 1649. A republican government known as the Commonwealth was established, and after Cromwell declared himself the "Lord Protector," he ran the government as a despot (treated in more detail below). His son Richard took over after Cromwell died in 1658.

The Long Parliament, which had been officially (though not actually) in session since 1640, met and dissolved itself in 1660. It then created a new Parliament that restored the monarchy by offering the crown to Charles II, the son of Charles I, thus accomplishing the "restoration" of the English monarchy.

THE ENGLISH BILL OF RIGHTS, 1689

After the restoration of the monarchy and the death of Charles II, Charles's brother, James II, ascended to the throne. In his short reign he tried, against the wishes of the Protestants, to reestablish Catholicism as a legitimate religion in England. The anti-James Protestants decided to wait out James's reign, after which his Protestant daughter, Mary, who was married to the Dutch William of Orange, would restore the Protestant ascendancy. But when a son was born to James, it appeared that he would have a Catholic heir to continue his pro-Catholic policies. William wanted the throne, based on his wife's claim as a direct descendant of Charles II, and he raised an army to invade England and capture power. James prepared to defend his kingship, but he began to act erratically, and members of Parliament concluded that he was incapable of fulfilling his duties as monarch. After much maneuvering, both Whigs and Tories in Parliament agreed to invite William and Mary to come to England to become co-monarchs. Before they were crowned, however, they had to accept a Declaration of Rights that was then passed by Parliament as the Bill of Rights of 1689.

The acceptance by William and Mary of the Declaration of Rights was another step on the road to a constitutional monarchy in England.

Among other rights, the Bill declared:

—"the pretended Power of Suspending of Laws or Execution of Laws by Regall Authority without Consent of Parliament . . . is illegal,"

—"dispensing with laws . . . is illegal,"

—the "levying money for or to the use of the Crown . . . without grant of Parliament . . . is illegal,"

—"the right of subjects to petition the king" is ensured,

—the king could establish no standing army "in time of peace . . . without consent of Parliament,"

—"election of members of Parliament ought to be free,"

—"freedom of speech and debates or proceedings in Parliament" shall not be questioned in court,

—no "excessive bail . . . nor excessive fines . . . nor cruel and unusual punishments [shall be] inflicted,"

—"Parliaments ought to be held frequently."[14]

The most important principles established in the Bill of Rights were that the king could not rule without the cooperation of Parliament and that the king was not above the law. The assertion of these rights was echoed in the U.S. Constitution. In the twenty-first century, George W. Bush, in effect, suspended laws concerning habeas corpus (covered in chapter 5) and he "dispensed" with the Foreign Intelligence Surveillance

Act (FISA) in his secret surveillance of citizens without warrants (covered in chapter 7). In his signing statements (covered in chapter 8), he threatened to "suspend" many of the provisions of laws and not to execute the law. It is also arguable that in encouraging harsh interrogations, he encouraged or condoned cruel and unusual punishment. Thus President Bush was attempting to exercise prerogative powers that were wrested from the king of England in 1689.

The Rise of Parliament

The assertion of individual rights of barons, nobles, and the people of England constituted in principle important limits on the authority of the king. The reality, of course, was that these rights were not always respected. Yet the declaration of the principles created a basis upon which firmer guarantees of the rights of Englishmen could be established. At the same time that the rights of individuals were established, the power of the crown was also being limited by the assertions of the rights of Parliament. As with individual rights, the asserted rights were not always respected by the king, but the assertions established the principles that gradually, over several centuries, led to a sovereign Parliament within a constitutional monarchy. The highlights of those developments will be briefly reviewed.

In theory as well as practice, the king had been the seat of sovereignty since the Norman invasion of 1066. Of course, the king's actual (effective) power ebbed and flowed depending on the particular historical circumstances, but the monarch was generally recognized among the people as sovereign in temporal affairs as well as the representative of God on earth. The pope was considered God's vicar—that is, until the reign of Henry VIII, when the king claimed ecclesiastical as well as temporal authority.

Despite the acceptance of the king's supreme authority, some limits on the complete discretion of the monarch were accepted, as various aspects of the common law were formalized and agreed to by the crown, in practice. Later, these rights became formalized in legal documents and laws, such as Magna Carta, the Bill of Rights, the habeas corpus statute, and others. The other main limit to the power of the executive that developed in tandem with the accretion of individual rights was the rise of the influence of Parliament, first as a legitimate limit on the power of the monarch and many centuries later as the seat of sovereignty of the realm.

This section will trace the development of Parliament from informal collections of barons who petitioned the king for recognition and redress of grievances to the sovereign body that could establish the laws of the land even if the monarch disagreed. The main tools of power won by Parliament over the centuries were control of government personnel (primarily through impeachment), control of the purse (that is, the raising of money through taxes), and control of policy (through responsible government). In the twenty-first century, President Bush denied that he was bound by laws that he thought impinged on his constitutional powers as president. In effect, he claimed powers that kings of England enjoyed before centuries of bloody battles and civil wars wrested them from the crown and limited them by law and the authority of Parliament.

The gradual establishment of Parliament as the sovereign in English constitutional law began humbly. In the several centuries before the Norman Conquest, the territory that is now England was ruled by kings who were chosen by groups of local notables called the *witans*. Witans comprised religious leaders, powerful barons, and members designated by the Anglo-Saxon kings in England. After the Norman Conquest and the establishment of a hierarchical, feudal system, England was ruled by monarchs who claimed to be absolute rulers whose authority flowed from their hereditary status and was derived from God through the divine right of kings. Medieval English kings, when they chose, called councils to confer with nobles and religious leaders. These local leaders had a feudal relationship with the king and no independent, legal authority. Yet they provided the king with support that was useful.[15]

By the early thirteenth century the barons chafed under King John's rule, and in 1215 they forced him to accept Magna Carta. John's son, Henry III (1216–1272) upset the barons of the kingdom by exacting heavy taxes from them. In response the barons, led by Simon de Montfort, the Earl of Leicester, forced Henry, through the Provisions of Oxford in 1258, to accept a permanent council of barons. This council constituted the first Parliament of England and had the authority to control some of the king's appointments. When Henry tried to renege on his agreement to heed the council, de Montfort organized resistance and invited the burgesses (commoners) to participate in the Parliament. This was the first representation of the common people in the English government.

The establishment of parliamentary power in England grew through its assertion of the right to impeach and remove from office ministers of the king. At the same time parliamentary control of the purse grew in fits and starts. Finally, in the eighteenth and nineteenth centuries, full parliamentary sovereignty was established through the responsibility of the executive ministers to Parliament rather than to the crown.

The gradual development of parliamentary power in England began when the king called and consulted with local barons. It was increased with de Montfort's insistence that Henry III recognize the council of barons and commoners. The powers of Parliament were expanded over the next several centuries, in part, through the practice of impeachment, which was established during the fourteenth century. In 1341 the lower house of Parliament, consisting of knights and burgesses, began to meet separately from the upper house, Lords. But more important, during the reign of Edward III (1327–1377), the precedent was set that the king could not impose taxes without the consent of Parliament.[16]

Despite the establishment of the principles of individual rights and the prerogatives of Parliament, the kings of England effectively controlled the government and were able to exact taxes, control land, fight wars, and imprison their domestic enemies. This royal power reached a peak during the reign of the Tudors and was only finally overcome as a result of the Civil War of the 1650s. The development of parliamentary rule on the way to sovereignty continued with the power of impeachment and control of the purse strings.

CONTROL OF PERSONNEL: IMPEACHMENT

Impeachment, that is, the ability of Parliament to depose (and sometimes to execute) ministers of the king, began as an intermittent and blunt instrument to curb the power of the crown. Its legitimacy was by no means always accepted by the crown, but it was established in English common law in the late medieval period.[17] Since the king was considered to have been anointed by God, the doctrine that the king could do no wrong developed in the twelfth and thirteenth centuries. The reality, of course, was that much wrong was done in the king's name by his ministers. The problem was how to punish wrongdoing if the king directly represented God. The legal fiction that the king could do no wrong was useful because the acts of his ministers could then be separated from the king's unquestioned authority, and the ministers could be punished for wrongdoing without questioning the king's divine authority.

As a consequence of this legal fiction, the king's ministers were not allowed to defend themselves by claiming (even truthfully) that they were acting according to the king's orders. The principle that the king could do no wrong was upheld, but redress was still possible through punishing his ministers. By 1341 the king's ministers were, in principle, answerable for their behavior, and in 1376 the practice of impeachment began with the Good Parliament. The legal power of Parliament to impeach ministers of the king could be based on the "notoriety of their reputation."[18] By the end of the fourteenth century, the power to impeach the king's ministers for their misdeeds was accepted in principle by both Parliament and king.

The principle that Parliament could impeach most of the king's ministers, however, was limited by the actual attitude and power of the king. For instance, when one of Richard II's ministers was challenged by Parliament in 1386, Richard said that he would not discharge even one of the "scullions" in his kitchen at Parliament's request.[19] Nevertheless, during the years 1376 to 1397, the House of Commons impeached eighteen officers of the king, and they were all convicted by the House of Lords.[20]

Impeachment, though established, was a blunt instrument that could be used only occasionally, but it was an important point in the gradual rise of Parliament. Henry IV (1399–1413) in 1406 agreed to the demand of the Commons that the king's ministers had to act according to the law, even if the king ordered otherwise.[21] In effect the king no longer had complete and unquestioned control of the counselors and ministers of the crown, though in practice, the king had much more power than Parliament.

THE TUDORS: PARLIAMENT GAINS AUTHORITY BUT DOES NOT USE IT

By the time the Tudors consolidated the control of the monarchy over England, the powers of Parliament had been established as legitimate in principle. In practical reality, however, parliamentary power was in eclipse, and Parliament only met when called into session by the king.

Parliament was seldom able to resist the crown effectively during the Tudor period; on the other hand, it did not often try. By the beginning of the reign of Henry VII, the first Tudor (1485–1509), several constraints on the power of the crown had been established:

—New taxes were assessed only with the assent of Parliament (effectively respected for the previous century);

—All new laws had to be approved and enacted by Parliament, rather than merely being announced by the king;

—No one could be imprisoned except by way of a legal warrant, and the accused was entitled to a speedy and public trial and had the right to be judged by his peers;.

—The officers or ministers of the crown could be held responsible for their actions and brought to justice through the criminal process.

But Parliaments did not constitute an essential part of the working of government, and the king was essentially sovereign. Though the power of the king in Tudor England was not absolute in theory, in fact the king dominated the country.[22]

Henry VII was determined to establish the supremacy of the crown over the nobles of England and effectively went about consolidating political control through the shrewd use of patronage and financial and administrative control of the realm.[23] Henry's son, Henry VIII, succeeded him and proceeded to aggrandize the power of the English crown to a zenith of personal control and domination. Through the Act of Supremacy of 1534, Henry convinced and coerced Parliament to declare him not only supreme in temporal matters but also the direct representative of God on earth, and as such, supreme in all ecclesiastical affairs. Henry thus replaced the Catholic Church with the Church of England, of which he was head, and confiscated all Church property, greatly increasing his wealth and power. This combination of powers temporal and spiritual led eventually to a series of civil wars that tore England apart and came to a close only after the accession of William and Mary in 1689.

The role of Parliament during Henry's reign was that of cheerleader and facilitator. It did his bidding without cavil, passed the laws Henry desired, and aided him in his domination of the realm by his personal will. But in doing so Parliament came to be accepted as legitimate in its exercise of the lawmaking power, though it never confronted the king by contesting its will against his. In passing laws concerning a wide range of areas, precedent for the broader jurisdiction of Parliament was established. Later, this wider jurisdiction could be resurrected to assert parliamentary authority.

Parliament continued to be compliant during the reign of Edward VI (1547–1553) and Mary (1553–1558) and particularly during the reign of Elizabeth I (1558–1603). Parliament again passed an Act of Supremacy (of the crown over ecclesiastical matters) in 1559 for Henry's daughter Elizabeth I, which she used to reverse the laws that Mary had passed favoring Catholics. Elizabeth had full support from Parliament because she was a strong ruler at a time when England was threatened by Spain. When the attempted invasion of England by Spain in 1588 was thwarted by unfavorable winds, Elizabeth received credit for the wreck of the Spanish Armada and for saving the kingdom. Though Parliament occasionally took issue with Queen Elizabeth, she was able to outmaneuver them and assert her own will effectively.

By the end of the Tudor period, two additional developments would add to the limits on monarchical power. The first was that the personal household of the crown, through which the monarch had administered his or her policies, had been transformed into the beginnings of public administration. That is, the crown's ministers were no longer personal servants of the monarch, but rather civil servants serving the nation.[24] Second, the House of Commons had emerged as an independent assembly that was determined to protect its own constitutional prerogatives. In the future when ministers were to be held accountable, they would be held to account by the House of Commons, not the crown.[25]

Thus under the Tudors, Parliaments were active in the passing of laws and working with the crown on public policy.[26] The House of Commons gradually began to establish its independence from the crown and became more important than the House of Lords as the center of parliamentary power, even though it did not often act independently.[27] Parliament established its power by choosing not to challenge royal prerogatives, but rather by supporting the crown in all important matters of state. By the end of the Tudor era, the sovereign in England had become the king-in-Parliament, rather than merely the king.[28] In its support of the crown, Parliament laid the groundwork for its independent legitimacy as a policy body, which it began to exercise independently against the crown in the seventeenth century.

THE STUARTS AND THE ENGLISH CIVIL WAR

The doctrine of the divine right of kings had prevailed in England in principle since the Norman Conquest. The Tudors continued to assert their divine prerogative, but in addition to the asserted principle, the Tudors effectively asserted the power of the crown and made it supreme in fact as well as principle. The principle of divine sanction took a blow when Elizabeth had her sister, Mary Queen of Scots, beheaded for treason. If a royal heir could be killed like a common person, the divine origin of monarchical rule might not be as certain as it had been in the past.[29]

Up to the time of the Civil War, the crown held the bulk of power in England. Kings could veto bills that Parliament had passed; they could pardon violators of the law; they could exempt individuals from obeying the law; they could suspend the laws for certain persons or purposes; they controlled most of the ministers and judges of the realm; and of course, they could take the kingdom to war. This was to change after the Glorious Revolution in 1688 when James was banished and William and Mary ascended to the throne.

The Stuart kings came to power believing in their absolute and divinely derived authority, and for the first half of the seventeenth century, they attempted to assert aggressively their claimed power. However counterpressures grew, both in theory and in power politics, that brought Parliament to the undreamed of point of regicide in 1649.

At the death of Queen Elizabeth in 1603, King James I (1603–1625), the first Stuart and son of Mary Queen of Scots, ascended to the throne. James believed firmly in the divine authority of the monarchy. In his own words, "The State of MONARCHIE is the supremest thing upon earth: For Kings are not onely GODS Lieutenants upon earth, and sit upon GODS throne, but even by GOD himselfe they are called GODS."[30] When he proclaimed England and Scotland to be one country and established himself as the king of Great Britain, he was able to prevail, but he incurred substantial costs as a result of the union and was forced to ask Parliament for tax revenues. When his demands were rejected by Parliament, James resorted to indirect taxation in order to meet his financial obligations. By this time, however, Parliament had established itself as a legitimate partner in making public policy and was ready to assert its control of the purse. James and Parliament struggled to a stalemate. At James's death in 1625, his son Charles I became king.

Charles's belief in his divine right to rule as an absolute monarch was even greater than his father's.[31] He insisted that his word was law and that neither Parliament nor the courts could challenge his authority.[32] Charles's wars with France and Spain were costly and unpopular in the kingdom, and in 1628 he had to call on Parliament to approve tax increases. With the unwillingness of Parliament to provide him with the tax revenue that he sought, Charles disbanded Parliament and decided to raise money by himself through forced loans, threats, and by forced quartering of troops in the homes of citizens. One of the most unpopular taxes was the "ship money." Originally imposed on port cities to pay for naval ships that protected them, they were extended by Charles to inland areas. This expansion of taxes yielded significant funds for his royal purposes without the inconvenience of consulting Parliament, but it also generated resentment throughout the kingdom.

After an eleven-year hiatus in sessions of Parliament, Charles needed money to put down a religious rebellion in Scotland, and in April of 1640, he was forced to call Parliament into session again. But Parliament would not provide Charles the money without significant concessions to its authority, so he dismissed the "Short Parliament" after only one month. By August 1640 Scottish troops were in England, and Charles was forced to recall the "Long Parliament" in order to raise taxes for military forces. Before they would approve of his taxes, he had to agree to many of Parliament's demands, including a demand that Parliament could not be dissolved without its consent.

Charles was rumored to be the tool of a Catholic conspiracy to take power in England, and he was presented by Parliament with "The Grand Remonstrance," a list of 200 demands. The document, which passed in Parliament by a narrow vote, specified many of Charles's arrogations of power and charged him with aiding or condoning the Catholic conspiracy. As a result, Charles decided to confront Parliament by arresting several MPs, and he personally went to Parliament to demand their surrender. When Parliament refused to deliver the members, Charles was shown to be extreme in his demands as well as incapable of enforcing his will. Parliament then took control of the government.

The aims of Parliament began as a demand of, in effect, a constitutional monarchy, with the king subject to parliamentary control. But Charles would not accept such an outcome, and the radical Protestants, under the leadership of Oliver Cromwell, also refused to compromise. Thus a war between Charles's Royalists and Cromwell's Roundheads began in 1644. Cromwell, leading the newly professionalized New Model Army, crushed Charles's troops. The king was taken into their control in 1647. After more fighting, the radicals again refused to compromise with Charles or those favoring a constitutional monarchy. The Protestant radicals then purged the moderates from Parliament, and with the support of the New Model Army, a "Rump" Parliament of 150 took complete control. Cromwell and the radicals in Parliament then condemned Charles to death, and he was beheaded on January 30, 1649. Parliament then abolished the monarchy and proclaimed itself the supreme ruler of England. Cromwell, after conquering Scotland and Ireland, became a more dictatorial ruler than most kings had been, and when he did not get everything he wanted, he, too, disbanded Parliament.

At Cromwell's death, his son Richard assumed the title of Lord Protector, but he was unable to control the army or Parliament, and he resigned his office in May of 1659. King Charles's son Charles II was in exile in the Netherlands, and the Parliament that was elected in 1660 offered Charles the throne. Accepting the offer, Charles returned to England in triumph, to the relief of the war-weary country. The restoration of the Stuart monarchy was an admission that England needed a king, but a king that was bound by traditional limits on royal authority. Despite the restoration of the monarchy, religious disagreements still plagued England, and Charles II (1659–1685), believing in the divine right of kings, moved England toward Catholicism and an alliance with Catholic France.

Charles continued to rule and asserted his royal authority, especially in his last four years, during which Parliament did not meet.[33] He was, however, widely distrusted by Protestants for his Catholic sympathies. His rejection by royal veto of three exclusion bills (which would have barred Catholics from holding office) provided evidence of his pro-Catholic sympathies. Before he died in 1685, he formally converted to Catholicism, confirming the suspicions of many Protestants. He was succeeded by his strongly Catholic brother, James. Ironically, the Catholic James became the head of the Protestant Church of England.

Like his father, Charles II, James II (1685–1688) decided to confront Parliament, and when Parliament refused to provide him with the taxes that he sought, he persuaded judges to rule that he could collect the taxes himself. Judges also declared that "the laws of England are the King's laws," so that he could "dispense with penal laws in particular cases," and that the king was sovereign.[34] Wishing to convert England to Catholicism, James wanted to expand his dispensing power, by which he could waive the law in individual cases, into a suspending power, in which he could suspend the law itself. After a civil war that had supposedly ended the absolute power of kings, James had brought the country back to an assertion of virtually absolute power.

Nonetheless Protestant England thought that the Catholic James could be endured in order to preserve the principle of hereditary succession. Protestants were comforted that after James's death, his Protestant daughter, Mary, who was married to William of Orange of the Netherlands, would accede to the crown and England would again be in safe Protestant hands. But this prospect was upset when James's wife unexpectedly bore a son in 1687. Now the likely future was another Catholic king and the continued persecution of Protestants. At this prospect, William began to raise an army in order to invade England and claim the throne in the name of his wife, Mary, who was safely Protestant, and the heir apparent.

Concluding that another war was not desirable, seven MPs, both Whigs and Tories, signed an invitation for William to assume the throne. As William's troops were welcomed in London, James fled and escaped to France. Because James had abandoned his and his son's claims to the throne when he fled to France (with the aid of William's forces), Mary was next in succession to the throne. But William had raised the army to drive James out, and his demands to be crowned could not be ignored. So Parliament decided to grant the crown to both equally, and they would reign as "William and Mary." In making this decision, Parliament decided that James had abdicated and that his infant son, James Francis, was ineligible as an heir to the throne because he was Catholic.

The implication of these changes was that Parliament, not divine heredity, determined who would rule England. Parliament had, in effect, made itself the sovereign power by its decision to determine succession to the crown. In order to establish its power formally, Parliament insisted that William and Mary agree to the Declaration of Rights before they were crowned. After the coronation in 1689, Parliament passed the Declaration as the Bill of Rights. The Bill of Rights declared, among other things, that

—the monarch could not suspend the laws;

—no taxes could be collected without Parliament's consent;

—there could be no standing army without parliamentary consent;

—the monarch could not be Catholic;

—Parliament would be chosen by free election;

—Parliament would be called into session frequently.

When they accepted the crown, both William (1689–1702) and Mary (1689–1694) swore to govern "according to the statutes in parliament agreed on," and religious toleration (except for Catholics) was established throughout the realm.[35] Thus, through this bloodless "Glorious Revolution," England was finally rid of the claim of the divine right of kings and had become a constitutional monarchy. The power to suspend the law that William and Mary ceded in 1689 was asserted by George W. Bush in the twenty-first century when he refused to obey the FISA law and issued signing statements.

The Rise of Responsible Government

The Dutch William was not well liked as king, but his popular wife, Queen Mary, was seen as the native, English part of the crown. William formed a grand alliance to go to war against France, and though he did not lose, neither was he able to achieve victory. Mary died in 1694, and when William died in 1702, the crown passed to Mary's sister, Anne (1702–1714).

Parliament passed the Act of Union in 1707, formally joining Scotland and England as Great Britain. The agreement provided some independence for Scotland's legal system, education, and the Presbyterian Church along with Scottish representation in Parliament. Queen Anne led Britain to military victory over France, but her son, William, died in

1700. When she died in 1714, the succession had to be established again. The Act of Succession provided that the succession to the crown would go to the House of Hannover in Germany. Since no Catholic could be king, Parliament passed over more than fifty Catholic hereditary descendants of the royal bloodline in order to find a royal Protestant.[36]

Queen Anne was succeeded by George Ludwig of Hannover, who became George I of England (1714–1727). Though George became King of England, his interests remained in his native Hannover. He never learned English, and he spent as much time as he could in his former home. George's lack of the English language and his preoccupation with Hannover provided the opportunity for further parliamentary independence and the development of responsible government. The Whig Robert Walpole came to dominate Parliament and was also close to King George, thus becoming the first prime minister of England. Since King George spent so much time away at Hannover, Walpole was able to frame issues to suit his own purposes, and he became rich and powerful. When George died in 1727, his son, George II (1727–1760), became king, but this George was angry at Walpole for being loyal to his father, with whom George II often disagreed. Walpole was, nevertheless, able to retain his influence through George's wife, Caroline.

At the time of the accession of George I to the throne, Parliament had come to play a much more important role in English government than ever before. The Glorious Revolution of 1688 had come to full fruition, and Parliament now dominated national policy. The king reigned, but Parliament ruled.[37] The transformation of the status and power of Parliament from the Tudors to the Hanoverians can be summarized by contrasting the advisory role of Lord Burghley to Queen Elizabeth I with that of Sir Robert Walpole to George I. Burghley's power depended exclusively on the Queen's favor, while Walpole needed the support of Parliament as well as the king. The Queen's pardon could get Burghley out of trouble, but Walpole could not afford to lose parliamentary support.[38]

Walpole's influence depended upon the confidence of both king and Parliament; thus he had to have the support of a working majority of the House of Commons. Thus began the ministerial responsibility to both king and Parliament. Previous ministers answered to the crown, though their influence with Parliament was important. But by Walpole's time,

Parliament had acquired enough power that the king's ministers, and especially his prime minister, had to answer to both king and Parliament. Despite Walpole's power and influence with both king and Parliament, he narrowly won a vote in Parliament in 1742 and had to resign because the margin of his majority was too small to govern effectively. His loss of the confidence of Parliament determined his fate, and the decline in royal power was confirmed. By the time of Walpole's death, Parliament had succeeded in dominating public policy and was well on the way to full sovereignty and responsible government.

The next great parliamentary leader was William Pitt, who rose to power as an enemy of Walpole and as champion of building the navy and an overseas British empire. But George II loathed Pitt and thought that foreign policy was his personal, royal realm. During the war with France, George II, despite his hatred for Pitt, was forced to appoint him prime minister because of his vision and consummate executive skills. Thus Pitt rose in power in spite of, not because of, royal favor, and he was able to prevail despite the king's opposition. In one famous speech, Pitt declared that he had come to office "by his sovereign," but also "by the voice of the people." The public recognition that part of his power was based on popularity with the people marked a turning point in royal power. As George II complained, "Ministers are Kings in this Country."[39]

George II died in 1760, and his grandson George III (1760–1820) took over the crown. Unlike his two predecessors, he was thoroughly English and became known as the Patriot King. When Parliament decided to tax the American colonies to pay the war debts incurred fighting the French and driving them from North America, the colonists rebelled. They rebelled in the name of the British Whig principle that governments were established on the consent of the governed. The colonists had no representation in Parliament, and they were no longer willing to accept British rule. Parliament was determined to quash the nascent American rebellion, and it had the full support of George III, who declared that he fully supported Parliament. Going further than his predecessors, he declared, "I will at all times consult my ministers and place in them as entire a confidence as the nature of this government can be supposed to require of me."[40]

It would be another century before Parliament became fully sovereign, with ministers responsible to Parliament alone, with no reference to the will of the king. Ministerial responsibility exclusively to Parliament was fully achieved in 1841, when Sir Robert Peel "formed a government that did not possess the confidence of the Queen."[41] Responsible government means that ministers, that is, executive officials, are fully responsible and accountable to Parliament rather than to the king.

George III became the symbol of the tyranny under which the colonists felt they suffered. The Declaration of Independence asserted that "The History of the present King of Great-Britain is a History of repeated Injuries and Usurpations, all having in direct Object the Establishment of an absolute Tyranny over these States." Since the Americans saw George III as a tyrant, they affirmed their distrust of executive power in the composition of their first government. They designed their first government, the Articles of Confederation, without a separate executive. They also reflected Whig principles and John Locke's thinking when they declared that governments are created to preserve the rights of the governed and that governments derived "their just Powers from the Consent of the Governed."

Conclusion

When the Americans established their constitution in 1789, they reasserted many of the rights of Englishmen that had been wrested from kings of England centuries ago. When he denied the right of habeas corpus and due process to those who were declared "enemy combatants," President Bush was asserting a monarchical prerogative that Magna Carta (1215), the Petition of Right (1628), the Habeas Corpus Act (1679), and the common law had taken away from English kings over the centuries. His denial of habeas corpus and oversight by Congress or by the courts placed him above the law and beyond the constraints of the Constitution. By establishing military commissions outside of the law providing for them (the Uniform Code of Military Justice), President Bush was, in effect, declaring martial law by suspending the due process requirements for trial and refusing to allow U.S. courts to oversee the process. Given the lack of due process that some of the Combatant Status Review Tribunals exhibited (see chapter 5), they might have seemed to resemble the Court of Star Chamber before Charles I was forced to abolish it in 1640.

The right of the people to be represented by Parliament and the authority of the laws passed by Parliament to bind the king came only after centuries of often bloody struggle. The framers of the Constitution went even further than the English had in providing for a legislature with significant political power. They rejected the British unity of power in both Parliament and king and created a separation of powers system that made the legislature independent from the executive and able to limit presidential power through law. Article I gives Congress "All legislative Powers," and Article II of the Constitution provides that the president "shall take Care that the Laws be faithfully executed."

During his two terms in office, President Bush challenged fundamentally the principle that the president could be bound by laws passed by Congress. He ignored the Foreign Intelligence Surveillance Act that required the executive branch to obtain a warrant before spying on people in the United States (covered in chapter 7). And when his secret program was exposed, he claimed that he was not bound by the law because he said that it impinged on his authority as commander in chief. In his frequent use of signing statements, he intimated that he would not execute those provisions of law that he thought were inconsistent with his executive power. These claims by the president fundamentally challenged the authority of Article I and the Constitutional legislative process. Although he went to Congress for laws on habeas corpus, torture, and surveillance when he was forced to politically, he did not admit that he could be bound by laws he deemed to conflict with his own constitutional powers. His use of signing statements threatened the very basis of the rule of law and the role of Congress in the constitutional system.

The next chapter will examine how the British principles of individual rights and legislative authority were translated by the framers into the U.S. Constitution. The rest of the book will explain how George W. Bush presented a fundamental challenge to this constitutional framework.

CHAPTER FOUR

THE AMERICAN CONSTITUTION

"A republic, if you can keep it."
> —Benjamin Franklin, on being asked whether the Constitutional Convention had created a republic or a monarchy

"Cato correctly concluded that in the realm of practical politics, the president's authority under the Constitution did not differ in important measure from that of the king."
> —John Yoo

When designing the U.S. Constitution, the framers adopted many of the limits on governmental and executive power that had been achieved in England over the preceding several centuries. The centuries of British struggles to limit the power of the monarchy with respect to individual rights and to establish the legitimate authority of Parliament were well known to the designers of the U.S. Constitution. The path to these achievements made by the British government by the eighteenth century was neither smooth nor direct. However, important progress along this path was made, and the principles that limited executive power were firmly established in England, even if practice did not always conform to theory. It was these principles—of individual rights and parliamentary prerogatives—that George W. Bush challenged in the twenty-first century.

The framers adopted significant limits on government and executive power by establishing the Bill of Rights and a separation of powers system. Despite their distrust of governmental chief executives, the framers of the Constitution designed an independent executive to balance legislative power, and they established for the first time an independent judiciary. This separation of powers system was intended to prevent the domination of the national government by any one faction or branch of government.

Of course legislative dominance is no formula for wise governance. Parliaments often acted arbitrarily, and the dominance of Parliament won during the English Civil War ended up with Cromwell's dictatorship of the Protectorate. Later the American Colonial assemblies and the state legislatures under the Articles of Confederation often abused their power when they came to dominate the American states. Nevertheless the framers, in creating a republic, gave Congress primary control of public policy.

The following analysis is intended to illuminate the importance of a legislative check on executive power. Although the architects of the Constitution expected that the legislature of the new republic would dominate governmental policymaking, during the twentieth century, with few exceptions, presidents have come to dominate the government, particularly in national security policy. This domination reached a peak under the presidency of George W. Bush, which will be examined in the subsequent chapters of this book. My intention is to explore the extraordinary claims to executive power that President Bush made in several areas of national security policy and to argue that the delicate balance, created by the framers and maintained throughout most of U.S. history, was threatened by President Bush's claims to extraordinary constitutional authority. If left to stand, these precedents may very well undermine the republican nature of American government. Madison's statement in *Federalist* No. 51, "In republican government, the legislative authority necessarily predominates," has been reversed.

Ideas of the Framers about Power and Government

Under the United States Constitution, the sovereign power, in principle, is vested not in a king or Parliament, president or Congress, but in the people. As Gouverneur Morris said: "This [U.S.] Magistrate is not the King, but the prime-minister. The people are the King."[1] For practical purposes the people act through the government, and the exercise of sovereignty in the U.S. government resides in all three branches, not exclusively in one of them.

Although the engineers of the Constitution drew heavily on the establishment of individual rights in England, when they turned to the structure of their new government, they firmly rejected the English model. First, they intended to design a republic—not a monarchy or even a constitutional monarchy. The U.S. government would be responsible to the people, not to a monarch. In rejecting the British governmental structure of their time, the framers intended to create a republic, which meant that, in the words of the Declaration of Independence, the government would derive its "just Powers from the Consent of the Governed."[2]

The framers' ideas about human nature and government were derived from an array of sources. In political philosophy they admired Locke, Montesquieu, and the legal scholar William Blackstone. They were also students of history, from the Bible to the classical experience of Greece and Rome, to the more contemporary history of Europe and especially of England. From their experience and study of history, they learned the dangers of executive power; from Greece they learned of the advantages and dangers of democracy; and from Rome they were cautioned about decadence and the decline of the Republic. In English history they hearkened to the myth of pre-Norman, Anglo-Saxon liberties, and in a sense, they saw themselves as striving to restore those ancient liberties.[3]

They were most aware of and familiar with the development of English government over the previous century. They remembered the often bloody struggles between the monarchy and Parliament over the limits to executive power that peaked during the English Civil War and culminated in the Glorious Revolution of 1688. One important lesson they took away from that era was that monarchs tended to accumulate power and often abused it.

Many of the colonists who left England for the new world of America had chafed under the power of the crown and particularly wanted freedom to pursue their own religious convictions (and often to exclude those who did not accept their doctrines). They were individualistic and predisposed to be suspicious of governmental power. Their experience as colonists under royal governors reinforced their distrust of executive power. Yet their experience under the Articles of Confederation convinced them that an executive with some independence from the legislature was necessary for efficient and effective government.

THE COLONIAL EXPERIENCE

The royal governors and their councils, appointed by the king of England as well as the chartered colonies, began with almost complete governmental authority, including judicial and legislative functions. But over the decades, as the local assemblies gradually gained power, they began to take some of that governmental power away from the royal governors, gradually acquiring legislative and judicial powers.[4]

The range of the powers of royal governors included an absolute veto over measures of the locally elected assemblies, the authority to appoint and dismiss judges and other officers of the government, the authority to grant pardons, and the ability to convene, dismiss, or dissolve the legislative bodies entirely. The main, effective powers that the assemblies exercised—similar to the powers of Parliament in previous centuries—were those concerning revenue, taxation, and appropriation of funds. Like the parliaments of England over the previous several centuries, the power of the purse constituted a significant, though not always efficacious, tool for the assertion of power independent of the crown. Royal governors had to depend on their assemblies for funds because Parliament did not subsidize the governors from the royal treasury; it granted them authority, but the governors were required to raise their own funds from their colonies. Thus by skillful exercise of their control of the purse, over the years, assemblies gained increasing control over the royal governors.[5]

Technically, the legitimacy of the governments of the colonies depended upon royal grants or charters. But the colonists began to see their elected assemblies and control of taxes as part of their own rights as Englishmen and not dependent on the acquiescence of the king, Parliament, or the royal governors. By 1748 the colonial legislatures had gained control over most of the governmental powers formerly exercised exclusively by the royal governors. They came to see the edicts of Parliament, such as the Stamp Act (1765) and the Townsend Duties (1767), as acts of oppression from a Parliament across the ocean in which they had no representation. Up until the Revolutionary War, the colonists saw Parliament as their oppressor and themselves as loyal subjects of King George III. When they chafed under British control, they appealed to the king to right the wrongs perpetrated on the colonies by Parliament. When King George personally denounced the American rebels and ordered military action (including the use of German mercenaries) against the colonies, the colonists turned their wrath toward the king also.[6]

Thus the Declaration of Independence stated, "The History of the present King of Great-Britain is a History of repeated Injuries and Usurpations, all having in direct Object the Establishment of an absolute Tyranny over these States." The writings of Thomas Paine, especially *Common Sense,* articulated the colonists' distrust of monarchy. The asserted violation of their rights by the monarchy and their revolutionary experience implanted in the colonists a profound distrust of executive power. Their subsequent experience as citizens of the United States under the Articles of Confederation, however, would extend some of that suspicion of governmental power to the legislative branch and temper their opposition to executive power in general.

Experience under the Articles of Confederation

The newly independent states established the Articles of Confederation to govern themselves. The Revolutionary War created a Continental Congress of thirty representatives but no separate executive. The members of the Congress were appointed by state governments, not elected by citizens, and executive powers were exercised by committees of the Congress. The state governments also were designed to minimize executive power. Most states chose their governors by legislative election and limited their executives to one-year terms; most governors did not have a veto, and Pennsylvania did not even have a chief executive.[7] Thus the states were hampered in the public administration of government by the lack of effective and competent executive power. This experience had important consequences for those who created the Constitution in 1787.

In addition to the lack of effective execution of state governmental power, the states suffered from the excesses and abuses of their legislatures. State legislatures often acted arbitrarily, issued paper money at inflated values, and allowed debtors to settle their debts at reduced rates. There were also riots and mob actions, such as Shays's Rebellion, that the states had trouble suppressing. The prospect of uprisings, mob rule, abolition of debts, and the distribution of property effectively focused the minds of the upper-class framers of the Constitution.[8]

In addition to the problems of the state governments, the central government did not possess sufficient power to govern the country. The powers of the Continental Congress were restricted to those that were clearly national, including the authority to conduct war, make foreign policy, negotiate treaties, create a postal service, and regulate money. But the ability actually to exercise these powers was hampered by their lack of clear authority over the states.

The power to regulate money was limited by the central government's inability to impose taxes on the states; it could merely assess charges against the states and could not force payment. The debt from the Revolutionary War still hung over the new government, and the economy was doing poorly. However, the states often refused to recognize each other's currency and imposed tariffs on goods coming into one state from the others. The central government did not have the authority or power to solve these serious problems. The authority to make foreign policy was put in jeopardy when Great Britain threatened to negotiate the end of the Revolutionary War with individual states, independently, rather than through the central government. Contributing to these difficulties was the lack of an independent executive that could take vigorous action to address any of the problems.

The legislatures of the states, which had gradually encroached upon the powers of the royal governors during the colonial period, continued their assertions of power, particularly over control of spending. Appointments to state governmental offices were made by the legislatures.[9] Legislatures also sought to exercise judicial powers, in part because of the misuse of the judiciary by the royal governors, who had the authority to appoint and remove judges. But governors often did not exercise the appointment power responsibly, and the legislatures intervened in individual cases and at times reduced the salaries of judges who were not responsive to them.[10] These legislative actions helped convince the framers to create an independent judiciary in the Constitution.[11]

The distrust of executive power that the framers acquired from political philosophy, their study of history, and their colonial experience under royal governors was balanced by the disappointing experience with the state legislatures after the Revolution. Thomas Jefferson remarked of the Virginia legislature, "All the powers of government, legislative[,] executive and judiciary, result to the legislative body."[12]

Madison argued in *Federalist* No. 48 (and during the Convention) that "the legislative department is everywhere extending the sphere of its activity and drawing all powers into its impetuous vortex. . . . Executive powers had been usurped." The exception to the relegation of executives to legislative control was the state of New York, which had a strong and independent executive elected by citizens, not appointed by the legislature. New York was to provide the model for some of the characteristics of the new government and its executive.

When they met in Philadelphia in 1787, some of the framers were convinced that to create an effective government, it must have a stronger and more independent executive. The majority of delegates, however, still held a strong distrust of executive power that would only be mitigated by deliberation during the summer of 1787.

Creation of the Presidency

The British Constitution was based on the idea of a balance or mixed structure of government in which the three key components represented different strata in society; the monarch for the royalty, the House of Lords for the aristocracy, and the House of Commons for the general population. The colonies, though their individual governmental structures differed, were closer to the mixed structures than to a pure separation of powers system.[13] The U.S. Constitution transformed this balance of powers among different elements of society embodied in the British government by separating the functions of government and assigning them to separate bodies: legislative, executive, and judicial—thus transforming the idea of a government balanced with respect to social class to one separated into different functions.[14]

SEPARATION OF POWERS

A strong consensus in favor of separation of power grew in the states between the American Revolution and the Constitutional Convention. And when the framers met, they were aware of Montesquieu's dictum that "When the legislative and executive powers are united in the same person, or in the same body of magistrates, there can be no liberty. . . . Again, there is no liberty, if the judiciary power be not separated from the legislative and executive."[15] They were also familiar with and quoted

William Blackstone, the respected jurist and interpreter of the laws of England. Blackstone was an advocate for separating governmental powers. "The total union of them [executive and legislative], we have seen, would be productive of tyranny. . . . And herein indeed consists the true excellence of the English government, that all of the parts of it form a mutual check upon each other."[16] The framers, however, rejected the British model and created a government with much greater separation than the British government at that time.

Despite the reality of legislative supremacy in the states, many of the designers of state governments believed strongly in separating the powers of government. One of the clearest statements of the separation of powers doctrine was contained in the Constitution of Virginia: "The legislative, executive and judiciary departments shall be separate and distinct, so that neither exercise [sic] the powers properly belonging to the other: nor shall any person exercise the powers of more than one of them at the same time."[17] The Maryland Declaration of Rights of 1776 stated: "The legislative, executive and judicial powers of government, ought to be forever separate and distinct from each other."[18]

The framers of the Constitution, based on their experience with colonial status and the Continental Congress, assumed implicitly that the creation of their government would be based on the principle of separation of powers. Even though their deliberations in 1787 were suffused with debates over how to separate powers, the principle of separation of powers per se was explicitly addressed by the convention only once. On the second day of the convention, a resolution was passed that stated: "that a national government ought to be established consisting of a supreme Legislative, Judiciary, and Executive."[19]

The men at the Constitutional Convention needed to create a government with sufficient power to govern—for example, to raise revenues, maintain an army, control foreign trade, establish internal control, and encourage a dynamic economy. But in order to convince the delegates from the different states to approve a governmental design, they had to construct a government that did not threaten state sovereignty and that gave the member states sufficient representation. In addition, the delegates who were convinced that an independent executive was essential to an effective government had to convince the others that an independent executive would not degenerate into a tyranny. They accomplished this goal, after great deliberation, by creating a government of separated powers.

The difference of interests between the small states and the large states, however, had to be resolved first, and the Connecticut Compromise, proposing different sources for the members of the two houses of Congress, was the crucial agreement that allowed the framers to design the rest of their government. With the abuses of executive power by King George and his royal governors fresh in their minds, the first governmental design adopted was the Virginia Plan, in which the legislature would be dominant. The Virginia Plan's provision for choosing an executive called for election by the legislature. This provision for selecting the executive, which was approved by vote in the first week, was the presumed method of selecting the executive until September, when the selection of the executive was finally taken up again.

The level of power of a chief executive would depend on several factors, including: the number (single or plural), how chosen (by the legislature or popular election), length of term, eligibility for reelection, and of course the formal powers granted to the office by the Constitution. At the beginning of the convention, Benjamin Franklin and Edmund Randolph favored a plural executive in order to limit its power. But on June 1, James Wilson of Pennsylvania proposed that "a single person" would provide the "most energy, dispatch, and responsibility to the office."[20] The first reaction of the convention to his proposal was not enthusiasm but a "considerable pause." George Mason objected because "If strong and extensive powers are vested in the Executive, and that Executive consists only of one person; the Government will of course degenerate ... into a Monarchy."[21] Edmund Randolph of Virginia saw Wilson's plan as "the Foetus of Monarchy."[22] Nevertheless on June 4, the proposal for a single executive was approved by a vote of 7 to 3.[23]

For most of the convention, the assumption was that the chief executive would be chosen by the legislature, as Madison had proposed in the Virginia Plan. The planners who favored an independent executive argued that an executive chosen by the legislature would be completely dependent on it and controlled by the intrigues of legislative politics. Alexander Hamilton was initially an advocate of a monarchical type of president, elected for life, with an absolute veto, who would be commander in chief of the armed forces, and the sole appointer of heads of the Departments of Finance, War, and Foreign Affairs.[24] He would be referred to as "his Excellency." Later in the summer, Hamilton changed his mind in agreement with the other delegates, and in his analysis of the power of the executive in *Federalist* No. 68, he distinguished the powers of the president from the powers of the king of England: "And it appears yet more unequivocally that there is no pretense for the parallel which has been attempted between him [the president] and the king of Great Britain." Hamilton, however, did believe in a strong and independent president, and in *Federalist* No. 70 he declared that "energy in the executive is a leading character in the definition of good government."

When the convention adjourned on July 25, 1787, the chief executive was to be chosen by the legislature, but the term of office was not set nor was the question of eligibility for reelection settled. The Committee of Detail reported on August 6 this formula:

> The Executive Power of the United States shall be vested in a single Person. His Stile shall be, "The President of the United States of America;" and his Title shall be, "His Excellency." He shall be elected by ballot by the Legislature. He shall hold his Office during the term of seven Years; but shall not be elected a second time.[25]

But there were objections that a president chosen by the legislature would be too indebted to it and thus not sufficiently independent. For this reason both James Wilson and Gouverneur Morris argued for election by the people.[26]

On August 24 the convention returned to the puzzle of executive power and retained the method for choosing the president by both houses of Congress and disapproved of a motion to choose the president by electors who were chosen by the people.[27] It also approved of a seven-year term without eligibility for reelection. After further deliberation the final provisions for the executive power were agreed to on September 6. Executive powers would be exercised by a president who would be commander in chief of the armed forces and faithfully execute the laws. He would be chosen by electors selected in accord with provisions of state legislatures and would eligible for reelection.

The deliberations about the office of the presidency were facilitated by the assumption on the part of all that the universally acclaimed George Washington would be elected as the first president of the Republic. The

framers were thus willing to give the office of the presidency more independence and power than they might have, had they not been confident
that Washington would be its first occupant.

The authority of Congress was spelled out in detail in Article I, but
only a brief statement of the authority of the president was provided in
Article II. It was, however, the third branch, the judiciary, that was a
unique contribution of the framers to the political theory and governmental reality of the separation of powers doctrine. While Montesquieu
suggested that the independence of the judiciary from the other two
branches is necessary for the evenhanded administration of justice, it was
the architects of the Constitution who first made the judiciary a fully separate and independent branch of government, with its members protected through lifetime appointments.

This innovation in the structure of government created a true separation of powers system. It was not, however, a system of completely separated powers, but rather a system of shared powers, with each branch
having the ability to check the others.[28] As Madison made clear, each
branch was given some means by which to affect the others. In making
this argument in *Federalist* No. 47, he made use of the analysis by "the
oracle who is always cited and consulted on this subject . . . the cele-
brated Montesquieu." Montesquieu made the point that if the separate
governmental powers are united in the same person, tyranny would
result. But as Madison argued, "he did not mean that these departments
ought to have no *partial agency* in, or no *control* over, the acts of each
other" (italics in original). Madison further illustrated how the constitutions of the thirteen states often mixed the separate powers and concluded that the sharing of powers in the new Constitution did not undermine the separation of powers principle that the same persons should not
possess the full powers of more than one branch.

Thus Madison in *Federalist* No. 47 refuted the future assertions by
the Bush administration that the president has exclusive control of the
"unitary executive" (to be discussed further in chapter 8). The president
can propose legislation, possesses a limited veto, and can appoint
judges. The judiciary can interpret the law, pronounce on the constitutionality of laws, and compel the executive to take certain actions. The
Congress provides appropriations for the other two branches, can affect
the jurisdiction of the courts, and can "make laws necessary and

proper" for carrying out the constitutional powers of the other two branches. Article I, Section 8, of the Constitution spells out the ways in which the war powers are divided between Congress and the president.

THE BILL OF RIGHTS

After the framers had drafted the Constitution, it had to be ratified in the states, and there was some important opposition to the Constitution as it stood. The primary concern of the anti-Federalists was that the central government would have too much power, but another and related objection was that it contained no bill of rights. The framers were familiar with the English Bill of Rights passed by Parliament in 1689, which specified a large number of constraints on the monarchy, prerogatives of Parliament, and rights of individuals. The Federalists, who were in favor of the new Constitution, argued that specifying particular rights would imply that any right that was not specified would be presumed not to exist. The anti-Federalists, however, were dubious about the power that the new, central government would have and insisted that individual rights be spelled out. Enough people held this view to force the drafters to promise that a bill of rights would be appended to the Constitution in the form of several amendments.[29] Several of the conventions in the states ratified the Constitution with recommendations that a bill of rights be passed by the first Congress.

Sentiment in favor of a bill of rights rested on a long history of the rights of Englishmen in common law and statute. Magna Carta of 1215, the Petition of Right of 1628, and the Bill of Rights of 1689 all specified individual rights that were echoed in the Fourth, Fifth, and Sixth Amendments. The provisions of those amendments included prohibitions against unreasonable searches and seizures, searches without warrants specifying probable cause, double jeopardy, and self-incrimination. The government was prohibited from taking life, liberty, or property without due process of law and also prohibited from imposing cruel and unusual punishments. Individuals accused of crimes were assured the right to a speedy and public trial, to be informed of charges against them, to examine evidence against them, to confront witnesses, and to be represented by counsel.

For purposes of this book, the rights that have been put in jeopardy by President Bush will be examined in more detail in subsequent chapters. Chapter 5 will examine the denial of the right to a writ of habeas corpus to detainees during the war on terror, insofar as it denies due process of law for prisoners. Chapter 6 will examine President Bush's claim to constitutional authority to deny even minimum due process to suspects in the war on terror, such as the right of accused individuals to be informed of the charges against them, to be able to confront witnesses against them, and the right to counsel (even though some of these rights were later granted to suspects). Chapter 7 will examine President Bush's claim to the constitutional authority to search the communications of people in the United States without a warrant, in violation of the law. The argument of these chapters and this book as a whole is that these actions by President Bush not only violate the rights of the individuals involved, but in his claim to constitutional authority to do so, he also threatens the future of these fundamental rights. If his actions are not challenged by Congress and the Supreme Court, all future presidents will have the implicit claim to the same authority that President Bush assumed. These arrogations of authority by the executive pose a threat to constitutionalism and the rule of law.

The Commander-in-Chief Authority

The framers thought the Articles of Confederation provided insufficient power to the national government, which had been the primary reason for their creation of a new government. They also agreed that the new government should have an independent executive rather than the executive by committee that existed under the Articles. But in creating an independent executive, they did not intend to give that office the authority to take the nation to war. From their reading of history and their assumptions about human nature, they concluded that executives were most likely to benefit from war, and thus they firmly lodged many aspects of the national security and war authority in Congress, leaving to the executive alone the commander-in-chief authority, to be exercised only to repel sudden attacks or pursuant to congressional authorization.

THE FRAMERS' DISTRUST OF EXECUTIVE POWER

Although the framers of the Constitution were optimistic about their ability to form a new government based on rationalism and individual freedom—principles of the Enlightenment—they were also realists and suspicious of human motives. They knew their history well enough to realize that people were self-serving, and they had witnessed aggrandizement and abuse of power by governmental leaders. So their design for the new government was tempered by their skepticism about human nature. In a letter to Thomas Jefferson in 1788 James Madison said, "Wherever the real power in a government lies, there is the danger of oppression. . . . Wherever there is an interest and a power to do wrong, wrong will generally be done. . . . There is a tendency in *all* governments to an augmentation of power at the expense of liberty . . ."[30] (emphasis in original). The year before the Constitutional Convention, Washington remarked on human failings: "We have, probably, had too good an opinion of human nature in forming our confederation."[31] As Benjamin Franklin told the Convention: "There are two passions which have a powerful influence on the affairs of men. These are ambition and avarice; the love of power and the love of money."[32]

Thus the framers set out to design a government that would take into account the negative side of human nature by trying to ensure that power would not be concentrated in one person or department, particularly the war powers. Hamilton said in *Federalist* No. 75: "The history of human conduct does not warrant that exalted opinion of human virtue which would make it wise in a nation to commit interests of so delicate and momentous a kind, as those which concern its intercourse with the rest of the world, to the sole disposal of a magistrate created and circumstanced as would be a president of the United States." In a letter to Jefferson, Madison observed: "The constitution supposes, what the History of all Govts demonstrates, that the Ex. is the branch of power most interested in war, & most prone to it. It has accordingly with studied care, vested the question of war in the Legisl."[33] During the Convention, George Mason stated that he was "agst giving the power of war to the Executive, because not [safely] to be trusted with it. . . . He was for clogging rather than facilitating war."[34]

THE BRITISH ALLOCATION OF THE WAR POWERS

The practical exigencies of government often give executives wide latitude, particularly with respect to national defense. But admitting that an executive is usually better suited to conduct a war does not entail agreeing that the framers placed the decision to go to war, or to control all of its incidents, in the executive.[35] Nor does the executive's superior ability to conduct a war imply that the decision of whether to go to war ought to be entrusted to the executive. The architects of the American Constitution decided to separate the decision of going to war from the conduct of war. They explicitly rejected the British model of royal power and created a republic in which the legislature shared important aspects of the war powers, including the decision of whether to commence war (aside from emergencies and repelling sudden attacks). Despite the historical reality that presidents have often dominated national security policy, repeated violation of the provisions of the Constitution do not make them constitutional.

For most of British history, the crown had the authority to take the nation to war, although the king's ability to do so was sometimes circumscribed by Parliament's authority to approve tax collections to support wars. After the Glorious Revolution, Parliament gradually gained control of all governmental powers and, in effect, now exercises sovereignty. But the war power, even in contemporary times, continues to reside constitutionally in the executive arm of the government, which is now a prime minister rather than a king. In examining the role that Parliament should play in going to war, the House of Lords recently explained: "Under the Royal prerogative powers, the Government [prime minister and cabinet] can declare war and deploy armed forces to conflicts abroad without the backing or consent of Parliament." The prime minister also has the authority to conduct the war once it has begun. "It is commonly accepted [that is, part of the British Constitution] that the prerogative's deployment power is actually vested in the Prime Minister, who has personal discretion in its exercise and is not statutorily bound to consult others, although it is inconceivable that he would not do so in practice." [36] The British model, ancient and contemporary, was rejected by the framers of the U.S. Constitution.

When the framers were designing the Constitution, they often referred to William Blackstone, whom they quoted approvingly on individual rights, such as habeas corpus, but whose prescriptions for war powers they rejected. Blackstone clearly considered the full range of war powers to be the prerogative of the king alone. In rejecting the British monarchical model and creating a republic, the framers explicitly lodged important parts of the war powers in the legislature. Whereas Blackstone placed the power of war and peace with the king, the framers gave the president only the authority of commander in chief.

Blackstone asserts that in the British constitution, "the king has also the sole prerogative of making war and peace"; the king possessed this authority because sovereignty was embodied in the monarch. "In England the sovereign power . . . is vested in the person of the king," and "the right of making war . . . is vested in the sovereign power."[37] In contrast, in the United States, sovereignty is lodged in the national government (and ultimately in the people) and shared among the three branches.

Blackstone attributes to the king, in addition to the authority to take the nation to war, other war powers that were given by the framers to Congress. In England the king could direct "ministers of the crown to issue letters of marque and reprisal upon due demand; the prerogative of granting which is nearly related to, and plainly derived from, that other of making war."[38] In contrast, the U.S. Constitution gives to Congress the authority to "grant Letters of Marque and reprisal." The king, according to Blackstone, was the "generalissimo" of the military: "In this capacity, therefore, of general of the kingdom, the king has the sole power of raising and regulating fleets and armies."[39] Although the Constitution makes the president commander in chief, the framers gave Congress the authority to "raise and support Armies" and to "provide and maintain a Navy." In addition they gave to Congress the British executive power to "make Rules for the Government and Regulation of the land and naval forces." In these important areas of British executive powers, the designers of the Constitution explicitly decided that Congress would share the war powers.

John Yoo, who wrote some of the Bush administration's most important documents claiming plenary power in national security matters for the president, quotes Blackstone approvingly and argues that the framers intended to follow the British monarchical model of giving to the executive all war powers. "Given their conclusion that Parliament and Congress controlled the 'sinews of war,' and that the King and the President directed the military, they had every reason to believe that the new Constitution would produce a war-making system similar to Britain's."[40] With respect to the war powers, Yoo agrees with the characterization of presidential power asserted by the anti-Federalists: "Cato correctly concluded that in the realm of practical politics, the president's authority under the Constitution did not differ in important measure from that of the king."[41] In Yoo's interpretation, the framers intended to give the president monarchical authority with respect to the war power. His arguments, however, are undercut by the words of Hamilton in *Federalist No. 69*, in which he argues against the anti-Federalists: "There is no pretense for the parallel which has been attempted between him [the president] and the king of Great Britain."

The Bush administration made much of the authority of the president as commander in chief, and some of the most sweeping assertions of presidential prerogative are based primarily on the commander-in-chief clause of Article II. For instance, a memorandum drafted by John Yoo and signed by Jay Bybee asserts that the president's authority as commander in chief can supersede any law. "The President enjoys complete discretion in the exercise of his Commander-in-Chief authority and in conducting operations against hostile forces."[42] But in the eyes of the framers, the presidential role as commander in chief of the army and navy did not convey authority other than the direction of the armed forces and only when authorized to do so or in repelling sudden attacks. The term *commander in chief* had been used by the British since the seventeenth century to denote the top military commander in a theater of battle and did not imply sweeping authority over all war powers. Most important, the term implied that the military authority was subordinate to civil authorities. The Duke of Wellington declared, "The commander in chief cannot move a Corporal's Guard from one station to another, without a route countersigned by the Secretary of War. This is the fundamental principle of the Constitution of the British Army."[43] Thus the British did not consider the office of commander in chief to include fundamental decisions about whether or not to go to war.

When the Continental Congress appointed George Washington commander in chief in 1775, he was ordered by that civil authority "punctually to observe and follow such orders and directions, from time to time, as you shall receive from this, or a future Congress of the United Colonies or Committee of Congress."[44] As David Adler argues in his history of the commander-in-chief title, the use of the term by the framers was to ensure that civil authority was superior to military authority and to ensure unity of command. The fact that they debated, sometimes heatedly, the powers of the president in general and the war powers in particular, but not the title of commander in chief, indicates that they did not attach to the title the sweeping scope claimed for it by the Bush administration.[45]

THE FRAMERS REJECT THE BRITISH MODEL

In John Yoo's analysis, the framers intended that presidential authority in national security issues would closely parallel that of the king of England. He argues that in eighteenth-century England the king had plenary authority over Locke's federative or national security powers, and he quotes Blackstone and others to that effect. The only control over war and peace left to Parliament was its power to authorize taxes and impeach ministers of the crown. "Naturally, then, when the Framers allocated war powers between the President and Congress, they used as their baseline the separation of powers they believed to exist between King and Parliament."[46]

Yoo is correct with respect to the war powers of the king of England. But he then goes on to argue that since the framers were very familiar with the constitutional authority of the king, they intended for the president of the United States to possess similar powers and that the only authority with respect to war left to Congress were the power of the purse and impeachment: "Thus, while the revolution may have represented a rebellion against the presence of the Crown, it was not an assault on the relationship between executive and legislative powers in war."[47] The framers "had every reason to believe that the new Constitution would produce a war making system similar to Britain's."[48] This book, to the contrary, argues that the framers explicitly rejected the British allocation of most war powers to the king and consciously placed many war powers with Congress.

Yoo argues that in giving Congress the authority to "declare" war, the framers were referring merely to the authority to give a particular war official legal status and that they intended to give the president the authority to decide when to go to war. "Thus, a declaration of war served the purpose of notifying the enemy, allies, neutrals, and one's own citizens of a change in the state of relations between one nation and another. In none of these [British] situations did a declaration of war serve as a vehicle for domestically deciding on or authorizing a war."[49] He then presents from British history examples of declarations of war not closely connected with the commencement of war.

Yoo is correct that formal declarations of war in Britain did serve the notification and legal functions he mentions, but when the framers deliberated over the war powers, they had in mind the decision to commence war in addition to the other legal functions that a declaration of war would serve. Alexander Hamilton in 1801 expressed the framers' meaning of the word "declare" in the Constitution: "The Congress shall have power to declare war, the Plain meaning of which is, that it is in the peculiar and exclusive province of Congress, *when the nation is at peace* to change that state into a state of war" (emphasis in original).[50] Hamilton also drew a distinction in *Federalist* No. 69: "The President is to be commander-in-chief of the army and navy of the United States. In this respect his authority would be nominally the same with that of the king of Great Britain, but in substance much inferior to it."

John Yoo's understanding of the meaning of the "declare war" phrase in Article I of the Constitution is further undermined by Madison's explanation for the reason that the framers separated the authority to declare war from the commander-in-chief power. The framers feared that executives might abuse their power and engage in war for their own self-interest, so they did not place the war powers in one branch alone. James Madison in 1793 wrote, "Those who are to *conduct a war* cannot in the nature of things, be proper or safe judges, whether a war ought to be *commenced, continued, or concluded.* They are barred from the latter functions by a great principle in free government, analogous to that which separates the sword from the purse, or the power of executing from the power of enacting laws" (emphasis in original).[51]

Although the failings of humans to act in enlightened ways had relatively minor consequences at the individual level, the framers argued that when an individual held executive power, the temptation to abuse executive authority was significant. John Jay expressed the framers' suspicions of executives in *Federalist* No. 4: "Absolute monarchs will often make war when their nations are to get nothing by it, but for purposes and objects merely personal, such as a thirst for military glory, revenge for personal affronts, ambition, or private compacts to aggrandize or support their particular families or partisans. These and a variety of other motives, which affect only the mind of the sovereign, often lead him to engage in wars not sanctified by justice or the voice and interests of his people." Madison argued that military glory is the true nurse of executive aggrandizement. . . . In war, the honours and emoluments of office are to be multiplied; and it is the executive patronage under which they are to be enjoyed. It is in war, finally, that laurels are to be gathered; and it is the executive brow they are to encircle. The strongest passions and most dangerous weaknesses of the human breast; ambition, avarice, vanity, the honourable or venal love of fame, are all in conspiracy against the desire and duty of peace.[52]

Such arguments are as applicable in the twenty-first century as they were in the eighteenth.

Yoo leaves for Congress merely the powers of the purse and impeachment if it wants to affect national security policy. By declaring that the contemporary Congress can act only with the extreme measures of cutting off funding for a war or by impeaching the president, Yoo presents a scenario that, for practical purposes, is not likely to occur. Thus Yoo can pretend to honor legislative authority in national security matters while at the same time realizing that Congress can seldom gather the consensus to cut off funding for a war or impeach a president over national security matters.

Those who argue that the president possesses virtually all of the war authority granted in the Constitution also often make a functional argument. That is, they argue that the executive, because of its unity of command, ability to keep secrets, and its more complete information, is better suited to make decisions about war than a bicameral Congress of more than 500 individuals. However valid that argument might be, it is beside the constitutional point. In establishing the legitimate constitutional authority of the president, we must rely on the Constitution itself supplemented with the intentions of the framers, not an abstract argument about the functional difference between executives and legislatures.

Yoo's arguments that the framers intended to give the war powers to the executive stretch the text of the Constitution and the deliberations of the framers beyond reasonable interpretation.

Congress and National Security Authority

The framers brought their doubts about the motives of executives with them to the Constitutional Convention. In an early version of the Virginia

Plan, just before the beginning of the Convention in 1787, Madison had suggested that the executive should have the rights possessed by the Continental Congress under the Articles of Confederation. James Wilson objected, however, saying that he "did not consider the Prerogatives of a British Monarch as a proper guide in defining the Executive powers. Some of these prerogatives were of a Legislative nature. Among others that of war & peace &c."[53] Since Wilson was one of the strongest advocates for a strong executive, his judgment that war and peace were legislative in nature is an important indicator of the intent of the framers. After Wilson's statement, Madison changed his mind and agreed with him, saying that "executive powers *ex vi termini* [by the force of the term, that is, by definition], do not include the Rights of war & peace &c."[54]

Even Hamilton, the most forceful advocate for a strong executive and an admirer of the British system of government, proposed in his plan for the executive that the commander in chief merely "have the direction of war, when authorized or begun." In Hamilton's earlier plan, the Senate would "have the sole power of declaring war."[55] In *Federalist* No. 69, Hamilton distinguished presidential powers from those of the English monarch. Commenting on the power of commander in chief, he said, "It would amount to nothing more than the supreme command and direction of the military and naval forces, as the first general and admiral of the Confederacy; while that of the British king extends to the *declaring* of war and to the *raising* and *regulating* of fleets and armies—all which, by the Constitution under consideration, would appertain to the legislature" (emphasis in original).[56] Hamilton defined the war powers: "*When the nation is at peace,* to change that state into a state of war; whether from calculations of policy or from provocations or injuries received: in other words, it belongs to Congress only, *to go to war* (emphasis in original)."[57] Charles Pinckney, commenting on a proposal that the president be given all of the executive powers that under the Articles were exercised by Congress, objected, saying that he favored "a vigorous Executive but was afraid the Executive powers of . . . Congress might extend to peace & war &c which would render the Executive a Monarchy, of the worst kind, to wit an elective one."[58]

An early draft of the Constitution provided that Congress be given the power to "make war." But on August 17, 1787, Elbridge Gerry and James Madison suggested that the word "declare" be substituted for "make," "leaving to the Executive the power to repel sudden attacks."[59] The deliberation of the framers that day indicated a consensus that the executive was not to be entrusted with the power to initiate war. Mr. Sherman added: "The Executive shd. be able to repel and not to commence war." In response to Butler's proposal for "vesting the [war] power in the President," Mr. Gerry responded that he "never expected to hear in a Republic a motion to empower the Executive alone to declare war." Mr. Elseworth replied: "It shd. be more easy to get out of war, than into it."[60] James Madison later wrote that the "fundamental doctrine of the Constitution" was

> that the power to declare war is *fully* and *exclusively* vested in the legislature; that the executive has no right, in any case, to decide the question, whether there is or is not cause for declaring war; that the right of convening and informing Congress, whenever such a question seems to call for a decision, is all the right which the Constitution has deemed requisite or proper . . . [for the President].[61]

There can be little doubt that the framers intended to give Congress and not the president the authority to decide about whether to go to war.

The president was given the authority to appoint and receive ambassadors, to negotiate treaties (both subject to the Senate's concurrence), and through the commander-in-chief clause, to conduct (or "make") war, once it is authorized. The president was also to "take care that the laws be faithfully executed." The framers, however, wanted to assure that many of the powers of war, which British monarchs possessed, would be exercised by Congress in the United States. Thus in Article I, Section 8, they specified the war powers entrusted to Congress, which has the authority to

—"define and punish Piracies and Felonies committed on the high Seas, and Offences against the Law of Nations,"

—"declare war,"

—"grant Letters of Marque and reprisal,"

—"make Rules concerning Captures on Land and Water,"

—"raise and support Armies" (with a two-year limit on appropriations for them),

—"provide and maintain a Navy,"

—"make Rules for the Government and Regulation of the land and navel forces,"

—"provide for calling forth the Militia to execute the Laws of the Union, suppress Insurrections and repel Invasions,"

—"provide for organizing, arming, and disciplining, the Militia, and for governing" (them when they have been called up), and to

—"make all Laws which shall be necessary and proper for carrying into Execution the foregoing Powers, and *all other Powers vested by this Constitution in the Government of the United States, or in any Department or Officer thereof*" (emphasis added).

Given the plain words of the Constitution, it is difficult to understand how some executivists can argue that the president can override laws with his authority as commander in chief and his leadership of the "unitary executive."

Advocates of executive authority often make much of the vesting of "the executive power" in the president. They argue that the powers specified for exercise by Congress are limits on congressional authority, but that by vesting the executive power in the president, the framers implied an authority much broader than either Article I or Article III conveys. Hamilton, in the Pacificus-Helvidius debate with Madison, argued that the congressional authority to declare war and the Senate's right to ratify treaties were "exceptions out of the general 'executive power'" vested in the President. Thus Hamilton—well after the Constitutional Convention—referring to the vesting clause, implied that declaring wars and ratifying treaties are merely exceptions to the executive power. Hamilton neglects all of the specified powers in Article I, Section 8, which are clearly executive in nature, such as raising and supporting armies and making rules for "captures on land and water."[62] All other exceptions listed above undercut the implication of his assertion.

Charles Thatch argued that the committee on style decided on the wording of Article II and that the vesting phrase was a "joker" clause. Thatch argues that "whether intentional or not, it admitted an interpretation of executive power which would give to the President a field of action much wider than that outlined by the enumerated powers."[63] Forrest McDonald argued that the vesting clause "presupposes that 'executive power' had an agreed-upon meaning. . . . It seems evident that some of [the framers], at least, thought of executive power as contingent and discretionary: the power to act unilaterally[,] . . . power corresponding to that of ancient Roman dictators."[64] McDonald argues that since the anti-Federalists were so upset about the monarchical possibilities of presidential power ("a positive, comprehensive, unspecified, and ominous grant of authority"), this fact constitutes evidence that granting those monarchical powers was the intent of the framers. As Jack Rakove points out, however, McDonald does not cite any evidence in the debates of the Convention or in the ratification debates to support his assertion.[65]

If what these advocates for enhanced executive power mean is that in an extreme emergency, the president can take actions normally not within the authority of the executive, or even against the law, they have a reasonable point. If there were a devastating attack on the United States, for example by a nuclear device, few would argue that the president could not, for instance, declare martial law, deny habeas corpus, withdraw money from the treasury, and respond militarily to the attack. Locke's prerogative power covers these circumstances. But if what these executivists mean is that the president can use his executive power to ignore the Constitution and the laws during circumstances that do not constitute an emergency, they are reading too much into the vesting clause.

David Adler raises the question that if the framers intended the president to have an expansive grant of executive power through the vesting clause, why did they specify in Article II that the president had the authority to "require the Opinion, in writing, of the principal Officer in each of the executive Departments"?[66] Certainly demanding an opinion from the heads of cabinet departments in the executive branch would normally be considered an essential executive function. That the framers took care to make the authority explicit in Article II is a strong indication that they had not, by the vesting clause, already given the president extensive executive powers not specified in the Constitution.

Those who weight the vesting clause with vast, unstated powers, prefer their own formulations of which powers the president ought to have to the plain words of the Constitution and the deliberations of the framers.

Supreme Court Decisions: Curtiss-Wright and Youngstown

The Supreme Court has occasionally spoken out on the division of powers between the president and Congress over national security policy. I will briefly characterize two iconic cases that are often posited by opposing sides in the executive power debate.

Justice Sutherland's decision in *U.S. v. Curtiss-Wright Export Corporation* (1936) is often quoted by advocates of extraordinary executive authority in foreign affairs. The Sutherland statement most often referred to states that the president "is the sole organ of the nation in its external relations." The *Curtiss-Wright* case was about whether Congress had delegated too much legislative power to President Roosevelt when it gave him authority to embargo the selling of weapons in South America. Sutherland's decision held that Congress was acting within its power and had not delegated too much power to the president. The case was not about presidential power but about how much discretion Congress could delegate to the president by enacting laws.

After stating the holding of the Supreme Court, Sutherland added a large section of *dicta,* stating, among other things, that the president was the "sole organ" in foreign affairs. Sutherland took the words "sole organ" from a statement by John Marshall on March 7, 1800, when he was a member of Congress and before he became chief justice. Marshall said that the president was "the sole organ of the nation in its external relations, and its sole representative with foreign nations." The issue in question was whether President John Adams, in extraditing a person to Britain, had acted properly in executing the treaty, which was the "supreme Law of the Land" (Article VI of the Constitution). Marshall argued that the president was the "sole organ" in communicating with and representing the United States to foreign countries, not that the president had extraordinary authority not specified in the Constitution.[67] Sutherland, in his *dicta,* incorrectly used Marshall's statement to claim that the president had extraordinary authority not specified in the Constitution. Using Sutherland's statement to justify broad presidential powers not specified in the Constitution misrepresents Marshall's meaning.

The other iconic Supreme Court case concerning presidential authority over national security is *Youngstown Sheet and Tube v. Sawyer,*[68] known as the "steel seizure case." In 1952 the United States was at war in Korea, and President Truman, in order to avert a strike in the steel industry, took control of the steel mills. Truman argued that continued production was essential to national security, and he asserted that his constitutional authority as president allowed him to take the action.

Justice Black wrote the Supreme Court's decision that held that presidential authority did not justify the seizure. There were five separate concurring decisions, all of which denied the president's claim that his authority during a national emergency (the Korean War) overcame the law, the 1947 Taft-Hartley Act.

Taft-Hartley required negotiations between the unions and the companies to try to settle their disagreements. The problem for Truman was that Congress had previously considered amending Taft-Hartley with a provision that would allow the president to seize private property in the event of a national emergency. The amendment was rejected by Congress. Thus Truman was asserting an inherent presidential authority act in a way that Congress had explicitly decided against. In effect he was asserting that his inherent authority as president trumped the law and will of Congress. Justice Black's opinion for the Court stated: "In the framework of our Constitution, the President's power to see that the laws are faithfully executed refutes the idea that he is to be a lawmaker. The Constitution limits his functions in the lawmaking process to the recommending [of] laws he thinks wise and the vetoing of laws he thinks bad. And the Constitution is neither silent nor equivocal about who shall make laws which the President is to execute."[69]

Justice Jackson concurred with the majority, arguing that the Constitution did not confer any inherent powers on the president. "The Solicitor General lastly grounds support of the seizure upon nebulous, inherent power never expressly granted but said to have accrued to the office from the customs and claims of preceding administrations. The plea is for a resulting power to deal with a crisis or emergency according to the necessities of the case, the unarticulated assumption being that necessity knows no law." Claims to inherent executive power were dangerous, he argued: "Such power either has no beginning or it has no end. If it exists, it need submit to no legal restraints." He finally concluded that "the executive action we have here originates in the individual will of the President and represents an exercise of authority without law."[70]

Justice Jackson also articulated in his opinion one of the most cogent formulations of presidential authority vis-à-vis Congress: "When the President acts pursuant to an express or implied authorization of Congress, his authority is at its maximum, for it includes all that he possesses in his own right plus all that Congress can delegate."[71] On the other hand, if Congress has legislated on a certain topic, thus expressing its will, the president cannot easily act contrary to the will of Congress. "When the President takes measures incompatible with the expressed or implied will of Congress, his power is at its lowest ebb, for then he can rely only upon his own constitutional powers minus any constitutional powers of Congress over the matter."[72] But if Congress has not addressed a particular issue, the president has more leeway to act. "When the President acts in absence of either a congressional grant or denial of authority, he can only rely upon his own independent powers." In such a situation, argued Jackson, the president's power was uncertain, and it constituted "a zone of twilight in which he and Congress may have concurrent authority, or in which its distribution is uncertain."

According to this formulation, President Bush's constitutional authority was at its lowest ebb when he suspended the Geneva Agreements, when he denied habeas corpus to detainees, and when he ordered the National Security Agency to listen in on U.S. communications without a warrant. The specific arguments and justifications President Bush used to defend his actions will be examined in the following chapters.

Conclusion

President Bush has made extraordinary claims to authority under the commander-in-chief clause of Article II; the plain words of the Constitution and the deliberations of the framers refute such claims. From their experience under the Articles of Confederation, the architects of the Constitution concluded that the new nation needed an independent executive. But as the debates at the Constitutional Convention demonstrate, the executive's power was intended to be balanced by the other two branches of government. The framers wanted to preserve their individual rights, and they embedded them in the Bill of Rights at the insistence of those who wanted to make them explicit. In writing the war powers into the Constitution, they divided authority between Congress and the executive.

Based on their study of history and their experience with overweening executives, they gave the president the title of commander in chief, but left most other war powers with Congress. Arguments by the Bush administration and others that the commander-in-chief power gives the president the authority to initiate war and nullify laws during times of conflict are vastly overdrawn. Certainly the president can act to repel sudden attacks and move quickly to defend Americans. In emergencies the executive can reasonably exercise further powers, such as quarantines or detentions. But these exercises of executive power are limited to special circumstances. The Bush administration, however, has used the president's commander-in-chief authority to justify ignoring laws and challenge the constitutionality of hundreds of provisions of enacted laws.

The argument by some scholars that foreign policy may be more conveniently and efficiently conducted by the executive may be reasonable, but that is beside the constitutional point. The principle established in the Constitution remains that authority over national security policy is shared with the legislature. The purpose of separation of powers was not the expediency of quick decisionmaking, but rather the limitation of power. As articulated by Justice Brandeis, "The doctrine of the separation of powers was adopted by the Convention of 1787, not to promote efficiency but to preclude the exercise of arbitrary power. The purpose was not to avoid friction, but, by means of the inevitable friction incident to the distribution of the governmental powers among three departments, to save the people from autocracy."[73] The next four chapters will examine the extraordinary claims of President Bush and how they have undermined the republican basis of the Constitution.

CHAPTER FIVE

THE POWER TO IMPRISON: HABEAS CORPUS

"The only thing I know for certain is that these are bad people."
—President Bush

"First they came for the Jews. I was silent. I was not a Jew. Then they came for the Communists. I was silent. I was not a Communist. Then they came for the trade unionists. I was silent. I was not a trade unionist. Then they came for me. There was no one left to speak for me."
—Attributed to Martin Niemöller

"The subjecting of men to punishment for things which, when they were done, were breaches of no law and the practice of arbitrary imprisonments have been, in all ages, the favorite and most formidable instruments of tyranny."
—Alexander Hamilton, *Federalist* No. 84

The purpose of the "Great Writ" of habeas corpus over the centuries has been to allow a person imprisoned by the executive to argue before an independent authority (a judge) that he had been unjustly incarcerated. This centuries-old protection requires that an independent judge concur with the executive's reasons for depriving a person of liberty or that he be set free. If a judge grants a writ of habeas corpus, the executive must explain the grounds for concluding that the person has in fact broken a law and thus has been justly put in jail. If the judge is convinced that the executive has a reasonable case that the law has been broken, the executive will be allowed to keep the person in jail and take him to trial. But if the judge is convinced that the executive does not have reasonable grounds for imprisoning the person, the person must be set free.[1]

This chapter will first review the development of habeas corpus as a fundamental right of individuals and a limit on governmental power. The development of this basic right will be traced from its English origins, through the framers of the Constitution, up through more recent precedents. It will then take up the Bush administration's assault on this fundamental liberty.

In 2003 and 2004 the Bush administration incarcerated hundreds of persons who were suspected of cooperating with the Taliban regime in Afghanistan and fighting U.S. troops. The administration argued that those incarcerated had no right to appeal to U.S. courts for writs of habeas corpus and that the courts had no jurisdiction to judge these executive branch actions. President Bush, in denying the writ of habeas corpus to citizens in the United States (few) and aliens held at Guantánamo (many), was asserting authority that had been denied English kings since before Magna Carta, in principle and in practice since the Habeas Corpus Act of 1648. This claim was consistent with President Bush's other claims to unilateral executive authority based on Article II of the Constitution and the commander-in-chief clause. Through military orders the administration claimed that its decisions could not be reviewed outside of the executive branch. When the Supreme Court ruled that U.S. courts had jurisdiction to hear habeas corpus appeals from Guantánamo detainees and citizens, the administration pushed a law through Congress stripping the courts of much of their jurisdiction.

Many people in the United States questioned why we should grant rights to terrorists. Why should they be able to enjoy the advantages of our judicial system? Justice Scalia articulated the sentiment: "War is war, and it has never been the case that when you capture a combatant you have to give them a jury trial in your civil courts. Give me a break."[2] Although no one had suggested that people picked up on a battlefield be tried in civil courts in front of juries, Scalia spoke for many Americans. But the whole point of habeas corpus is to determine whether the captive is, in fact, a terrorist and thus justly held by the executive.

Undoubtedly, many detainees in Guantánamo did fight against U.S. soldiers and their tribal allies in Afghanistan, and some were admittedly terrorists. But some had undeniably been sent to Guantánamo by mistake. Only 5 percent of the detainees in Guantánamo were actually taken into custody directly by U.S. troops, and many of them were not captured on a field of battle.[3] Many detainees denied that they had fought U.S. forces and that the circumstantial evidence used to support their incarceration was incorrect. That is why the "wrong man problem" is so important. The second part of this chapter will document several cases of genuinely innocent people incarcerated by the executive and sometimes subjected to torture.

After studying unclassified Combatant Status Review Tribunals (CSRT) records, Benjamin Wittes estimates that there were serious cases against about one third of the detainees in Guantánamo. Another third have denied (with various amounts of credibility) any complicity in fighting against the United States or its allies. And a third have made no statement at all. Wittes also points out that a large number of detainees had already been released.[4] He thus chides the critics of the Bush administration's policies at Guantánamo for exaggerating the number of innocent detainees at Guantánamo. But he also admits that the policies and secrecy of the Bush administration have invited confusion. It adopted policies suitable for captured troops in a war, but the government argued that it can continue to hold these detainees indefinitely.[5] The point of this chapter is not about the number or status of detainees at Guantánamo; it is about the principle of whether the executive branch should be able to lock persons up indefinitely with no judicial oversight.

That so many remaining detainees (in 2008) have declared their innocence and so many have already been released by the military indicates that at least some of those remaining may not be guilty of terrorism. In a conventional war with a specific end point, this would not be a problem. But the Bush administration argues that it can keep detainees deemed to be enemy combatants indefinitely. With the internal reviews so deficient in due process, the only resort that detainees have is to petition U.S. courts for a writ of habeas corpus.

The purpose of the Great Writ of habeas corpus over the centuries has been to allow an independent authority to confirm that a law has been broken and that the executive had reasonable cause to put a person in prison. Habeas corpus oversight for Guantánamo detainees is important to ensure that the wrong man is not incarcerated and punished. That is why the Constitution guarantees the right of habeas corpus to people in the United States. The constitutional implications are profound: if to President Bush is conceded the authority to deny habeas corpus to those whom he classifies as "enemy combatants" and to incarcerate them indefinitely, then all other future presidents can plausibly claim the same authority to deny habeas corpus to those they deem to be threats to the security of the nation. The writ of habeas corpus, established as a fundamental right over the centuries, is at stake here, and the citizens of the United States should not give it up lightly.

The British Origins of Habeas Corpus

The writ of habeas corpus (Latin for "you have the body") has for centuries provided individuals with the opportunity to challenge their imprisonment by the government. It originated in ancient Anglo-Saxon common law several centuries before Magna Carta was issued. The writ was originally used to compel the appearance of a person in a court to establish rightful jurisdiction, and during the Elizabethan era, the writ was often used to challenge the jurisdiction of one of the royal courts or commissions.[6] Over time, it came to be used as a defense against false imprisonment through a legal demand that the king's ministers demonstrate to an independent judge that the person was being imprisoned in accord with the law and with reasonable evidence that he had in fact committed the crime with which he was charged.

Over the centuries habeas corpus came to be seen as one of the most important bulwarks of individual liberty in the face of the overwhelming power of the state. The British legal scholar William Blackstone called it "the great and efficacious writ, in all manners of illegal confinement."[7] The scholar William Holdsworth called it "the most effectual protector of the liberty of the subject that any legal system has ever devised."[8]

The principle of habeas was stated in Magna Carta, which provided that: "No free man shall be seized or imprisoned, or stripped of his rights or possessions, or outlawed or exiled, or deprived of his standing in any other way, nor will we [the king] proceed with force against him, or send others to do so, except by the lawful judgment of his equals or by the law of the land."[9] Thus if a person were imprisoned without a lawful reason or due process, a judge could command that he be set free.

In the Stuart era, Charles I began to coerce "loans" from landowners to raise money. When five knights refused to give loans to Charles, he had them imprisoned. They filed for a writ of habeas corpus in the Court of King's Bench, challenging the king's right to imprison them solely upon Charles's own command and not based on the common law. Their lawyer, John Seldon, argued that Magna Carta guaranteed them the right to be judged through "the law of the land" and that the king's command alone was not the equivalent of the law of the land. The court refused to rule in their favor, but the arguments in the case represented an important development in connecting habeas corpus to Magna Carta.[10]

In Darnel's Case (1627), King Charles I by virtue of his "special command" (prerogative) imprisoned several men as enemies of the state.[11] The king refused to allow any questions about the legal or factual basis for imprisonment of the men. The court in this case upheld the king's prerogative to block any inquiry and set off a constitutional crisis that led to the Petition of Right of 1628.[12] In the petition, King Charles was accused of imprisoning people without showing sufficient cause: "Your subjects have of late been imprisoned without any cause showed . . . and their keepers commanded to certify the causes of their detainer, no cause was certified, but that they were detained by your Majesty's special command . . . and yet were returned back to several prisons, without being charged with anything to which they might make answer according to the law."[13] During the war on terror, President Bush imprisoned hundreds of men in Guantánamo without charging them with crimes or allowing them to appeal for writs of habeas corpus. Several Supreme Court cases (considered later in the chapter) challenged the Bush administration's right to hold people indefinitely without charge or benefit of habeas corpus.

King Charles's contempt for Parliament and claims to absolute authority led to the English Civil War and his beheading. After the Commonwealth period of legislative rule and the restoration of the monarchy, Charles II again violated English tradition by imprisoning subjects without due process of law. Parliament reacted against Charles II by passing the Habeas Corpus Act of 1679. The act stated:

> WHEREAS great delays have been used by sheriffs . . . in making returns of writs of habeas corpus to them directed . . . contrary to their duty and the known laws of the land, whereby many of the King's subjects have been and hereafter may be long detained in prison.
>
> For the prevention whereof, and the more speedy relief of all persons imprisoned for any such criminal or supposed criminal

matters. . . . That whensoever any person or person shall bring any habeas corpus directed unto any sheriff . . . shall within three days after the service . . . bring or cause to be brought the body of the party so committed or restrained, unto or before the lord chancellor . . . and shall then likewise certify the true causes of his detainer or imprisonment.[14]

Sir William Blackstone, in his *Commentaries on the Laws of England* in 1765, after quoting Magna Carta, declared: "Of great importance to the public is the preservation of this personal liberty: for if once it were left in the power of any, the highest, magistrate to imprison arbitrarily whomever he or his officers thought proper . . . there would soon be an end of all other rights and immunities."[15]

He further explained how habeas corpus relates to due process of law:

To make imprisonment lawful, it must either be, by process from the courts of judicature, or by warrant from some legal officer, having authority to commit to prison; which warrant must be in writing, under the hand and seal of the magistrate, and express the causes of the commitment, in order to be examined into (if necessary) upon a *habeas corpus*. If there be no cause expressed, the gaoler is not bound to detain the prisoner. For the law judges in this respect . . . that it is unreasonable to send a prisoner, and not to signify withal the crimes alleged against him.[16]

Thus, argued Blackstone, one of the core tenets of limited government is the requirement that if the government is going to imprison a person, it must have sufficient evidence that the person ought to be imprisoned and it must follow due process in doing so. This right against arbitrary imprisonment must be enforced by judgment of an independent authority, that is, by an official independent of the executive authority "who shall determine whether the cause of his commitment be just."[17]

The U.S. Framers and Habeas Corpus

Although the framers clearly rejected British constitutional doctrine with regard to the power of the crown in making war, they built into the Constitution the ancient individual liberties that they felt had been their right as British citizens. The new Constitution would specify many of these rights explicitly in the Bill of Rights. That the right to a writ of habeas corpus was not included in the Bill of Rights was not an oversight. Rather, it reflected the consensus that the right was unquestioned and had been protected from easy governmental abuse in Article I of the Constitution. The right of habeas corpus to the colonists was so important that some states (Massachusetts and Georgia) adopted approximately the same wording as the English Habeas Corpus Act of 1679 into their own laws.[18]

This fundamental right of free people was carried forward in England and the United States and remains a key protection from arbitrary imprisonment by the government, particularly the executive. In the United States the requirements of the writ were implied in the Constitution in the Fifth and Sixth Amendments, which provide for due process of law in any imprisonment and other rights of the accused. The right to a writ of habeas corpus was so taken for granted that the Constitution explicitly refers to it only once when it provides in Article I, Section 9, that "The Privilege of the Writ of Habeas Corpus shall not be suspended, unless when in Cases of Rebellion or Invasion the public Safety may require it." The Constitution's reference to the "privilege" implies that the right was not created in the Constitution but was a right assumed to be possessed by all, and only in special circumstances could the government deny the protections of the right to individuals.

According to Madison's account, habeas corpus was first mentioned at the convention on August 20, 1789. Charles Pinkney proposed that "The privileges and benefit of the Writ of habeas corpus shall be enjoyed in this Government in the most expeditious and ample manner, and shall not be suspended by the legislature except upon the most urgent and pressing occasions, and for a limited time not exceeding [___] months."[19] The words "most urgent and pressing occasions" were very broad, and the final wording in the Constitution much more tightly circumscribed the conditions under which the writ could be suspended. By August 28, the clause was essentially in its final form, when Pinkney proposed "that it should not be suspended but on the most urgent occasions, [and] then only for a limited time not exceeding twelve months." Rutledge, however, was for declaring habeas corpus inviolable. Wilson "doubted whether in any case (a suspension) could be necessary." In the end, approval of the provision in its final form won by a vote of 7 to 3, with the three dissenting votes cast by those states that thought there should be no provision for suspending habeas corpus whatsoever. [20] In the debates over ratification of the Constitution, the writ of habeas corpus did not feature significantly. When the issue did arise, the discussion revolved around the question of whether the suspension clause protected the writ effectively enough.

The decision of the framers to allow only Congress to suspend the writ is based on its placement in Article I, although the words of the clause do not specifically mention Congress. The decision to allow Congress to suspend the writ in the exceptional cases of danger to the nation caused by invasion or rebellion may have been based on Blackstone's analysis that it was only the legislature in England that could suspend the writ.

> And yet sometimes, when the state is in real danger, even this [that is, executive detention] may be a necessary measure. But the happiness of our constitution is, that it is not left to the executive power to determine when the danger of the state is so great, as to render this measure expedient; for it is the parliament only, or legislative power, that, whenever it sees proper, can authorize the crown, by suspending the *habeas corpus* act for a short and limited time, to imprison suspected persons without giving any reason for so doing . . . this experiment ought only to be tried in case of extreme emergency; and in these the nation parts with its liberty for a while, in order to preserve it for ever. [21]

Thus, argued Blackstone, one of the core tenets of limited government is the requirement that if the government is going to imprison a person, it must have sufficient evidence that the person ought to be imprisoned and it must follow due process in doing so. This right against arbitrary imprisonment must be enforced by judgment of an independent authority, that is, by an authority different from the one imprisoning the man.

In debates over ratification of the Constitution, some used the presence of the writ in Article I in order to argue that the specification of other rights should be included in the Constitution. These arguments were part of the debates that led to the creation of the Bill of Rights. Other objectors argued that the suspension clause was not a strong enough protection, but those who supported the Constitution argued that the suspension clause provided sufficient protection of the writ and that habeas corpus did not need to be included in the Bill of Rights.[22] There was consensus enough on the importance of the writ that the framers did not feel a need to include it as a separate right in the Bill of Rights.[23] The arguments were not about whether the right to habeas corpus was an essential element of liberty, the arguments were about whether that right, which was accepted as fundamental, was sufficiently protected in the Constitution.[24]

After the Constitutional Convention, Hamilton asserted in *Federalist* No. 84: "The establishment of the writ of *habeas corpus,* the prohibition of ex post facto laws . . . are perhaps greater securities to liberty and republicanism than any [the New York constitution] contains." Hamilton argued further: "The practice of arbitrary imprisonments have been, in all ages, the favourite and most formidable instruments of tyranny." He then goes on to quote Blackstone:

> "To bereave a man of life (says he) or by violence to confiscate his estate, without accusation or trial, would be so gross and notorious an act of despotism, as must at once convey the alarm of tyranny throughout the whole nation; but confinement of the person by secretly hurrying him to gaol, where his sufferings are unknown or forgotten, is a less public, a less striking, and therefore *a more dangerous engine* of arbitrary government." And as a remedy for this fatal evil, he is everywhere peculiarly emphatical in his encomiums on the *habeas corpus* act, which in one place he calls "the BULWARK of the British constitution."[25]

In addition to the constitutional provision in Article I, the United States has kept habeas corpus on the statute books since the Judiciary Act of 1789.[26]

It is important to remember that a writ of habeas corpus is not, and has never been, a "get-out-of-jail-free card." That is, judges do not lightly override executive branch decisions to imprison people; they most often give appropriate weight to evidence and reasons for imprisoning a person. Usually the executive branch is correct; it has sound grounds for imprisoning a person. In some cases, however, a person may be imprisoned by mistake or through malice. In these cases, which have happened many times, including during the war on terror, habeas corpus is one of the few ways for an innocent person to win a fair hearing. The writ then is an opportunity for a prisoner to present to an independent authority (a judge) arguments and evidence that his imprisonment is not based on law or sufficient evidence.

In the middle of the twentieth century, habeas corpus was also used to enforce constitutional guarantees of due process. In these cases, a conviction could be overturned if the government did not abide by the law when the person was apprehended and imprisoned as a suspect. In the case of Guantánamo detainees, however, the purpose of most habeas corpus cases was to determine whether or not the detainee was in fact a member of al Qaeda or a combatant against the United States.[27] That 95 percent of detainees in Guantánamo were not picked up by U.S. forces led to the possibility that not all were enemy combatants but rather victims of tribal rivalries in Afghanistan.[28] In addition, the detainees were concerned about more than their mere detention. Some of the detainees in Guantánamo were interrogated using harsh techniques that most of the world would consider torture. The section on "the wrong man problem" later in this chapter provides evidence that some of the detainees were not guilty of the crimes of which they were accused. Appeals of habeas corpus were one of the few ways that genuinely innocent detainees could make a case for their innocence.

Defenders of Bush administration policy in Guantánamo argue that habeas corpus is appropriate for U.S. citizens accused of crimes, but since the U.S. is engaged in a war on terror, the rules of war should apply and not criminal procedures such as habeas corpus. When enemy combatants are picked up on the battlefield and held as prisoners of war, it is entirely reasonable that U.S. troops imprison the enemy troops for the duration of the conflict, after which they will be released. The problem with detainees in Guantánamo is that there is no certainty that all of the detainees were in fact enemy combatants. Yet they were confined in very harsh circumstances, subject to aggressive interrogation—what most of the world would consider torture, and there is no likely end to the war on terror or to their imprisonment. A writ of habeas corpus is the only way that those who are genuinely innocent can present an argument to an independent judge.

LINCOLN AND HABEAS CORPUS

Those who are in favor of the prerogative of the executive to deny habeas corpus, or violate other express provisions of the Constitution, often point to President Lincoln's suspension of the writ of habeas corpus during the Civil War. When the war started in the spring of 1861, it was clearly a rebellion and Congress was not in session, so President Lincoln suspended habeas corpus in some areas, increased the size of the army, and called up the state militia. He reasoned that such measures were necessary to preserve the Union and that there was not sufficient time for Congress to return and consider the matter. As he explained, his actions, "whether strictly legal or not, were ventured upon under what appeared to be a popular demand and a public necessity, trusting then, as now, that Congress would readily ratify them." He added that "nothing has been done beyond the constitutional competency of Congress."[29]

Unlike President Bush, Lincoln did not claim exclusive constitutional authority to deny appeals through habeas corpus petitions. He claimed to act under the Constitution, but invoked the suspension clause in Article I. The beginning of the Civil War was clearly a case of rebellion as specified in Article I of the Constitution, and thus an appropriate justification for suspension by Congress. But since Congress was not in session, Lincoln invoked the suspension clause before Congress came back in session. He recognized that Congress had superior authority with respect to the actions he took.[30] In his dissent in *Hamdi* v. *Rumsfeld,* Justice Scalia argued: "President Lincoln, when he purported to suspend habeas corpus without congressional authorization during the Civil War, apparently did not doubt that suspension was required if the prisoner was to be held without criminal trial. In his famous message to Congress on July 4, 1861, he argued only that he could suspend the writ, not that even without suspension, his imprisonment of citizens without criminal trial was permitted." President Bush, in imprisoning detainees in Guantánamo, did not declare habeas corpus to be suspended, but he denied them the possibility of appealing to a court for a writ.

When Congress returned to Washington and came into session three months later, Lincoln asked Congress to approve of his actions through law. There was no question that his actions exceeded his constitutional authority, as both he and Congress recognized. The matter was debated at some length, and on August 6 Congress passed laws ratifying Lincoln's decisions, retroactively making them legal.

The key to the constitutional issue here is that Lincoln did not claim the unilateral authority to declare martial law, expand the army, and call up the state militias; he recognized that those powers were given to Congress alone. But he had to act with dispatch because of the military situation, and after taking the necessary actions, he came to Congress for approval, recognizing that he had taken actions that the Constitution allocates to Congress. This is much different from the assertion by President Bush that he has the constitutional authority to act unilaterally in these areas.[31] Chief Justice John Marshall declared in *Ex parte Bollman*: "If at any time the public safety should require the suspension of the powers vested by this act in the courts of the United States, it is for the Legislature to say so."[32] In March 1863 Congress passed a law authorizing Lincoln to suspend habeas corpus during the rebellion.[33]

Ex parte Merryman

John Merryman was suspected of giving aid to the South during the Civil War, and he was arrested on May 25, 1861, and put in prison at Fort McHenry in Baltimore.[34] He appealed for a writ of habeas corpus to Chief Justice Roger Taney, who was sitting as a circuit judge. Taney issued the writ to the commandant of Fort McHenry, and when General Cadwalader refused to honor it, Taney held him in contempt. When the U.S. marshal attempted to deliver the writ to the general, he was not permitted to enter the fort. Lincoln had ignored the order of the Supreme Court.[35] Nevertheless Judge Taney laid out his judgment on habeas corpus:

> I can see no ground whatever for supposing that the President, in any emergency or in any state of things, can authorize the suspension of the privilege of the writ of *habeas corpus,* or arrest a citizen, except in aid of the judicial power. He certainly does not faithfully execute the laws if he takes upon himself legislative power by suspending the writ of *habeas corpus.* . . . And if the President of the United States may suspend the writ, then the Constitution of the United States has conferred upon him more regal and absolute power over the liberty of the citizen than the people of England have thought it safe to entrust to the Crown.[36]

Congress has exercised the suspension authority only four times in U.S. history, and each time it has set a clear limit on its suspension: In 1863 during the Civil War, President Grant during reconstruction in the South, in 1902 for the Philippines war, and immediately after the attack on Pearl Harbor. These suspensions have always been explicit, with an end point specified—nothing like the Authorization to Use Military Force (AUMF) that President Bush cited to justify his denial of habeas corpus.[37]

EX PARTE MILLIGAN

American citizen Lambden Milligan was seized in Indiana by military order on suspicion of aiding the South during the Civil War and sentenced by a military tribunal to be hanged. His execution was delayed by President Lincoln but approved by President Johnson after Lincoln's assassination. Milligan appealed to a federal judge for a writ of habeas corpus, arguing that the military tribunal did not have jurisdiction over him. The case reached the Supreme Court after the war had ended, and in deciding the case, it agreed with Milligan. The Court reasoned that, since the civil court system in Indiana was functioning, military courts did not have jurisdiction. Justice Davis said that the issue of habeas corpus "involves the very framework of the government and the fundamental principles of American liberty."[38]

Davis acknowledged that under some circumstances, martial law without the right of habeas corpus was necessary. The government argued that the state of Indiana, though it was a loyal state, was in the theater of military operations and thus threatened by a possible invasion by the enemy, and so martial law was justified. But Davis countered that "The necessity must be actual and present; the invasion real, such as effectually closes the courts and deposes the civil administration" in order for the government's argument to prevail and habeas corpus legitimately denied to citizens.[39]

Despite the claim by the government that martial law should prevail, Davis declared that "it is the birthright of every American citizen when charged with crime, to be tried and punished according to law."[40] Davis further argued:

This nation, as experience has proved, cannot always remain at peace, and has no right to expect that it will always have wise and

humane rulers, sincerely attached to the principles of the Constitution. Wicked men, ambitious of power, with hatred of liberty and
contempt of law, may fill the place once occupied by Washington
and Lincoln; and if this right is conceded, and the calamities of war
again befall us, the dangers to human liberty are frightful to con-
template.[41]

FDR AND EX PARTE QUIRIN

Ex parte Quirin was a Supreme Court decision that retroactively justified the Roosevelt administration's sentencing to death of eight Nazi
saboteurs who had landed on the east coast of the United States in June
1942 with the intent to sabotage railroads and defense installations.[42]
The FBI was able to capture the men shortly after their landing and
before they had committed any sabotage because one of them turned
himself in to the FBI and gave them the necessary information to locate
the others.

The Roosevelt administration decided to try them by military tribunal rather than in the civil courts for two reasons. The administration
thought that criminal law did not provide for sufficiently harsh penal-
ties, in part because the Germans did not have time actually to commit
any sabotage; they merely had the equipment to do so. Second, the FBI
had been praised in the press for its vigilance and effectiveness, but the
public did not know that the real reason the saboteurs were caught so
quickly was that one of them turned himself in and told the FBI about
his comrades. In addition, Roosevelt did not want to publicize how easily the German U-boats were able to penetrate American defenses and
land the saboteurs on the east coast. The advantages of using a military
tribunal were that it could be conducted in secrecy according to rules
devised by the military, and it could punish the men much more harshly
(with the death penalty) than criminal law would have allowed.[43]

Just as the criminal law was avoided, so were the legal aspects of military law, such as the Articles of War and the procedure for military
courts-martial. President Roosevelt decided to proceed with a military
tribunal created by his own proclamation in which he appointed the
seven members of the commission and in which he would be the final
arbiter. He carefully arranged that there would be no avenue for the

saboteurs to appeal to the judiciary so that any habeas corpus appeal would be precluded. Nevertheless, the Supreme Court did agree to hear an appeal in late July 1942, and the government argued that the defendants did not have the right to a habeas corpus hearing because they were "armed invaders" who were not entitled to civil remedies. The Court heard oral argument over a two-day period and on the following day issued a brief *per curiam* opinion upholding the government's argument that the military tribunal had jurisdiction in the case. The full reasoning in the *Quirin* case was not issued until three months later, after the justices had time to work through their analysis.

Several of the justices felt uneasy about the legal basis for the government's interpretation of the Articles of War, and their opinion on October 29 concluded that, because of the secrecy in the case, they could not fully decide whether the president's proclamation establishing the tribunals squared with the Articles of War. Given that six of the men had already been executed, it would have been difficult for the Court to come to any decision that the tribunal did not measure up to the legal standards of the Articles of War. The Court held that since one of the men was an American citizen working for the enemy, he was subject to military jurisdiction. In addition, he was a spy and thus guilty of treason, which distinguished this case from *Milligan*.[44]

Constitutional scholar Louis Fisher argues that the trial of the saboteurs by military tribunal was an unnecessary concentration of power in the executive. All of those conducting the process—prosecutors, judges, defense counsel—were selected by the president, and he was the ultimate authority of appeal. The saboteurs could just as well have been tried under the regular military procedures of courts-martial with consideration of habeas corpus considered (and probably rejected) by the civil judiciary. The guilty verdicts would probably have been the same, though the sentences may have been less severe.[45]

In subsequent decades, the *Quirin* decision has been criticized and attributed to the atmosphere of fear surrounding World War II when it was decided. According to Justice Felix Frankfurter (who was on the Court for the *Quirin* case), *Quirin* "was not a happy precedent."[46] Justice Scalia, in his dissent in *Hamdi*, echoed Frankfurter: "The case [*Quirin*] was not this Court's finest hour."[47]

President Bush and Habeas Corpus

One of the challenges stemming from 9/11 concerned how to deal with suspected terrorists or members of al Qaeda. When U.S. forces captured terrorists, they had to be imprisoned in a location controlled by the United States and easily accessible to U.S. officials. The U.S. naval base at Guantánamo Bay, Cuba, seemed to be an ideal location. The base had been leased from Cuba for an indefinite time period and was under complete U.S. military control. The Bush administration was concerned that if the prisoners were held in the United States, they would have access to the federal court system and be able to raise legal objections to their incarceration. Since Guantánamo was not technically U.S. territory, the executive branch reasoned it was exempt from oversight by federal courts.

On November 13, 2001, President Bush issued a military order concerning the detention and trial of al Qaeda terrorists. The order declared that in accord with his commander-in-chief authority and in light of the national emergency created by the terrorist attacks of 9/11, suspected terrorists could be detained and put on trial for violations of the laws of war.[48] The development of this policy decision by President Bush, however, excluded cabinet level officers who normally would have been able to advise the president on its issuance. On November 6, John Yoo of the Office of Legal Counsel of the Justice Department prepared a draft of the order and determined that the State Department did not need to see the draft. On November 10 John Ashcroft went to a meeting on the draft memo that was chaired by Vice President Cheney. Ashcroft argued that the Justice Department should oversee the prosecution of terrorists, but Vice President Cheney wanted to keep the trials of terrorists out of the U.S. court system and did not take Ashcroft's advice. Three days later the document was taken to President Bush, who signed it immediately.[49]

The order was carefully guarded so that other White House staff or cabinet secretaries would not see it, and it was handled so that the president would not know that the draft was finalized by the vice president. National Security Adviser Rice and Secretary of State Powell were quite upset at the lack of a regular policy process because, as two of the highest level presidential advisers that should see such a document before the president's signature, they were not informed. Upon hearing on CNN that the order had been signed, Colin Powell's reaction was, "What the hell just happened?"[50]

The order applied to non-U.S. citizens who were members of al Qaeda or "engaged in, aided or abetted" it or who "knowingly harbored" members of al Qaeda. The order called for the secretary of defense to detain such persons, treat them humanely, provide them with the necessities of life, honor their religious beliefs, and have them "detained in accordance with such other conditions as the Secretary of Defense may prescribe."[51]

Within a year, the base at Guantánamo held about 600 detainees, most of whom were captured in Afghanistan by the tribal allies of the United States and handed over to U.S. troops. The administration intended eventually to try some of them by military tribunal for war crimes and punish them accordingly. But before the tribunals were established and began trying suspects, several of the detainees challenged their imprisonment in federal court, arguing that they had engaged in no terrorist acts and had not been combatants against the United States.

RASUL v. BUSH

In 2003, sixteen Guantánamo detainees appealed for writs of habeas corpus and argued that they were not guilty of terrorism but were innocent civilians who had been turned over to U.S. troops by bounty hunters.[52] Two lower courts agreed with the administration that they did not have jurisdiction to hear the pleas because *Johnson v. Eisentrager* established that foreign nationals captured outside the United States could not appeal to U.S. courts.[53] In *Eisentrager,* the Supreme Court decided that German soldiers who had been seized by U.S. forces in China after World War II for continuing to fight after Germany had surrendered could be tried by military commission and did not have the right to appeal to civilian courts for writs of habeas corpus. In order for U.S. courts to have jurisdiction, alien appellants had to be present in the sovereign territory of the United States. Thus the courts could not interfere with the military decision to try the Germans by military commission.[54]

When the appellants appealed to the Supreme Court to hear the case, the government argued that "aliens detained by the military abroad [only have rights] determined by the executive and the military, and not the courts."[55] The government relied on *Eisentrager*, in which Justice Jackson wrote: "We are cited to no instance where a court, in this or any other country where the writ is known, has issued it on behalf of an alien enemy who, at no relevant time and in no stage of his captivity, has been held within its territorial jurisdiction."[56] In dissent, Justice Black, joined by Douglas and Burton, argued "That we went on to deny the requested writ, as in the *Quirin* case, in no way detracts from the clear holding that habeas corpus jurisdiction is available even to belligerent aliens convicted by a military tribunal for an offense committed in actual acts of warfare. . . . The Court is fashioning wholly indefensible doctrine if it permits the executive branch, by deciding where its prisoners will be tried and imprisoned, to deprive all federal courts of their power to protect against a federal executive's illegal incarcerations."[57]

In June 2004, however, the Supreme Court in *Rasul* v. *Bush*[58] overturned the two lower court decisions and ruled that federal courts did have jurisdiction to hear habeas corpus cases from detainees in Guantánamo. The Court based its decision on the status of Guantánamo. Even though Guantánamo was on the island of Cuba, "By the express terms of its agreements with Cuba, the United States exercises 'complete jurisdiction and control' over the Guantánamo Bay Naval Base, and may continue to exercise such control permanently if it so chooses."[59] That the detainees were not U.S. citizens did not matter; they were persons being held in a location over which the United States exercised complete control. The Court distinguished *Eisentrager* by noting that the WWII *Eisentrager* appellants had already been tried and convicted of crimes. In contrast the Guantánamo detainees claimed they were innocent and "have never been afforded access to any tribunal, much less charged with and convicted of wrongdoing"[60] The appellants had been held for more than two years without any charges having been made against them and were no longer in a combat zone. The Court therefore decided that "Aliens held at the base, no less than American citizens, are entitled to invoke the federal courts' authority."[61] The Court noted that it was not deciding on a constitutional right of the appellants but rather on the statutory grounds of the habeas jurisdiction of the courts.[62]

Hamdi v. Rumsfeld

Yaser Esam Hamdi traveled from Saudi Arabia to Afghanistan in the summer of 2001 and was later captured on a battlefield by the Northern Alliance, turned over to U.S. forces, and sent to Guantánamo. When it was discovered that he had been born in the United States and was thus an American citizen (though having left at age three), he was moved from Guantánamo, put in a Navy brig in South Carolina, and held in solitary confinement. Hamdi appealed for a writ of habeas corpus, and the federal district judge ordered that Hamdi be given access to a lawyer. The Fourth Circuit Court of Appeals, however, overruled the district court and decided that Hamdi could be held in the United States without access to a lawyer and that the government did not have to charge him with a crime. Later, the full Fourth Circuit, sitting *en banc,* decided that special deference was owed to the president in making decisions about imprisoning enemy combatants and that Hamdi was not entitled to a writ of habeas corpus.

When the decision was appealed to the Supreme Court, Solicitor General Theodore Olson argued that the court did not have jurisdiction: "Courts have an extremely narrow role in reviewing the adequacy of the government's return on a habeas action, such as this, challenging the quintessentially military judgment to detain an individual as an enemy combatant in a time of war."[63] The Court, however, ruled that although Congress had authorized the war against al Qaeda and the military could detain enemy combatants to prevent them from returning to the battlefield, "indefinite detention for the purpose of interrogation is not authorized."[64] Justice O'Connor wrote for a plurality of the Court and noted that the government claimed that "the Executive possesses plenary authority to detain pursuant to Article II of the Constitution." The opinion did not address that issue but reasoned that Congress had authorized the executive to engage U.S. forces in the war and that "detention to prevent a combatant's return to the battlefield is a fundamental incident of waging war."[65] Thus holding prisoners to prevent them from returning to the battlefield was reasonable. But the "indefinite" detention for the purpose of interrogation that, given the nature of the war on terrorism, might very well last for the rest of Hamdi's life, was not authorized by Congress.

In deciding against the Bush administration's contention that it could hold U.S. citizens indefinitely without charging them, Justice O'Conner said:

> The most elemental of liberty interests [is] the interest in being free from physical detention by one's own government [without due process of law]. . . . History and common sense teach us that an unchecked system of detention carries the potential to become a means for oppression and abuse of others who do not present that sort of threat. . . . We reaffirm today the fundamental nature of a citizen's right to be free from involuntary confinement by his own government without due process of law.[66]

She argued that "we must preserve our commitment at home to the principles for which we fight abroad" and that a citizen "must receive notice of the factual basis for his classification and a fair opportunity to rebut the Government's factual assertions before a neutral decision maker." This requirement of due process does not apply to "initial captures on the battle field," but "is due only when the determination is made to *continue* to hold those who have been seized."[67]

In a rebuke to the Bush administration's argument that the courts do not have jurisdiction over cases concerning detainees, Justice O'Connor declared,

> We necessarily reject the Government's assertion that separation of powers principles mandate a heavily circumscribed role for the courts in such circumstances. . . . We have long since made clear that a state of war is not a blank check for the President when it comes to the rights of the Nation's citizens. . . . Unless Congress acts to suspend it, the Great Writ of habeas corpus allows the Judicial Branch to play a necessary role in maintaining this delicate balance of governance, serving as an important judicial check on the Executive's discretion in the realm of detentions."[68]

After determining that Hamdi had the right to argue his case before an independent judge, the case was remanded to the court of appeals for further proceedings.

In a strongly worded dissent, Justice Scalia, one of the most conservative justices who often sided with the executive, argued that the majority did not go far enough in protecting habeas corpus and its role in assuring individual liberty (quoted earlier in the chapter). Joined by Justice Stevens, Scalia began his argument by asserting that habeas corpus has been fundamental to Anglo-American jurisprudence. "The very core of liberty secured by our Anglo-Saxon system of separated powers has been freedom from indefinite imprisonment at the will of the Executive." He went on to argue that due process rights "deemed necessary before depriving a person of life, liberty, or property . . . have historically been vindicated by the writ of habeas corpus. In England before the founding, the writ developed into a tool for challenging executive confinement."

In this case, Scalia saw a clear challenge to what he took as one of the fundamental rights protected by the Constitution. He noted that some people concede that *inter arma silent leges* (during war the laws are silent), but "that view has no place in the interpretation and application of a Constitution designed precisely to confront war and, in a manner that accords with democratic principles, to accommodate it." Scalia concluded: "It follows from what I have said that Hamdi is entitled to a habeas decree requiring his release unless (1) criminal proceedings are promptly brought, or (2) Congress has suspended the writ of habeas corpus."[69] Hamdi was subsequently sent to Saudi Arabia with the provision that he renounce his U.S. citizenship.[70] The key to Scalia's opposite judgment in *Rasul* was that Hamdi was a U.S. citizen detained on U.S. soil, whereas Rasul was an alien imprisoned in Guantánamo, which Scalia argued did not fall under U.S. sovereignty.

Military Commissions

When the administration was preparing President Bush's Military Order of November 13, 2001, it felt that normal trials would afford too many legal protections to terrorists, and were "not practicable" (sec. 1 f), so the order required that military commissions be established entirely within the executive branch to try them.[71] In the order, President Bush declared that any noncitizen "whom I determine" (sec. 2 a) is a terrorist or abetted one could be "detained at an appropriate place" by the secretary of defense and tried by military tribunals created by the secretary of defense.[72] When lawyers for the judge advocate general found out about the order, some were upset and believed that the procedures for courts-martial should have been used.[73] The order also declared that no court would have jurisdiction to hear any appeal of a decision or for a writ of habeas corpus (sec. 2 a). Any evidence would be admitted that would "have probative value to a reasonable person" (sec. 7 [2]). Evidence obtained through torture might be considered reasonable to a presiding officer.

It may be reasonable to use lawfully established military commissions to try enemy belligerents. However, the procedures set out by the Department of Defense (DOD) in Military Commission order no. 1 (March 21, 2002) contained a number of problems.[74] They provided no independent authority, other than the president's decision, to establish military tribunals. Military commissions that have been established by previous presidents were created pursuant to acts of Congress, which has the constitutional authority to "define and punish . . . Offenses against the Law of Nations" (Art. 1, Section 8, Clause 10). Neither did the commissions provide for any review outside the executive branch. That is, the person would be indicted by a subordinate of the president based on evidence provided by subordinates of the president; the defendant would be tried by subordinates of the president; the defendant would be sentenced by subordinates of the president; and the only appeal would be to the president.

In passing the Detainee Treatment Act (DTA) of 2005,[75] Congress banned the torture of detainees by U.S. forces anywhere in the world (discussed in the next chapter). But in addition the Bush administration was able to append a restriction barring habeas corpus relief to any Guantánamo detainee. The act said that

> no court, justice, or judge shall have jurisdiction to hear or consider . . . an application for a writ of habeas corpus filed by or on behalf of an alien detained by the Department of Defense at Guantánamo Bay, Cuba; or any other action against the United States or its agents relating to any aspect of the detention, transfer, treatment, trial, or conditions of confinement of an alien who is or was detained by the United States.[76]

The act required the Defense Department to set up what were called Combatant Status Review Tribunals (CSRTs) to determine whether each detainee was properly classified as an enemy combatant and whether he was entitled to POW status. The set of procedures in the CSRT was expected to substitute for the writ of habeas corpus in that they allowed the detainee to argue that he was not an enemy combatant. The law allowed only limited appeals to the D.C. Circuit contesting whether the procedures of the CSRT hearings were followed or concerning the constitutionality of the act itself (section 1005). Thus, as with the military commissions, the whole set of procedures were conducted by the executive branch and by executive branch personnel, and the only substantive appeal (for example, on the merits of the argument or the facts) was to executive branch personnel.

HAMDAN v. RUMSFELD

Salim Ahmed Hamdan was a Yemeni national who was captured in Afghanistan in November 2001 and turned over to U.S. forces. He was transported to Guantánamo, where he was charged with conspiracy to aid al Qaeda (as Osama bin Laden's driver) and was going to be tried by a military commission established by President Bush. Hamdan filed a habeas corpus petition, arguing that he was entitled to be tried under the requirements of Common Article 3 of the Third Geneva Convention. The district court granted Hamdan's petition for habeas corpus, but the Court of Appeals for the D.C. Circuit reversed the district court. When the Supreme Court heard the appeal, the Bush administration argued that the Detainee Treatment Act, discussed above, denied jurisdiction to any U.S. court.

Justice Stevens, who wrote for the Court, ruled that the DTA stripped courts of jurisdiction only for future appeals, not for those already pending when the law was signed, which Hamdan's was.[77] The Court concluded that the military commissions and procedures established by President Bush were not authorized by the Constitution or any U.S. law (not the Authorization to Use Military Force, the Detainee Treatment Act, or the Uniform Code of Military Justice). The UCMJ restricts the use of military commissions to those that comply with the provisions of the UCMJ and common law of war. Thus the president had to comply with existing U.S. laws. In making his argument Stevens quoted Chief Justice Chase in *Ex parte Milligan*: "Congress cannot direct the conduct of campaigns, nor can the President, or any commander under him, without the sanction of Congress, institute tribunals for the trial and punishment of offenses, either of soldiers or civilians, unless in cases of a controlling necessity." That necessity did not exist in the *Hamdan* case, Stevens argued, so the procedural rights of courts-martial must apply, and the "commission's procedures are illegal."[78] He concluded that the "the military commission convened to try Hamdan lacked authority to proceed because its structure and procedures violate both the UCMJ and the Geneva Conventions."[79]

With respect to elements of a fair trial, the procedures created by the Defense Department by Military Commission order no. 1 had a number of defects.[80] For instance:

> the detainee, though presumed innocent, had the burden of proof to show that the allegations of the government are incorrect (sec. 5[b]);
>
> the detainee is limited in ability to gather and present his own evidence (sec. 6[D][5 and 9]);
>
> coerced testimony can be used against the detainee (sec. 6[D][1]);
>
> civilian defense counsel may be denied access to evidence (6[b][3]).[81]

In addition, the accused could be excluded from being present or being told of the evidence used against him. Importantly, there was no provision for the decisions of the commissions to be appealed outside of the executive branch; the president, not a federal court, would hear the final appeals.

The commissions thus violated the Geneva Convention Common Article 3, which provides that detainees "as a minimum" are entitled to be tried "by a regularly constituted court affording all the judicial guarantees . . . recognized as indispensable by civilized peoples."[82] Stevens noted that the U.S. Army *Law of War Handbook* says Common Article 3 "serves as a minimum yardstick of protection in all conflicts, not just internal armed conflicts."[83] The military commissions lacked the judicial guarantees to the accused of being informed of charges, having the opportunity to rebut them, and to be represented by counsel.

The court did not say that Hamdan could not be detained for the duration of the hostilities, but if the government wanted to try him for a crime, it had to use regularly constituted courts that comply with minimal requirements of procedural due process to do so. The Court finally concluded: "Even assuming that Hamdan is a dangerous individual who would cause great harm or death to innocent civilians given the opportunity, the Executive nevertheless must comply with the prevailing rule of law in undertaking to try him and subject him to criminal punishment."[84]

The claim of President Bush that he had the constitutional authority to imprison terrorism suspects indefinitely without the due process of charging them and trying them in a regularly constituted court was repudiated by the *Hamdan* ruling. As a result of the Supreme Court's ruling in *Hamdan*, the administration convinced Congress to pass the Military Commissions Act, which denied the courts jurisdiction over pending habeas corpus appeals from Guantánamo inmates.

MILITARY COMMISSIONS ACT OF 2006

In order to overcome the roadblock that the Supreme Court decisions threw in the way of the administration's policy on military commissions, President Bush sought legislation that would authorize the creation of military commissions and spell out limits on the rights of detainees. In seeking this legislation, the administration wanted congressional authority to create military commissions, Combatant Status Review Tribunals (to determine if a detainee qualified as a prisoner of war or was an illegal combatant), and the leeway to use harsh interrogation procedures that would not be subject to prosecution under U.S. law. (The aspects of the MCA that deal with interrogation and torture will be covered in chapter 6.)

After several weeks of contentious debate between the two political parties, S. 3930 was passed by both houses of Congress, and President Bush signed the Military Commissions Act of 2006 (P.L. 109-366) into law. It gave the Bush administration most of what it wanted in order to enable it to deal with detainees in ways that had been invalidated by the *Hamdan* ruling. Most directly, the law authorized the president to establish military commissions to try alien detainees believed to be terrorists or unlawful enemy combatants. The law defined "enemy combatant" as "a person who has engaged in hostilities or who has purposefully and materially supported hostilities against the United States or its co-belligerents," or "a person who . . . has been determined to be an unlawful enemy combatant by a Combatant Status Review Tribunal" established by the president or secretary of defense (sec. 948[a]). These provisions seem to allow for the possibility that U.S. citizens, if declared so by the president, could be treated as enemy combatants.

The MCA provided that any appeals of the decisions of the commissions could concern only questions of law—for example whether the law is constitutional or in conflict with other laws—and not of fact. The act also amended the DTA's limits on jurisdiction by stripping courts of the right to hear any habeas corpus appeals of any alien in U.S. custody who had been declared an enemy combatant.[85] In addition, no court could consider any other challenge concerning "any aspect of the detention, transfer, treatment, trial, or conditions of confinement of an alien who is or was detained by the United States" (MCA, sec. 7). Thus it appeared that aliens could be held indefinitely without any access to the courts to challenge their status or treatment. The act also declared that the president could interpret the Geneva Conventions and that the military commissions set up by the act were in accord with Common Article 3 of Geneva, and thus regularly constituted courts.[86]

The court-stripping provisions of the act regarding habeas corpus were quickly challenged in court, and were upheld by the District of Columbia Court of Appeals in *Boumediene v. Bush* in February 2007.[87] The appeal challenged the court-stripping provisions of both the Detainee Treatment Act of 2005 and the Military Commissions Act of 2006. By a 2-1 majority, the Court ruled that the language and congressional intent of the laws were clear and that U.S. courts did not have jurisdiction to hear habeas corpus appeals from aliens held at Guantánamo and that aliens held outside the United States had no constitutional rights.

The habeas-related Supreme Court rulings in *Rasul* and *Hamdan* were based on statutory interpretation and did not reach the constitutional question of whether the two laws amounted to a suspension of habeas corpus. The Constitution allows the suspension only in cases of "Rebellion or Invasion" (Article I, Section 9). In *Boumediene v. Bush*, however, the Court of Appeals ruled that the alien inmates of Guantánamo did not have a constitutional right to habeas and thus the suspension clause was not violated by the MCA. The decision involved a constitutional ruling, and the Supreme Court was faced with the question of affirming or denying the decision of the appeals court. Even though the MCA denied alien detainees a writ of habeas corpus to challenge the evidence upon which they were declared enemy combatants, the CSRT process itself might be judged to be an adequate substitute for habeas corpus. In the fall of 2007 the Supreme Court heard the case.

The argument that aliens have a constitutional right to a habeas corpus hearing does not imply that they cannot be imprisoned by the military. It merely means that they can challenge the grounds of their imprisonment through a writ of habeas corpus and attempt to persuade a federal judge that the government was mistaken about the basis for their incarceration.[88] It is by no means certain that federal courts would agree with the arguments of detainees, but a hearing in court on the issue might disclose evidence about the conditions of their confinement. In addition to their defense of the CSRTs, the Bush administration did not want any public disclosure of the methods of interrogation to which the detainees at Guantánamo were subjected, arguing that to do so would disclose sensitive intelligence techniques to the enemy. If terrorists knew about the techniques used by U.S. personnel in interrogations, they would be able to train to resist them. Critics of the administration, however, argued that the reason that the administration did not want to allow public evidence about detainee treatment was that it did not want the harsh interrogation methods to be made public. Former detainees and public accounts had already disclosed most, if not all, of the techniques that the interrogators used.

GUANTÁNAMO LEGAL OFFICERS
CHALLENGE CSRT PROCEDURES

Questions about the procedures of the CSRTs and the military commissions were raised by two men who participated in their administration as military officers at Guantánamo. Lieutenant Colonel Stephen E. Abraham was an Army Reserve intelligence officer who was assigned to active duty (from September 9, 2004, to March 9, 2005) in the Office for the Administrative Review of the Detention of Enemy Combatants. He was assigned to gather information about detainees for the central computer depository. This evidence would be used in their CSRT hearings to determine whether or not they would be classified as enemy combatants.

In a statement to the Supreme Court in relation to a case on habeas corpus for Guantánamo detainees, Abraham criticized the process of information gathering and CSRT decisions. He said that the information used by CSRTs that established that detainees were enemy combatants was fragmentary, generic, outdated, and often not specific to the individuals in question or the circumstances of their capture. "The classified information was stripped down, watered down, removed of context, incomplete and missing essential information. . . . What purported to be specific statements of fact lacked even the most fundamental earmarks of objectively credible evidence."[89] In addition the detainees often had no means of disputing the general evidence provided or questioning statements from other detainees that might have been obtained under pressure.

Abraham reported that members of CSRTs felt pressure to decide cases quickly and to determine that detainees were in fact enemy combatants. "The prevailing attitude was 'if they're in Guantánamo, they're there for a reason'. . . . Anything that resulted in a 'not enemy combatant' would just send ripples through the entire process. The interpretation is, 'You got the wrong result. Do it again.'"[90] When Abraham himself was assigned to a CSRT, he and two other officers found that there was "no factual basis" for determining the detainee to be an enemy combatant. After their determination, they were ordered to reopen the hearing, but with no further evidence presented, they reaffirmed their first determination that the detainee was not an enemy combatant. Abraham was not assigned to another CSRT panel.[91] All detainees had CSRT hearings, and of 558 cases, thirty-eight were determined not to be enemy combatants.[92]

On October 4, 2007, Morris D. Davis, a career Air Force officer and the chief prosecutor for the military commissions, resigned from his position "because I felt that the system had become deeply politicized and that I could no longer do my job effectively or responsibly."[93] Davis explained that the secretary of defense had replaced a career military officer as "convening authority" with a political appointee. The convening authority oversaw the military commission's process, but rather than acting as a neutral supervisor of the process, the new appointee aligned herself with the prosecution, thus compromising the fairness of the process. In addition, the chief prosecutor (Davis) was placed in the direct chain of command under the DOD general counsel, William Haynes, who had been active in implementing the harsh interrogation policies of the Bush administration. Davis said that he had ruled out any evidence gained through waterboarding. Davis argued that if the tribunals were to be truly impartial military commissions "and not merely a political smoke screen," control of them should be given to professional military officers: "It is time for the political appointees who created this quagmire to let go."[94] Davis later said that William Haynes, the Pentagon general counsel, said, "We can't have acquittals; we've got to have convictions."[95]

These were serious declarations made by officers who participated in the Guantánamo CSRT and the commission's process in general, and in specific cases. Abraham, a lawyer, spent twenty-five years in the Army Reserve and was a political conservative; Davis was a career Air Force officer. These statements, based on personal experience, severely undercut any claim that the procedures of the CSRTs or commissions provided adequate hearings about the status or guilt of Guantánamo detainees.

BROADER SIGNIFICANCE OF MCA

The broader importance of the Military Commissions Act was that it allocated significant new powers to the president. It allowed the president or secretary of defense to decide unilaterally who is an enemy combatant; it allowed the executive to prosecute the person in a tribunal that allows the use of coerced testimony; and it purported to preclude any oversight or appeal of the actions of the executive by the judiciary.[96]

Critics of the administration argued that the new law would allow U.S. forces to capture anyone declared an "enemy combatant" anywhere in the world, including those thought to have purposefully supported hostilities against U.S. co-belligerents (for example a donor to a charity in Australia that has been suspected of aiding al Qaeda), and hold them indefinitely. These suspects could be held without charges being filed against them and subjected to harsh interrogation techniques with no recourse to the courts for writs of habeas corpus to correct possible mistakes by the military or the CIA. Thus there would be no check on executive actions that might have been mistaken or violated the rights of the suspects. Critics also questioned whether the MCA amounted to a constitutional suspension of habeas corpus.[97] The MCA represented a congressional ratification of executive power to set up unilaterally military commissions, conduct trials, preclude any appeal for habeas corpus, and sentence detainees with no judicial or congressional oversight. If it is allowed to stand, it represents an important expansion of presidential power.

In testimony before the Senate Judiciary Committee, Attorney General Alberto Gonzales called into question the right to a writ of habeas corpus in the United States. In response to a question from Senator Arlen Specter, Gonzales said, "There is no expressed grant of habeas in the Constitution. There's a prohibition against taking it away." Specter pressed him: "The Constitution says you can't take it away except in case of rebellion or invasion. Doesn't that mean you have the right of habeas corpus unless there's an invasion or rebellion?" Gonzales replied: "I meant by that comment the Constitution doesn't say every individual in the United States or every citizen is hereby granted or assured the right to habeas. Doesn't say that. It simply says the right of habeas corpus shall not be suspended except. . . ."[98]

The fact that the attorney general raised the issue in such a way called into question the commitment of the Bush administration to honor the right. Bush's executive order setting up military tribunals denied to detainees the writ. So Gonzales's saying that the habeas right does not apply "to every individual in the United States or citizen" indicated the perspective of the Bush administration that the president could deny the right to a writ of habeas corpus to certain individuals by detaining them indefinitely without charging them with a crime or allowing them to challenge the grounds of their incarceration before an independent judge.

It should be reiterated that a writ of habeas corpus does not mean that prisoners will be set free. It merely means that the executive must present reasonable evidence to a judge that the person has been imprisoned according to law and that there is sufficient evidence that the person committed a crime to keep him in jail until his trial.

The Wrong Man Problem

The premise of the Bush administration's argument that "aggressive interrogation," or in President Bush's words, "the program," was necessary is that the persons to be harshly interrogated (or tortured, depending on the definition) have valuable information, the knowledge of which would prevent future attacks on civilians in the United States. This justification for imprisonment and harsh interrogation breaks down if it is not certain that the victim is indeed a terrorist who possesses such knowledge. Thus the possibility of capturing the wrong person and subjecting him to torture to extract evidence presents a serious problem to the advocates of the Bush administration's detention policies. Unfortunately, there is abundant evidence that many prisoners held in Guantánamo, Abu Ghraib, or tortured at Bagram Air Force Base in Afghanistan were innocent bystanders or low-level functionaries. Such people would have no knowledge of any possible future attacks on the United States and may have been swept up by allied forces and handed over to U.S. forces. Evidence of the capture and incarceration of innocent individuals accused of being enemy combatants reinforces the importance of habeas corpus procedures in order to balance the zeal of executive branch personnel who genuinely want to punish the guilty or protect the security of the nation.

GENERAL EVIDENCE OF MISTAKEN IMPRISONMENT

Two professors of law at Seton Hall undertook an analysis of the more than 500 detainees held at Guantánamo in 2005.[99] They based their evaluation exclusively on official U.S. government documents and did not use any assertions of those who had been detained. In contrast to what Secretary Rumsfeld called "the worst of the worst," the Seton Hall Report found, among other facts, that (quoting the report):

1) Only 5 percent of the detainees were captured by United States forces. Eighty-six percent (86%) of the detainees were arrested by either Pakistan or the Northern Alliance and turned over to United States custody.

2) Fifty-five percent (55%) of the detainees were not determined to have committed any hostile acts against the United States or its coalitional allies.

3) Only 8 percent of the detainees were characterized as al Qaeda fighters. Of the remaining detainees, 40 percent have no definitive connection with al Qaeda at all and 18 percent have no definitive affiliation with either al Qaeda or the Taliban.[100]

They found further that 60 percent of the inmates were detained because they were "associated with" groups that are deemed to be "terrorist organizations." Only 10 detainees were charged with a crime regarding the laws of war.[101]

A study by the West Point Combating Terrorism Center, using the same DOD data, agreed with the Seton Hall study that only 5 percent of the detainees were captured by U.S. forces, but characterized the detainees differently than the Seton Hall study did. The West Point study found that 73 percent of the detainees (based on unclassified records) could be categorized as a "demonstrated threat" as an enemy combatant; 95 percent were a "potential threat;" 77 percent were associated with terrorist group members who posed a threat; and that 6 detainees (1.6 percent) posed no threat.[102]

In Iraq, investigations of Abu Ghraib by the International Committee of the Red Cross (ICRC) indicated that significant portions of the inmates probably did not fall into the category of those who might possess important information central to the protection of the United States from future attacks. The ICRC, after a visit to Abu Ghraib, stated: "Certain CF [Coalition Forces] military intelligence officers told the ICRC that in their estimate between 70 and 90 percent of the persons deprived of their liberty in Iraq had been arrested by mistake."[103]

One of the reasons that prisoners were of little intelligence value and may not have participated in hostilities toward the United States was the way in which they came to be prisoners of the United States. In Afghanistan, most U.S. soldiers did not know the language of their captives nor did they understand the nuances of violent tribal rivalries; thus they had to depend on Afghan locals to capture and interrogate suspected hostile forces. The Seton Hall report pointed out that the 95 percent of the detainees who were not captured by American forces were rendered to U.S. troops during the time that large bounties were offered for the capture of members of the Taliban or al Qaeda. One Afghanistan leaflet promised, "Get wealth and power beyond your dreams. Help the Anti-Taliban Forces rid Afghanistan of murderers and terrorists."[104] Another noted that those who helped capture Taliban or al Qaeda fighters would be rewarded with $4,285.[105] Secretary Rumsfeld said that leaflets advertising these offers were "dropping like snowflakes in December in Chicago."[106] With incentives like these, it does not take too much imagination to understand the temptation these bounty offers presented to turn in personal or tribal enemies. But it is also true that some of the detainees were captured by Pakistani forces who were not motivated by bounties.

In Guantánamo, the reality was that not all of the prisoners held were in fact enemy belligerents or knew information that the United States could use to prevent future attacks, and a number of them were released from Guantánamo. Major General Michael Dunlavey, who was in charge of interrogations at Guantánamo, estimated that up to half of the prisoners did not possess any intelligence of value to the United States.[107] Some U.S. personnel in Afghanistan tried to alleviate the problem by drawing up a list of detainees who were innocent, not dangerous, or who had little intelligence value. Interviews with military intelligence officers in Afghanistan and Guantánamo Bay and the reading of files by Los Angeles Times reporters in 2002 found that at least fifty-nine of the detainees had been judged by U.S. intelligence officers in Afghanistan to be of little or no intelligence value.[108]

Some of the captives were farmers, taxi drivers, workers, or persons who had been conscripted by the Taliban and were not fighting U.S. forces but were fighting for the Taliban against the Northern Alliance. In 2002 there were so many prisoners of little intelligence value that General Dunlavey actually went to Afghanistan to "chew us out," in the words of one U.S. officer. Dunlavey complained that many of those sent to Guantánamo were "Mickey Mouse" types in terms of military or intelligence value.[109] Despite documenting these cases of low-value (for intelligence purposes) captives, the danger of making even one mistake was so high that all of the fifty-nine ended up being flown to Guantánamo. And once in Guantánamo it was very difficult to get out, although many of the detainees were eventually released. Detainees were presumed to be guilty, had little opportunity to prove their innocence, and were denied the opportunity to present their cases to an independent judge through a writ of habeas corpus. U.S. officials in the Pentagon denied the presence of any detainees who should not have been in Guantánamo. "All are considered enemy combatants lawfully detained in accordance with the law of armed conflict," according to one Pentagon official.[110]

Given this evidence that many detainees in Guantánamo did not fight directly against U.S. forces or possess any intelligence of value, it is possible that habeas corpus hearings might have helped the military distinguish detainees of little intelligence value from those who actively supported al Qaeda. In addition to the general evidence cited above about the aggregate of detainees, some accounts of individuals who were

wrongly imprisoned present compelling evidence of the dire consequences that can result from mistakes by U.S. forces. The following sections will provide brief summaries of people captured in the war on terror who turned out not to be guilty of the crimes of which they were
accused: Maher Arar, Khaled el-Masri, Donald Vance, and Jose Padilla.

THE CASE OF MAHER ARAR

Maher Arar was a computer programmer who was a Canadian citizen of
Syrian origin. As he was transferring planes at Kennedy International
Airport in New York City in September 2002, he was seized by the FBI
and not given an opportunity to appeal his seizure to the courts because
he was not a U.S. citizen. Arar repeatedly denied that he was connected
with al Qaeda. After thirteen days of interrogations, U.S. authorities,
convinced that he was lying, put him on a plane and took him to Jordan.
He was then driven to Syria, where he was tortured over a ten-month
period and forced to confess that he had trained in an al Qaeda camp in
Afghanistan to fight the United States, which was not true. Arar said that
he was kept in a small underground cell with no windows and beaten
with heavy electrical cables, among other torments.[111]

When U.S. authorities finally realized that his designation as an
"Islamic extremist" resulted from the fabrication and incompetence of a
member of the Royal Canadian Mounted Police, he was released in
October 2003 with no apology or admission of fault by the United
States. Arar brought a lawsuit against the U.S. government for his false
imprisonment and torture in Syria, but the Bush administration invoked
the "state secrets privilege" to argue that the "intelligence, foreign policy and national security interests of the United States" would be jeop-
ardized by a court hearing.[112] A lawyer representing Arar said that the
government lawyers "are saying this case can't be tried, and the classified information on which they're basing this argument can't even be
shared with the opposing lawyers. It's the height of arrogance—they
think they can do anything they want in the name of the global war on
terrorism."[113] With this type of claim by the Bush administration, it will
be very difficult for citizens to make any firm judgment as to whether the
accounts of torture by many other detainees are true or not.

The Canadian government conducted an inquiry and officially apolo-
gized for Arar's ordeal, and the head of the Royal Canadian Mounted

Police resigned.[114] The head of the commission, Justice Dennis R. O'Connor, said after the report was released: "I am able to say categorically that there is no evidence to indicate that Mr. Arar has committed any offense or that his activities constituted a threat to the security of Canada."[115] Three other men of Syrian origin were picked up during visits to Syria and imprisoned for several years (one for only one month). They were released without any charge or explanation.[116]

THE CASE OF KHALED EL-MASRI

On December 31, 2003, Khaled el-Masri, who had been residing in Germany, was arrested when he was on vacation in Macedonia, interrogated for twenty-three days by Macedonian police, and then flown by the CIA to a prison in Afghanistan.[117] While there, he was imprisoned, shackled, beaten, tortured, and had drugs injected into him by U.S. personnel. Masri had a passport that had the same name as another person the CIA wanted to arrest.[118] In May of 2004 National Security Adviser Condoleezza Rice, after learning that it was a case of mistaken identity, ordered that Masri be released. He was taken to Albania, dropped off, and told that he could return home to Germany. In January 2007 the German government issued warrants for the arrest of twenty-five CIA personnel and one Air Force officer for kidnapping and inflicting bodily harm on Masri.[119]

When Masri sued the CIA, the district judge in Alexandria, Virginia, said that his case had to be dismissed because of the state secrets privilege, even though Masri had evidently been done a great injustice. On appeal to the Fourth Circuit, the Justice Department asserted that judges were bound to defer to executive branch claims that continuing with the case would reveal state secrets. The lawyer for the Bush administration said that CIA Director Porter Goss had filed a secret statement arguing that hearing the case would "have a cascading effect that will have devastating consequences" for U.S. national security. Masri's lawyer pointed out that President Bush had admitted on September 6, 2006, that the CIA established secret prisons in other nations ("black sites") and undertook rendition flights to them.[120]

Since judges routinely defer to executive branch claims that cases involving "state secrets" cannot be heard by judges, there is no way that the executive branch can be brought under any oversight in cases in which it invokes state secrets. The Bush administration argued that judges cannot be trusted to make responsible decisions about what information should be kept secret: "Even disclosures to judges carry risks," said Justice Department attorney Gregory Katsas.[121] Thus the Bush administration had a legal license to keep secret any case they thought might be embarrassing to the administration, since not much more than an assertion is sufficient to dismiss any case in which the executive claims the state secrets privilege.

Lest one think that being an American citizen would guarantee treatment in accord with the Constitution, consider the cases of Navy veteran Donald Vance and Brooklyn-born citizen Jose Padilla.

THE CASE OF NAVY VETERAN DONALD VANCE

Suppose you were a Navy veteran who went to Iraq to work for a contractor supporting U.S. troops. Suppose further that you began to suspect that the contractor for whom you were working was involved in selling arms to Iraqi militias or terrorists and that you were working with the FBI to investigate the corruption. Suppose that you became frightened that the contractor might find out that you were informing the FBI, and so you went to the United States Embassy to stay overnight. You might suppose that you would be safe, but you would be wrong.

This is what happened to twenty-nine-year-old Donald Vance in April 2006.[122] He had gone to Iraq as a security contractor and became a whistle-blower when he suspected corruption. He met with the FBI and set up a communications link so that they could investigate the contracting company. Fearing for his safety, Vance went to the American Embassy to stay overnight. Just before dawn, he was awakened, shackled with zip ties, blindfolded, and put in a Humvee. As he was being driven through Baghdad to maximum security prison Camp Cropper, he requested a helmet and flak jacket, but the Army refused. When he got to Camp Cropper, he was given a number and he was often referred to by his captors merely by the number.

He was eventually told that he was being held because he was associated with a contractor that was suspected of selling arms to terrorists. Of course, Vance knew this because he was the one who had exposed the firm to the FBI and told the military authorities where the weapons caches were. Vance, a resident of Chicago and a Navy veteran, had no language problem with his American guards. When his military captors contacted the FBI (after delaying three weeks), they continued to hold him because he "posed a threat."

Despite the obvious fact that he was an American and not a member of an Islamic militia or a terrorist group, he was treated harshly and without any respect for his rights as an American citizen or human being. He was explicitly denied the right to a lawyer to contest his detention at a hearing to decide whether he should continue to be imprisoned. Thus an American citizen was imprisoned by American officials and was denied due process and habeas corpus.

When he was taken from his 9-by-9-foot cell for interrogation, his hands and feet were shackled and he was blindfolded. He was interrogated by persons who were identified as being from the FBI, CIA, the Naval Criminal Investigative Service, and Defense Intelligence Agency. His pleas to them that he was innocent and an FBI informer were ignored by his interrogators; they evidently considered him part of the arms smuggling operation. His requests for a lawyer were continually refused. Bright lights were kept on in his cell twenty-four hour a day, and loud, heavy metal or country music was played outside of his cell. He was awakened at random times in the night and forced to stand in his cell, and he was not allowed to shield his eyes from the lights.

A Detainee Status Board met to consider Vance's case several times, but only once with him present. He was told that he was allowed to be present at his status review meetings because he was an American, but that all others were not allowed to be present at their review board meetings. He was told that he could not have a lawyer but could have a personal representative. When he asked that an associate, also wrongly imprisoned with him, be made his personal representative, the request was denied. At the board meeting that he attended, he was allowed to see some of the papers the board was using, but he was not allowed to see most of the papers the board consulted. (So much for being informed of the charges against him.) The members of the board wore Army uniforms, but without rank insignia or name tags.

Army spokesperson First Lieutenant Lea Ann Fracasso said that he had been "treated fair[ly] and humanely," and that the Army had no record that he had complained about his treatment. When he was finally released after ninety-seven days—with no explanation and no apology—

he was asked if he were going to contact an attorney or talk to the press. He interpreted this as a threat that he might not be released, so he merely said, "No, sir, I want to go home."

If innocent American citizens are treated this way by United States military personnel, imagine how they treat innocent victims whose language they do not understand and who, they are told by President Bush, Vice President Cheney, and Donald Rumsfeld, are "bad men" and the "worst of the worst." Vance later recalled his experience at the mercy of U.S. soldiers and his attempts to return to a normal life: "It's really hard. . . . I feel ashamed, depressed, still have nightmares, and I'd even say I suffer from some paranoia."

THE CASE OF JOSE PADILLA: A POSSIBLE RIGHT MAN

In the case of Jose Padilla, the Bush administration argued that it could imprison a citizen of the United States indefinitely without charging him and without allowing the courts to consider an appeal for a writ of habeas corpus. Because of court decisions, the administration was not able to act as it wanted to, and Padilla was eventually granted a trial.

Jose Padilla, a citizen of the United States and former resident of Chicago, was seized by U.S. marshals as he was reentering the country in May 2002. Attorney General John Ashcroft announced that Padilla was conspiring with al Qaeda to detonate a "radioactive dirty bomb" in the United States and that he had been trained in Pakistan in terrorist techniques. He was first held as a material witness, but in June of 2002, President Bush designated him an "enemy combatant" and ordered that he be placed in military custody, where he was denied access to a lawyer.

Padilla appealed for a writ of habeas corpus, and a district court ruled that it had jurisdiction to hear the case. The Second Circuit Court of Appeals declared that "the President lacks inherent constitutional authority as Commander-in-Chief to detain American citizens on American soil outside a zone of combat."[123] Padilla could not be held by the military and had to be turned over to civilian authority. The Supreme Court remanded the case on procedural grounds. Without reaching the merits of the case, the court ruled that Padilla had filed his petition in the wrong jurisdiction and had to seek a writ in South Carolina rather than New York.

In September 2005 the Fourth Circuit Court of Appeals ruled on the Padilla case and held that the president did have the authority to detain indefinitely American citizens, and the government did not have to file criminal charges against persons designated as enemy combatants. Padilla appealed to the Supreme Court and argued that the government could not legally hold him indefinitely without charging him with a crime. When faced with a potential loss in the Supreme Court, the Bush administration decided to indict Padilla in criminal court.[124]

Padilla was indicted in November 2005 (after four years in captivity) on terrorism and conspiracy charges unrelated to his alleged dirty bomb plans. His lawyers requested a competency hearing, arguing that his treatment by the government had rendered him unable to defend himself. Previously, Padilla had said that he was seriously abused during his more than three years in custody, including being forced to stand in stress positions, threatened with execution, and given "truth serums."[125] Padilla's lawyers said that he was denied counsel for twenty-one months and kept in isolation and sensory deprivation in his small cell in which the windows were blacked out. He had virtually no contact with other human beings other than his interrogators. His meals were passed to him through the slot in his cell door, and he slept on a steel plate after his foam mattress was taken from him. His lawyers say that he was subjected to threats of execution, assaults, stress positions, and hooding.[126]

Some insight about the way American citizens who are declared enemy combatants would be treated can be gleaned from a tape of his visit to the military dentist in 2006. On May 21, 2006, several guards in riot gear came to Padilla's cell and opened a small door at the bottom of his cell door. Padilla put his feet through the slot and the guards shackled them. Then he put his hands through another opening in the door and his wrists were handcuffed and attached to a metal belt. Blackened goggles were placed over his eyes and noise-blocking headphones placed over his ears. He was then taken to the dentist by the guards who had shaded plastic covering their eyes. There was no evidence that Padilla struggled or complained. Padilla was described to his lawyers by brig staff as "so docile and inactive that his behavior was like that of a 'piece of furniture.'"[127] A forensic psychologist who examined Padilla said that he was "an anxiety-ridden, broken individual who is incapacitated by that anxiety."[128]

As a result of his treatment, his lawyers argued that his mental capacity was compromised and that he could not assist in his own defense.

Although a government psychiatrist judged that Padilla could participate in his own defense, the director of forensic psychiatry at Creedmoor Psychiatric Center in Queens, New York, judged that "as a result of his experiences during his detention and interrogation, Mr. Padilla . . . has impairments in reasoning . . . complicated by the neuropsychiatric effects of prolonged isolation."[129]

The Pentagon denied any impropriety in Padilla's treatment. Lieutenant Colonel Todd Vician denied Padilla's claims about his treatment, and court papers show that the prosecutors "deny in the strongest terms" any accusations of torture; they say that he was treated humanely. The government prosecutors asked the judge to disallow any descriptions of Padilla's treatment during his trial for fear that they would "distract and inflame the jury."[130] Padilla, despite watching his lawyers defend him in court, did not fully trust them and thought that they might have been part of the government's prosecution team. This feeling is not irrational. Part of the practice of interrogation at times was to tell a victim that his lawyers were not to be trusted.

The Florida district court judge ruled that Padilla was competent enough to be tried in court. The prosecution argued that in 1998 he had left the United States, that he intended to commit terrorist acts abroad, and that he went to a camp in Afghanistan for training in terrorism. The jury convicted him of conspiracy to commit murder because he was in training in order to learn how to kill. The defense argued that the prosecution offered no evidence that he was connected to al Qaeda or that he planned to engage in any terrorist activities or return to the United States to do so.[131] In January 2008 Padilla was sentenced to seventeen years in prison.

Padilla's situation was symptomatic of the problems raised by the Bush administration's approach to its treatment of terrorism suspects and specifically American citizens who have been declared enemy combatants. If detainees are tortured or interrogated by harsh means, it is difficult to get a court to convict them on charges the evidence for which is obtained through coercive means. In addition, the government is often unwilling to take detainees to trial because the trial might include evidence of the treatment the detainees received while in custody. Administration lawyers said that revelations of interrogation techniques might reveal the methods and thus let terrorists learn how to resist those techniques most effectively. Critics of the administration argue that the administration was worried that the public would be outraged at the treatment individuals received at the hands of U. S. personnel, including what most nations would consider torture.

The unwillingness of the government to present evidence against Padilla, its shifting legal ploys over the years, and its alleged harsh treatment of Padilla that led to his questionable mental competence have combined to make it very difficult if not impossible ever to know whether Padilla was guilty of the crimes of which Attorney General John Ashcroft publicly accused him.

In April 2007, 385 detainees remained in Guantánamo, down from approximately 680 in May 2003. More than one fifth of these, eighty-two inmates from sixteen countries, had been cleared for release, but there was no immediate move to release them. U.S. officials said that they intended to try sixty to eighty of the remaining 300 for crimes and eventually to set the remaining detainees free. The difficulty in doing this, however, was illustrated by the slowness in releasing the eighty-two who had been cleared by May 2007.[132]

The problem, according to U.S. officials, was that it was difficult to find third-party nations that would accept the inmates. The United States would not repatriate detainees to their own nations if U.S. officials suspected that they might be subject to persecution or sent to a country that had been listed by the State Department for human rights abuses. A legal adviser to the State Department, said, "It often takes us months and months, or even years, to negotiate the human rights assurances that we are comfortable with before we will transfer someone to another country."[133]

In speculating about what might constitute those human rights abuses of which the State Department might be wary, one might include:
—torture,
—harsh interrogation methods and conditions of imprisonment,
—arbitrary imprisonment,
—indefinite incarceration without charge,
—denying prisoners the right to see the charges against them,
—denying prisoners the right to see a lawyer,
—severely limiting contact with lawyers for those who were represented,

—undermining trust in a lawyer by saying that the prisoner's lawyers were not genuine,

—not allowing inmates or lawyers the right to see evidence against them,

—not allowing a habeas corpus–type appeal to independent judicial officials,

—not allowing inmates to communicate with relatives, and

—keeping inmates hidden from the International Red Cross (that is, as "ghost detainees").

Of course, some of the above conditions pertained to some of the U.S. prisoners at Guantánamo itself. There is no small irony that after six years of treating some detainees as the United States did that U.S. officials should hesitate to release prisoners to other nations because they might be subjected to conditions similar to (though probably harsher than) those to which the United States had subjected them.

One reason that countries might not want to accept prisoners who have been incarcerated in Guantánamo is that officials in the countries might have believed the president, vice president, secretary of defense, and other U.S. officials who characterized individuals kept in Guantá-namo as the "worst of the worst." Other nations might think that the United States was merely reassuring them because it was unwilling to try them in order to prevent the conditions of their imprisonment from being made public. As of May 2007, only two detainees had been charged with crimes under the military commission system created by law in 2006. One of them, Australian David Hicks, had pleaded guilty to supporting terrorists in order to be released after a nine-month sentence.[134]

One possibility for releasing inmates whose home country might subject them to further abuse would be for the United States to grant them asylum. But military officials said that they were still classified as enemy combatants and, even though they have not been charged, they could not be released in the United States. This is one consequence of one's designation as an enemy combatant by the secretary of defense, a designation that cannot be challenged and which can be applied to U.S. citizens. According to the Military Commissions Act of 2006, U.S. citizens might be designated as "enemy combatants" and held indefinitely without charge or a habeas corpus hearing. This happened to Jose Padilla before he was finally charged with conspiracy.

Conclusion

From the beginning, the Bush administration fought to keep its policies and practices concerning detention of suspected terrorists secret. It set up the Guantánamo Base as a high-security facility and tried to deny inmates the assistance of counsel. It set up military commissions that denied minimal due process rights to detainees and allowed for no appeal outside the executive branch. When the Supreme Court in *Rasul* (2004) ruled that aliens had the right to a habeas corpus appeal, the administration used the DTA (2005) as a vehicle to deny, through law, future habeas corpus appeals. It sought to use CSRTs to substitute for habeas corpus hearings.

When the Supreme Court ruled in *Hamdan* (2006) that President Bush's military commissions were unlawful and that the Geneva Conventions applied to Guantánamo, the administration pushed the MCA through Congress, which amended the DTA in order to deny any pending appeals to the courts from Guantánamo detainees and gave the president the authority to interpret the Geneva Conventions. In April 2007 the Justice Department went to a federal appeals court to ask for the imposition of tighter controls on lawyers for Guantánamo inmates, arguing that communication between detainees and lawyers caused "intractable problems and threats to security."[135] After much public outrage, the administration revoked the request. In the spring of 2007 an assistant secretary of defense publicly implied that lawyers representing Guantánamo detainees were not loyal citizens.[136] After extensive media coverage and controversy, the individual was relieved of his position. When some cases did get to court, such as when Maher Arar brought a suit against the United States, the administration was concerned that a hearing or trial might disclose the conditions under which detainees were held. Consequently it used the official secrets privilege to stop judicial proceedings.[137]

In conclusion, we return to the fundamental importance of habeas corpus to a limited government under the rule of law. Even in a time of war, individual rights and freedoms must be protected. As Alexander Hamilton said in *Federalist* No. 8:

Safety from external danger is the most powerful director of national conduct. Even the ardent love of liberty will, after a time, give way to its dictates. The violent destruction of life and property incident to war; the continual effort and alarm attendant on a state of continual danger, will compel nations the most attached to liberty, to resort for repose and security to institutions which have a tendency to destroy their civil and political rights. To be more safe, they, at length, become willing to run the risk of being less free.

As shown in this chapter, it has taken centuries of struggle for executive power to be limited by habeas corpus. In the cases of the "wrong man" presented in this chapter, a writ considered by a judge might have saved individuals from years of incarceration and torture. But the longer-term threat to liberty comes from conceding to the executive the authority to deny the writ of habeas corpus at its own discretion. As Justice Scalia said: "The Founders warned us about the risk, and equipped us with a Constitution designed to deal with it." He continued:

Many think it not only inevitable but entirely proper that liberty give way to security in times of national crisis—that, at the extremes of military exigency, *inter arma silent leges*. Whatever the general merits of the view that war silences law or modulates its voice, that view has no place in the interpretation and application of a Constitution designed precisely to confront war and, in a manner that accords with democratic principles, to accommodate it.[138]

President Bush claimed constitutional authority to deny the writ of habeas corpus to those persons he determined to be enemy combatants. The DTA and MCA have given the patina of law to President Bush's actions. The combination of executive prerogative and the sanction of law presents a significant precedent that can be used by future presidents as they please. But as Madison said in *Federalist* No. 10, "Enlightened statesmen will not always be at the helm."

CHAPTER SIX

THE POWER TO TORTURE

"We conclude that for an act to constitute torture, it must inflict pain that is . . . equivalent in intensity to the pain accompanying serious physical injury, such as organ failure, impairment of bodily function, or even death."
> —Jay S. Bybee, Office of Legal Counsel, August 2002

"We do not torture."
> —President Bush

"When *I* use a word," Humpty Dumpty said, in a rather scornful tone, "it means just what I choose it to mean—neither more nor less." "The question is," said Alice, "whether you *can* make words mean so many different things." "The question is," said Humpty Dumpty, "which is to be master—that's all."
> —Lewis Carroll, *Through the Looking Glass*

Torture can be used for a number of purposes: for sadism, to punish, to obtain a confession, or to secure information. Torture has been sanctioned by governments throughout human history for all of these purposes, but the official justification of torture (or "robust interrogation") in the United States after 9/11 has been for purposes of obtaining information about possible future terrorist acts. A key distinction must be made between torture in general and torture under the color of law. The former is an individual or group crime (against law or nature, or both). Torture sanctioned by law, however, is particularly insidious because, by being authorized or warranted by law, it becomes legitimized and often institutionalized. Governmental sanctioning of torture is a license for sadists within the government or armed forces to inflict pain upon other humans and to believe that they are doing their duty according to law. Government-sanctioned torture also encourages individuals, who are not necessarily sadists themselves, to commit or enable torture in a systematic way.

The argument of this chapter is that the conditions that allowed a relatively small number of U.S. personnel to engage in torture were set by executive leadership. In reaction to the atrocities of 9/11, President Bush decided that the attacks had to be met with more than the ordinary military means. Since the enemy was spread throughout the world in small cells rather than being controlled by the hierarchy of an established state, U.S. forces needed nontraditional tools with which to gain information. His decision to suspend the Geneva Agreements with respect to members of al Qaeda allowed a cascading set of legal and operational decisions to set the conditions under which torture would be used. Since the enemy had used illegitimate methods by attacking civilians, the United States must, it was argued, be willing to use unconventional means to fight that enemy. Since the enemy did not play by the rules and was willing to kill civilians, the United States should not be squeamish about using torture to extract information from terrorists.

As far as we know, these decisions by President Bush were the first time in American history that the decision to torture enemy prisoners was connected to and defended by the president.[1] This chapter argues that the sanctioning of torture by President Bush and others in his administration has damaged the reputation of the United States throughout the world and has set dangerous precedents. It has also facilitated the recruitment of potential terrorists who are outraged at the humiliation of detainees of their own ethnicity or religion. Despite the resistance of many in the professional officer corps of the military services to President Bush's initial decisions about torture, the professionalism of the United States Army came into question. The U.S. Army Field Manual No. 2-22.3 (FM 34-52), "Human Intelligence Collector Operations," was revised in 2006, and the policies that allowed torture were set aside, returning the U.S. military to its traditional policy of abiding by the Geneva Conventions. In 2007, however, President Bush issued an executive order implementing the Military Commissions Act that authorized the CIA to continue to use "enhanced" interrogation techniques with suspects.[2]

This chapter begins with a review of some of the official reports that documented how abuse and torture were used at Guantánamo and Abu Ghraib. It will then take up the logic of torture and some of its ethical dimensions. The chapter will next examine how leadership and operational decisions set the conditions for torture. Finally it will lay out the legal arguments surrounding President Bush's decisions about coercive interrogation and changes in the law regarding torture. The conclusion will analyze the broader implications of torture for the United States, both internationally and domestically.

Torture and Inhumane Treatment of Prisoners

Since some citizens who have not examined the evidence may think that allegations of torture by U.S. personnel were merely reports of minor incidents disproportionately reported by the media and enemies of the United States, establishing that U.S. personnel (military, CIA, and contractors) did in fact subject detainees to torture is important. Some of the ample evidence of torture was documented in official reports commissioned by the Department of Defense and carried out by career military officers. This section will review some of the conclusions of reports by military officers as well as FBI agents and the International Committee of the Red Cross.

After U.S. forces invaded Iraq and defeated the military forces of Saddam Hussein, the notorious prison at Abu Ghraib, which had been the center for much of Saddam's torture and killing, was looted and stripped of any useful building materials. The U.S. occupying authority had the prison rebuilt and converted to use by U.S. occupying forces for the detention of prisoners.

Brigadier General Janis Karpinski took formal control of U.S. military prisons in Iraq on June 30, 2003, and the facility went into operation on August 4, 2003. A month later, General Geoffrey Miller, the commander of the U.S. detention center at Guantánamo Bay, Cuba, visited Abu Ghraib and recommended changes that would require the military police to assist military intelligence in its mission of extracting information from inmates of the prison. After this visit, particularly in October, November, and December of 2003, U.S. personnel engaged in the now notorious abuses that resulted in the humiliation, injury, and death of prisoners.

THE TAGUBA REPORT

After photographic evidence of abuse of prisoners was reported in early January 2004, Major General Antonio M. Taguba was assigned to investigate the abuses. General Taguba concluded that at Abu Ghraib "numerous incidents of sadistic, blatant, and wanton criminal abuses were inflicted on several detainees. This systemic and illegal abuse of detainees was intentionally perpetrated by several members of the military police guard force."[3] Taguba concluded that abuse of prisoners was often done at the request of military intelligence personnel and "Other U.S. Government Agencies' (OGA) interrogators" (that is, the CIA) in order to "set physical and mental conditions for favorable interrogation of witnesses."[4] After General Taguba issued the report on the abuse that he was tasked to investigate, his military career was essentially finished; he was shunned by fellow officers and encouraged to retire.[5]

ARMY INSPECTOR GENERAL REPORT

In July 2004 the Army released the report of its inspector general, Lieutenant General Paul T. Mikolashek. His team examined 125 reports of possible abuses at sixteen detention centers and concluded that ninety-four of them involved misconduct and that twenty incidents resulted in deaths. He concluded, "In the few cases involving the progression to more serious abuse by soldiers, tolerance of behavior by any level of the chain of command, even if minor, led to an increase in the frequency and intensity of abuse."[6]

FAY REPORT

General Fay reported on the behavior of the 205th Military Intelligence Brigade at Abu Ghraib.[7] Fay specifically identified forty-four instances of alleged detainee abuse that were committed by soldiers and civilian contractors at Abu Ghraib. The physical abuse involved slapping, kicking, restricting breathing, dislocating the shoulder of a detainee, and other harsh treatment. Dogs were used to "threaten and terrify detainees," and dogs were released in the cells with juvenile detainees. Although there are legitimate uses of isolation, Fay concluded, isolation and deprivation of sleep were used in inappropriate ways at Abu Ghraib. Fay reported a death at Abu Ghraib as well as several alleged sexual assaults. Fay argued that the abuses resulted from "systemic problems" and "intense pressure felt by the personnel on the ground to produce actionable intelligence from detainees."[8]

JONES REPORT

Lieutenant General Anthony R. Jones was instructed to investigate the possible involvement of personnel higher in the chain of command than the soldiers of the 205th Military Intelligence Brigade.[9] Jones distinguished two types of abuse that took place at Abu Ghraib. One type was "intentional violent or sexual abuse" that was due to "individual criminal misconduct," in clear violation of law, policy, and Army doctrine. The other type was "inhumane or coercive" treatment of detainees in violation of international or U.S. criminal law. This latter type of behavior included clothing removal, use of dogs, and improper imposition of isolation, and it was conducted by soldiers who may have "honestly believed the techniques were condoned."[10] Jones argued that "the events at Abu Ghraib cannot be understood in a vacuum." The causes of the abuses ranged from inadequate resources, to confusion about allowable interrogation techniques, to conflicting "policy memoranda," to "leadership failure."[11] Jones concluded that "leadership failure, at the brigade level and below, clearly was a factor in not sooner discovering and taking actions to prevent" the abuses.[12]

FBI REPORTS

In May 2004 FBI officials in Iraq sent e-mails to Washington headquarters to ask whether they should report certain harsh treatment as abuse.[13] They said that before policy was changed in May 2005, an "Executive Order signed by President Bush authorized the following interrogation techniques among others[:] sleep 'management,' use of MWDs (military working dogs), 'stress positions' such as half squats, 'environmental manipulation,' such as the use of loud music, sensory deprivation through the use of hoods, [and so forth]."[14] In August 2004 a FBI official at Guantánamo sent an e-mail reporting on "what I observed at GTMO." The official said that he had observed on several occasions detainees "chained hand and foot in a fetal position to the floor, with no chair, food, or water. Most times they had urinated or defecated on themselves, and had been left there for 18 [to] 24 hours or more." The temperature in the rooms was at times made extremely cold or "well over 100 degrees."[15]

THE INTERNATIONAL COMMITTEE
OF THE RED CROSS REPORT

The International Committee of the Red Cross (ICRC) visited 14 U.S. detention sites in Iraq between March and November 2003 and objected to many cases of what were, in its judgment, abuses of detainees.[16] The ICRC report catalogued a wide range of abuses and ill-treatment of detainees by U.S. and coalition forces. The main violations of the Geneva Conventions on treatment of those captured included: "Brutality against protected persons upon capture and initial custody, sometimes causing death or serious injury; absence of notification of arrest; physical or psychological coercion during interrogation; prolonged solitary confinement in cells devoid of daylight; excessive and disproportionate use of force."[17] The report then specified methods of ill-treatment that were most frequently alleged, including: hooding to disorient and interfere with breathing, handcuffing with flexi-cuffs that damaged wrists, beatings with hard objects, threats against family members, pressing the face into the ground with boots, solitary confinement without clothes, [and] acts of humiliation."[18] Perhaps most alarming in the ICRC Report is that "certain CF [Coalition Forces] military intelligence officers told the ICRC that in their estimate between 70% and 90% of the persons deprived of their liberty in Iraq had been arrested by mistake."[19]

More than 100 detainees have died while in U.S. custody (though thirty-six were due to enemy mortar attacks), and homicide was the cause in forty-three of those deaths. Although some of the homicides were the result of escape attempts or justifiable homicides, some were the result of physical mistreatment by U.S. personnel. Fifteen of those who died between December 2002 and May of 2004 were "shot, strangled or beaten" before they died. The circumstances surrounding a number of the deaths included "blunt force trauma," "strangulation," and "asphyxia due to smothering and chest compression," among other things.[20] In effect, they were tortured to death.

The Logic of Torture

In considering whether torture is ever justified, two questions must be answered: is it morally justified? And does it work? If either of these questions is answered in the negative, torture is not an appropriate public policy. This section will first take up the most common justification for torture, the "ticking time bomb" scenario; it will then examine the efficacy of torture: Is it effective in extracting accurate information?

THE TICKING TIME BOMB SCENARIO

The most popular argument that torture may be necessary as a tactic is the "ticking time bomb" scenario. Blanket condemnations of torture are often countered with a hypothetical situation in which a captive knows where a time bomb has been hidden and refuses to divulge the information.[21] In such a case, the argument goes, torture would be necessary in order to save many innocent lives and thus be justified.

This seductive scenario has been popularized in the TV show "24" in which intrepid terror fighter Jack Bauer foils fictional attempts to kill Americans with deadly weapons. Often he is forced to resort to extreme measures (and the torture is usually graphically depicted) to get the bad guy to answer his questions, which sometimes leads to saving innocent lives in the nick of time. Bauer is portrayed as the patriotic hero, and his brutal means are necessary to save the day.[22] The Secretary of Homeland Security, Michael Chertoff, lent the prestige of his office to the message of the TV program by visiting the actors when they were filming an episode in Washington, D.C.[23]

The American public may be convinced that such situations are often encountered by U.S. law enforcement, antiterrorism, and military officials. But the reality is that they are very rare. Even the creator of the show, Bob Cochran, concedes that "most terrorism experts will tell you that the 'ticking time bomb' situation never occurs in real life, or very rarely. But on this show it happens every week."[24] The show is so compelling that the dean of the U.S. Military Academy at West Point, Brigadier General Patrick Finnegan, went to see its creators in California to ask them to tone things down a bit. Military cadets were so enamored of the show that it was difficult to get them to accept the professional military doctrine on the rule of law and the laws of war. Finnegan said, "I'd like them to stop. They should do a show where torture backfires."[25]

The ticking time bomb scenario becomes less seductive, however, if the premises upon which such a scenario rests are examined carefully.[26] Below is a list of the requisites necessary for a ticking time bomb scenario to be genuine, along with potential flaws in the premises:

1. There must be a planned attack (the bomb is still ticking).
   Possible problem: There may be no attack planned.
2. The interrogators must capture the right person.
   Possible problem: There are examples of U.S. personnel torturing innocent persons.
3. The captive must know about the planned attack.
   Possible problem: The captive may not know of the attack.
4. Torture must be the only way to obtain the information.
   Possible problem: Nonviolent means may be more effective (as many experienced interrogators have argued).
5. The captive must provide accurate information.
   Possible problems:
   Captive may invent answers merely to stop the pain.
   Captive may deceive interrogators (as John McCain did in Hanoi).
   Captive may purposefully have been given false information.
   Captive may not be able to specify location of bomb.
6. Captive must divulge information quickly; that is, there must be time to defuse bomb.
   Possible problems:
   Many techniques and examples of torture take days.
   Torture may cause unintended death; thus potential information will be lost.
7. If the information is obtained, there must be effective means to defuse the bomb.
   Possible problem: Technical capacity or knowledge to defuse the bomb may not exist.

If any one of these problems is present, torture will not solve the problem. Thus even if one posits that torture would be justified in order to save innocent lives, as in the ticking time bomb scenario, most torture scenarios are ruled out. The further a situation is removed from the ticking time bomb scenario, the less torture would be justified.

Further problems with the ticking time bomb scenario concern the real world of torture. Presidents and generals may authorize torture, but they do not carry it out. The first problem is that junior personnel may get carried away and let sadistic urges take over their interrogations, as happened at Abu Ghraib. The second problem flows from the first. If in fact there is a weapon of mass destruction, such as a nuclear bomb, hidden, amateurs might not be able to extract the information quickly enough or may kill the detainee before gaining the correct information. Thus in order to be prepared for such an eventuality, personnel in large organizations (for example, the CIA) must be trained in torture techniques. The professionalization of torture is a very serious step that any nation ought to undertake only after carefully considering its insidious and corrupting consequences.

I will concede for purposes of argument here, that in a genuine ticking time bomb situation, torture might be justified to obtain specific information that would almost certainly save innocent lives. But if the preconditions for the ticking time bomb situation mentioned above are not rigorously adhered to, any tactical situation could lead to torture. Any enemy captive might conceivably have information that might help one side, and thus torture might be justified by any nation in any armed conflict. This likely justification for the use of torture to extract tactical information is the reason that rules of warfare have developed over the centuries and why the United States is a party to the Geneva Conventions. The generally accepted rules of warfare thus forbid torture and provide for the humane treatment of enemy captives. Without these rules, all armed forces would be vulnerable to torture if captured by the enemy; therefore all sides have a stake in limiting the use of torture.

The implication of these arguments is that torture ought not to be authorized in law or policy. If a genuine ticking time bomb situation does occur, whoever carries out the torture should be able to use necessity as a defense for breaking the law. If indeed the reaction to the situation was legitimate, a jury or court martial would probably accept the defense of necessity and not convict the person of a crime. Thus the person who would inflict the torture would have to understand that he might have to convince a jury that his actions were necessary, and so would think very carefully before inflicting torture on a detainee.

The ticking time bomb scenario did not apply with respect to Abu Ghraib since the detainees were Iraqis who did not have knowledge of future planned attacks on the United States by al Qaeda. Although some detainees were involved with the insurgency, many were ordinary criminals, and some were innocent civilians detained by mistake. What the U.S. interrogators seemed to want was tactical intelligence about the Iraqi insurgency, presuming that the detainees had such information and that it would help U.S. forces tactically suppress the insurgency and avoid casualties.

THE EFFICACY OF TORTURE: DOES IT WORK?

One of the key elements of the ticking time bomb scenario is the ability to get a person to divulge crucial information to save innocent lives. While there is a wide range of interrogation techniques, from seemingly friendly trickery to the most extreme infliction of pain, the results are mixed.[27] No doubt torture works in some cases, but approaches that work with some people do not work with others.[28] Even if people are forced to talk, they may or may not tell the truth. They may say whatever it takes to stop the pain. Willie J. Rowell, an Army Criminal Investigation Division (C.I.D.) agent for thirty-six years, is dubious: "They'll tell you what you want to hear, truth or not truth."[29]

The Army Field Manual on interrogations states: "Army interrogation experts view the use of force as an inferior technique that yields information of questionable quality. The primary concerns, in addition to the effect on information quality, are the adverse effect on future interrogations and the behavioral change on those being interrogated."[30] Before Congress in March 2005, CIA Director Porter Goss testified, "As I said publicly before, and I know for a fact, that torture is not—it's not productive. . . . That's not professional interrogation. We don't do torture."[31] Several concrete examples illustrate the problems with taking confessions induced by torture at face value. When John McCain was in captivity in Hanoi, his torturers wanted him to divulge the names of others in his squadron. McCain gave them the names of the offensive line of the Green Bay Packers. There is no reason to believe that members of al Qaeda are not capable of the same sort of deception.[32]

In February of 2002 the Defense Intelligence Agency (DIA) reported that Ibn al-Shaykh al-Libi, a bin Laden aide, had recanted his confession about cooperation between al Qaeda and Iraq. He had probably confessed because he was being tortured by the Egyptians, to whom he had been rendered by the United States. The DIA was suspicious of his confession because he could not specify the places he had met with the Iraqis, the names of the people with whom he had dealt, or the types of weapons he discussed with them. Despite this finding of the DIA, President Bush used al-Libi's allegations in his war speech of October 7, 2002, when he said that Iraq had been given training in "poisons and deadly gases" by al Qaeda. Al-Libi's statement was made subsequent to "aggressive interrogation techniques" intended to get him to talk.[33] Thus possibly one of the Bush administration's reasons for war with Iraq was based on false evidence coerced by aggressive interrogation of an al Qaeda operative. According to retired FBI agent Dan Coleman, who had worked closely with the CIA for ten years on terrorism directed against the United States, "It was ridiculous for interrogators to think Libi would have known anything about Iraq. I could have told them that. He ran a training camp. He wouldn't have had anything to do with Iraq. Administration officials were always pushing us to come up with links, but there weren't any. The reason they got bad information was that they beat it out of him. You never get good information from someone that way."[34]

In another case three British detainees at Guantánamo said that they were tortured in order to force them to "confess" that they went to Afghanistan to fight a holy war and that they were in a video of Osama bin Laden in 2000. They denied that they had been involved in these activities, but said that they confessed to stop the pain and ill-treatment. Torturing prisoners to confess falsely is even less defensible than revenge as a rationalization and is reminiscent of the worst of Soviet prisons and the Grand Inquisition. British intelligence later produced evidence that the accused men were in Britain at the time the video was made and thus could not have been photographed with bin Laden.[35]

According to a Defense Department report, Mohammed al Qahtani gave information about thirty people who, he said, were Osama bin Laden's bodyguards. But according to the report, al Qahtani was subjected to sleep deprivation, sensory deprivation, sexual humiliation, and intimidation by dogs, and he was interrogated for seven weeks for twenty hours a day.[36] Obviously it is reasonable to infer that a person subjected to such prolonged and intense torture might say things that were not true in order to please his torturers or that he might attest to dubious assertions out of exhaustion or delirium.

In December 2006, a 374-page report by the Intelligence Science Board called into question the efficacy of torture in gaining accurate information. After an exhaustive review of the evidence and scientific literature, the board concluded that there is little evidence that torture can produce truthful answers to questions and that torture might even inhibit gaining intelligence. In the words of Colonel Steven M. Kleinman, who had been one of the military's senior officers on intelligence and survival training, "The scientific community has never established that coercive interrogation methods are an effective means of obtaining reliable intelligence information."[37] The commander of the American military in Iraq, General David Petraeus, wrote: "Some may argue that we would be more effective if we sanctioned torture or other expedient methods to obtain information from the enemy. They would be wrong. Beyond the basic fact that such actions are illegal, history shows that they also are frequently neither useful nor necessary."[38]

Torture as Public Policy: Leadership and Command Responsibility

In addition to official memoranda and executive directives, leadership was also provided in public statements by high-level public officials, especially those at the top of the chain of command. Even if low-level perpetrators of torture do not directly hear the statements of their superiors, the impact of authoritative public statements is far-reaching. High-level officials in the administration and the military take the statements seriously as expressions of the policy direction and attitudes of the highest levels of leadership of the country. These officials pass down the chain of command the attitudes conveyed in public statements. In this case, public leadership was effective in conveying the administration's point of view on detainees and the type of treatment they were expected to receive.

President Bush, in talking about the detainees at Guantánamo in July of 2003, declared, "The only thing I know *for certain* is that these are bad people"[39] (emphasis added). In 2005 he again stated, "They're dangerous and they're still around, and they'll kill [at] a moment's notice."[40] Vice President Cheney said, "These are the worst of a very bad lot. . . . They are very dangerous. They are devoted to killing millions of Americans, innocent Americans, if they can, and they are perfectly prepared to die in the effort. And they need to be detained, treated very cautiously, so that our people are not at risk."[41] On January 27, 2002, Secretary of Defense Donald Rumsfeld said just before he left for Guantánamo, "These are among the most dangerous, best trained vicious killers on the face of the earth. And that means that the people taking care of these detainees and managing their transfer have to be just exceedingly careful for two reasons. One, for their own protection, but also so these people don't get loose back out on the street and kill more people. This is a very, very serious business and it ought to be treated in that manner. . . . They are not POWs[;] they will not be determined to be POWs."[42]

Statements like these, coming from those who were the most authoritative government officials in the nation and who should be the most knowledgeable about the war on terror, were likely to dispose U.S. personnel to treat the detainees as if they were complicit in the 9/11 atrocities and actively seeking to kill American civilians. In combination with official changes in policy, and other factors described in this chapter, these statements helped to create the conditions in which torture was tolerated.

In addition to statements by the Bush administration leadership, changes in policy set the conditions under which torture took place. The argument here is that formal changes from previous policy make a difference; memoranda are read and acted upon by civilian and military leaders; public statements by the president and other administration officials are heard; and pressure from above for "actionable intelligence" is taken seriously. These actions, together or separately, constituted Bush administration policy with respect to the treatment of detainees.

Personal visits to Abu Ghraib by personnel at high levels of the administration impressed upon intelligence personnel the importance placed on actionable intelligence. For instance, the visit of a "senior member of the National Security Council staff" to Abu Ghraib in November 2003 sent a strong signal that intelligence in Iraq was valued at the highest levels of the United States government.[43] Army Lieutenant Colonel Steven Jordan, head of the Joint Interrogation and Detention Center at Abu Ghraib, said that he felt pressure to produce more actionable intelligence from senior officials who told him the reports were read by Secretary Rumsfeld and particularly from the visit of Fran Townsend, deputy assistant to President Bush and one of the top aides to Condoleezza Rice on the NSC staff.[44]

Several key changes in the operation and organization of U.S. forces with respect to U.S. prisoners were made that allowed the abuses at Guantánamo, Bagram Air Force Base, and Abu Ghraib to occur. According to the Schlesinger Report, special techniques of interrogation were allowed at Guantánamo, these techniques and procedures were then transferred to Afghanistan, and the techniques and personnel were transferred from Afghanistan to Abu Ghraib.[45]

GUANTÁNAMO

In January 2002, prisoners were brought to Guantánamo, which was under the command of Military Police General Rick Baccus, who had prisoners treated "by the book" of Geneva rules. Baccus gave prisoners copies of the Qur'an and posted rights of prisoners.[46] But this approach did not satisfy the Defense Department leadership, and in October of 2002, Baccus was replaced by General Geoffrey Miller, a military intelligence officer. This change of control of the detention center from military police to military intelligence foreshadowed the change in control of Abu Ghraib that would occur in 2003 and lead to the abuse publicized worldwide in photographs.

The Army Field Manual describes a number of techniques that could be used to induce cooperation from a detainee. The techniques generally involve developing a rapport with the prisoner and using positive and negative psychological techniques to get the prisoner to reveal information that may be useful. None of these techniques approaches torture.[47] On October 11, 2002, Lieutenant Colonel Jerald Phifer at Guantánamo requested approval of three categories of interrogation techniques beyond those specified in the Army Field Manual.[48]

The techniques in category 1 included yelling at the detainee and convincing the detainee that the interrogator is from a country that practices torture. Category 2 included using stress positions (like standing in awkward and painful positions) for four hours, isolation for up to thirty days, deprivation of light and auditory stimulation, hooding, interrogations up to twenty hours, removal of clothing, and use of special fears, such as dogs. Category 3 included "use of mild, non-injurious physical contact," exposure to cold weather or water, convincing the detainee that "death or severely painful consequences are imminent for him and/or his family," and the use of pouring water on a wet towel over the detainee's face (waterboarding) to induce the "misperception of suffocation."[49]

According to one military official, "We'd been at this for a year-plus and got nothing out of them," so it was concluded that "we need to have a less-cramped view of what torture is and is not."[50] Major General

Michael E. Dunlavey forwarded the requested changes and justified them by arguing that the normal field manual techniques "have become less effective over time."[51] His request was forwarded to Secretary Rumsfeld by Defense Department General Counsel William J. Haynes II on November 27, 2002, with the recommendation that seventeen new techniques in several categories be authorized.[52]

In December of 2002 Secretary Rumsfeld approved all seventeen techniques of interrogation included in categories 1 and 2 and only one in category 3 that allowed noninjurious physical contact.[53] Then, after some of the techniques were actually used in Guantánamo, concern was expressed by some military officials, and Rumsfeld on January 15, 2003, rescinded his December decision.[54] Three months later he officially approved a list of twenty-three techniques that included sixteen in the Army Field Manual and included the warning that some of the other techniques may be considered to be prohibited by the Geneva Conventions.[55] The Schlesinger Report concluded that "It is clear that pressure for additional intelligence and the more aggressive methods sanctioned by the Secretary of Defense resulted in stronger interrogation techniques."[56]

Some of the techniques approved at Guantánamo as specified in these documents violated the Geneva Conventions, such as stress positions, up to thirty days of isolation, and removal of clothing.[57] Most of the techniques did not amount to torture, though some of them were harsh and might amount to torture, depending on the intensity and application (for example, thirty days of isolation, sensory deprivation, twenty hours of interrogations, and noninjurious physical contact).[58] According to the *Wall Street Journal,* techniques that were used included deprivation of food, deprivation of sleep (for up to ninety-six hours), deprivation of clothes, and shackling in stress positions.[59] The problem, of course, is that in the actual practice of interrogations, as was evident at Abu Ghraib, guards and interrogators can easily get carried away and move beyond the bounds specified in the legal memoranda. Ensuring that this kind of misconduct does not happen is the obligation of leadership. It was after General Miller "Gitmo-ized" Abu Ghraib that the abuses and systematic humiliation occurred there.

Despite the use of additional interrogation techniques at Guantánamo, no ticking time bomb plots were discovered (that were made public), though some useful intelligence was discovered. According to some defense officials, of the approximately 600 men imprisoned at Guantánamo, only one-third to one-half of the inmates seemed to be of value.[60]

ABU GHRAIB

After the initial combat phase of the invasion was completed, the ensuing looting made Abu Ghraib unusable as a U.S. detention facility. Prisoners were temporarily detained at Camp Cropper near the Baghdad airport, which was designed for 250 prisoners but which held up to 1,000 at times. At the same time Camp Bucca in southern Iraq held up to 7,000 detainees. On June 30, 2003, Brigadier General Janis Karpinski took command of the 800th Military Police Brigade, which was in charge of all military prisons in Iraq, and on August 4 Abu Ghraib was opened for use by U.S. military police. The prison was undermanned, and the MPs were operating under very harsh conditions, with about 450 MPs policing 7,000 inmates. In the fall of 2003, most of the prisoners were common criminals.[61]

The lack of personnel and resources played an important role in creating the conditions that allowed the abuse and torture to occur. The low-level MPs were overworked, ill trained, and without proper supplies to carry out their mission. The stress created by these conditions contributed to the unacceptable behavior of the guards, although it does not excuse it.

Under Secretary of Defense for Intelligence Stephen Cambone, in August, had his deputy, Lieutenant General William (Jerry) Boykin, organize a visit of Guantánamo commander General Geoffrey Miller to Abu Ghraib with a view toward improving its operation and increasing the collection of intelligence about the uprising against U.S. forces. Miller favored employing some of the procedures used at Guantánamo, and his conclusion was that MPs should be actively involved in intelligence collection by "setting the conditions" for prisoner interrogation by military intelligence troops (and CIA and contractor personnel). General Karpinski said that she objected to Miller's assertion of authority and his intention to "Gitmo-ize" the facility for which she was officially responsible. His response, according to her was, "You can do this my way, or we can do it the hard way."[62] The subsequent changes in the methods of interrogation, according to Colonel Thomas Pappas, Commnander of the 205th Intelligence Brigade, were "enacted as the result of a specific visit by Major General Geoffrey Miller."[63]

Other actions by Miller were intended to change the role of MPs from their official mission of detaining and caring for prisoners to helping military intelligence actively extract information from the prisoners. Although Miller maintained that it was necessary to provide a safe and humane environment, his assessment also stated that "it is essential that the guard force be actively engaged in setting the conditions for successful exploitation of the internees."[64]

The problem with General Miller's transfer of the interrogation techniques and other procedures from Guantánamo to Abu Ghraib, according to the Taguba Report, was that the two detention facilities had different functions and different types of detainees. Guantánamo was intended to hold members of al Qaeda who potentially had information related to possible future terrorist attacks on the United States, while those in Abu Ghraib held large numbers of "Iraqi criminals" and individuals involved in the uprising against U.S. forces. In addition, according to Army doctrine, the role of MPs should remain distinct from that of military intelligence personnel.[65]

MPs reported that military intelligence personnel encouraged them to abuse the detainees and praised them when they did. For instance, the MI personnel were quoted as saying, "Loosen this guy up for us. Make sure he has a bad night. Make sure he gets the treatment." When they did what MI wanted, they were praised: "Good job, they're breaking down real fast. They answer every question. They're giving out good information. Keep up the good work."[66] When asked about the abusive techniques, one MP said, "I witnessed prisoners in the MI hold section, Wing 1A being made to do various things that I would question morally. In Wing 1A we were told that they had different rules and different SOP [standard operating procedure] for treatment. I never saw a set of rules or SOP for that section[,] just word of mouth."[67] Taguba found that the MPs at Abu Ghraib "had received no training in detention/internee operations," and that they had little or no instruction on the Geneva rules for the treatment of detainees, which officially did apply to the Iraq conflict.[68]

In August 2003 there was no formal policy for interrogation at Abu Ghraib aside from the standard Army Field Manual.[69] After Miller's visit in early September, according to Karpinski, Colonel Pappas formally asked General Sanchez to "escalate" the level of interrogations.[70] In a memo dated September 14, 2003, General Sanchez relayed the specific interrogation techniques memo. The transmittal memo stated that the "Counter-Resistance Policy" was "modeled on the one implemented for interrogations conducted at Guantánamo Bay," but modified to take into account the Geneva Conventions. He further instructed that "my intent is to implement this policy immediately."[71] The techniques included "dietary manipulation," "adjusting temperature," "isolation" (though for more than thirty days required special permission), use of "military working dogs" (muzzled), "sleep management" of up to twenty hours a day, "loud music and light control," and "stress positions."[72]

After the objections by officials at U.S. Central Command in Florida, Sanchez on October 12 rescinded some of the tactics on the list and insisted that the use of some of them required his direct approval. These included the use of dogs, more than thirty days' isolation, and maintaining stress positions for forty-five minutes. At the same time, an "Interrogation Rules of Engagement" memo of October 9 said, "At no time will detainees be treated inhumanely nor maliciously humiliated."[73] The Schlesinger Report found that Lieutenant General Sanchez's command, "reasoning from the President's memorandum of February 7, 2002," believed that the presence of "unlawful combatants" justified more aggressive interrogation techniques.[74] Schlesinger also concluded that these changes caused confusion among U.S. personnel at Abu Ghraib as to which techniques were acceptable and which were not.[75]

Military Intelligence was officially given control of Abu Ghraib on November 19, 2003, which formalized the replacement of military police control with military intelligence control. This change was criticized by the Taguba Report as being "not doctrinally sound" and confused the roles and missions of the two different types of units: the MPs to hold and care for prisoners and MI to extract as much information as possible.[76] It was during the October–December period that the abuses at Abu Ghraib were photographed.

Laying the Legal Groundwork for Torture

The Bush administration went to great lengths to insulate itself from possible accountability for the actions of its interrogators. It argued that the president was not bound by the Geneva Conventions, by U.S. law, or by customary international law. This section will first present an account of

President Bush's decision to suspend the Geneva Conventions with respect to the Taliban and al Qaeda. It will then explain the constraints the United States agreed to when it signed and ratified the Geneva Conventions. Next, United States laws as well as international law on torture will be examined. The argument is that the president of the United States is in fact bound by these laws and conventions, despite the arguments of the Bush administration that the commander-in-chief authority exempts the president from obeying the law.

Legal efforts to shield the Bush administration from liability for its interrogation practices began immediately after 9/11 and continued throughout the Bush administration. John Yoo in the Office of Legal Counsel of the Justice Department and David Addington in the vice president's office prepared legal memoranda that construed the law so as to exempt the president from constitutional law, criminal law, international law, and customary international law.

These legal efforts would not have been necessary if President Bush had intended to comply with the normally accepted requirements of the Constitution, criminal law, and international law.[77] In effect, the intense efforts to construct legal justifications for harsh interrogations, combined with the secrecy with which they were developed and carried out, signaled the intentions of the administration. These legal documents foreshadowed the actions the administration was going to take with regard to the treatment of prisoners and the interrogation of suspected terrorists and other detainees.

In laying the legal groundwork to protect the administration and U.S. personnel from possible prosecution, the administration made several arguments:

1) The Geneva Conventions do not apply to the war on terror;
2) The laws of the United States do not apply;
3) The president is not bound by international law; and
4) The president's commander-in-chief authority can override any law.

President Bush Decides to Suspend the Geneva Conventions

The Geneva Conventions were agreed to in 1949, and they were ratified by the United States in 1955. They were intended, in part, to assure the humane treatment of captives during times of war and to prevent the recurrence of some of the worst practices of the Nazis and Japanese during World War II. But the requirements of the Geneva Conventions seemed to preclude some of the actions that President Bush saw as essential to the war on terror after 9/11. This led President Bush to make an early decision in the war on terror that he would suspend the Geneva Conventions for captives who fought for the Taliban and al Qaeda.

The question of whether President Bush should declare that the Geneva Conventions did not apply to al Qaeda or the Taliban was the subject of a series of memoranda in early 2002. On January 9 Deputy Assistant Attorney General John Yoo wrote a memorandum concluding that the Geneva Conventions did not protect members of al Qaeda, in part because they were non-state actors and had not signed the Geneva Accords. In addition the war on terror was a new type of war that was not fought between traditional nation-states. Yoo argued that the drafters of the Geneva Conventions "could not have" contemplated a conflict between a nation-state and a "transnational terrorist organization."[78] He thus concluded that the Geneva Conventions should not apply to the treatment of al Qaeda prisoners. This Yoo memo was followed by a memorandum by Assistant Attorney General Jay S. Bybee that argued that the treaties concerning the laws of armed conflict (particularly Geneva Convention III concerning prisoners of war) do not protect members of al Qaeda because they were "non-state" actors.[79]

Then on January 25, 2002, Counsel to the President Alberto Gonzales wrote a memo that affirmed the reasoning of the Department of Justice memos and recommended that Geneva Convention III on Treatment of Prisoners of War should not apply to al Qaeda and Taliban prisoners. He reasoned that the war on terrorism was "a new kind of war" and that the "new paradigm renders obsolete Geneva's strict limitations on questioning of enemy prisoners." Gonzales restated the memos' arguments that exempting captured al Qaeda and Taliban prisoners from the Geneva Convention protections would preclude the prosecution of U.S. soldiers under the U.S. War Crimes Act. "A determination that GPW [Geneva prisoner of war] is not applicable to the Taliban would mean that Section 2441 [War Crimes Act] would not apply to actions taken with respect to the Taliban."[80]

Secretary of State Colin Powell objected to the reasoning of the Justice Department and the president's counsel. In a memo of January 26,

2002, he argued that the drawbacks of deciding not to apply the Geneva Conventions outweighed the advantages because "It will reverse over a century of policy . . . and undermine the protections of the law of war for our troops, both in this specific conflict and in general; it has a high cost in terms of negative international reaction. . . . It will undermine public support among critical allies."[81] Powell also noted that applying the Geneva Conventions "maintains POW status for U.S. forces . . . and generally supports the U.S. objective of ensuring its forces are accorded protection under the Convention[s]." The memo also addressed the intended applicability of the Geneva Conventions to nontraditional conflicts: "The GPW was intended to cover all types of armed conflict and did not by its terms limit its application."[82]

Despite Powell's memo, and in accord with the Justice Department and his counsel's recommendations, President Bush signed a memorandum on February 7, 2002, that stated: "Pursuant to my authority as Commander in Chief [I have determined] that none of the provisions of Geneva apply to our conflict with al Qaeda in Afghanistan or elsewhere throughout the world because, among other reasons, al Qaeda is not a High Contracting Party to Geneva." The memo argued that the Geneva Conventions apply only to states and "assume the existence of 'regular' armed forces fighting on behalf of states," and that "terrorism ushers in a new paradigm," that "requires new thinking in the law of war." The memo also stated that "as a matter of policy, the United States Armed Forces shall continue to treat detainees humanely and, *to the extent appropriate and consistent with military necessity,* in a manner consistent with the principles of Geneva" (emphasis added).[83] This determination allowed the use of aggressive techniques of interrogation by the CIA and military intelligence at Guantánamo that were later, in the fall of 2003, transferred to the prison at Abu Ghraib.[84]

The changes in policy regarding the status of prisoners at Guantánamo upset top-level military lawyers in the Judge Advocate General Corps (JAG), including lawyers in the chairman of the Joint Chiefs of Staff's office.[85] A memorandum from Major General Thomas J. Romig (JAG Corps, U.S. Army) raised several problems with the administration's policy. He argued that the position (taken by the administration) that presidential decisions can exempt the nation from customary international law "runs contrary to the historic position taken by the United

States Government concerning such laws and, in our opinion, could adversely impact DOD interests worldwide." He further argued that it opened the United States to criticism that the "[United States] is a law unto itself," and that the policy would harm the country by "putting our service personnel at far greater risk and vitiating many of the POW/detainee safeguards the [United States] has worked hard to establish over the past five decades."[86] In 2003 a group of JAG officers went to visit the New York City Bar Association's Committee on International Human Rights. They were concerned about "a real risk of disaster," a concern that later proved to be prescient.[87]

The president's decision led to the expansion of interrogation techniques that were used at Guantánamo. Secretary of Defense Rumsfeld expanded the range of interrogation techniques allowed. He appointed officers (especially Geoffrey Miller) to oversee interrogations and apply the techniques used at Guantánamo to Abu Ghraib in Iraq, which the United States considered to be covered by the Geneva Conventions.[88]

THE GENEVA CONVENTIONS

On the face of it, President Bush arguably acted against his duties and oath of office, as set out in the Constitution. Article VI of the Constitution declares that "This Constitution, and the Laws of the United States which shall be made in Pursuance thereof; and all Treaties made, or which shall be made, under the Authority of the United States, shall be the supreme Law of the Land." Article II of the Constitution declares that the president "shall take care that the laws be faithfully executed." Thus, although presidents have some leeway in interpreting treaties, President Bush acted in a way incompatible with his constitutional authority in unilaterally suspending the Geneva Agreements.[89] The Supreme Court's *Hamdan* decision rejected the arguments of the administration and ruled that the United States was bound by Common Article 3 of the Geneva Conventions.[90]

The four Geneva Conventions of 1949 were designed to protect individuals who are captured or at the mercy of enemy forces during times of war. The articles assume that fighting in a war is not illegal. Different parts of the Conventions cover different classes of those who fall under the control of the armed forces of a nation during times of war. Geneva Convention I covers the sick and wounded on land. Convention II covers those shipwrecked at sea. Convention III covers those who are prisoners of war, and Convention IV covers civilians. The protections of Article III for POWs are available to those who are lawful belligerents in warfare, and they are given the highest level of protection. Geneva Convention III provides that prisoners must be treated humanely, and that if interrogated, they cannot be forced to reveal information beyond their name, rank, date of birth, and serial number.[91] The convention does not forbid interrogation, but it limits the methods that can be used to those that are humane.[92] The conventions apply to those countries that have signed the treaty. This includes Iraq and arguably Afghanistan.

In order to qualify as a prisoner of war, individuals must be soldiers of a state that has signed the treaty and must (among other things): belong to an organized group that is a party to the conflict that is commanded by a responsible person; they must wear a "distinctive sign" identifying them as a combatant; and they must carry arms openly.[93] If there is some doubt as to whether a detainee is entitled to status as a prisoner of war, Geneva Convention III, Article 5, requires that the person is to be treated with POW status until a properly constituted tribunal has determined the person's status. The person is entitled to some procedural rights in order to act in his own self-defense. The United States recognized as prisoners of war those captured by U.S. forces in the Korean and Vietnam and first Gulf Wars.

Even if the Convention III, Article 5, tribunal determines that the person is not a covered belligerent and thus not a POW who is entitled to the full protections of Geneva III, the person may be covered by Geneva Convention IV, which applies to civilians. Article 4 of this convention applies to: "those who, at a given moment and in any manner whatsoever, find themselves, in case of a conflict or occupation, in the hands of a Party to the conflict." Article 27 of Convention IV provides that these persons are entitled to "respect for their persons," shall be "humanely treated," and be protected "against all acts of violence or threats thereof and against insults and public curiosity." Many of the prisoners at Abu Ghraib fell into the category of civilian detained by an occupying power.

Each of the four Geneva Conventions has several identical articles. Common Article 3 prohibits certain practices in the treatment of those persons under the control of military forces. Section (1) of the article requires that detained persons be treated "humanely," and it prohibits "violence to life and person, in particular murder of all kinds, mutilation, cruel treatment and torture," and "outrages upon personal dignity, in particular, humiliating and degrading treatment." Thus all captives of the United States were entitled to the protections of Common Article 3. Alberto Gonzales wrote in an article in the *New York Times* in 2004 that Iraq had signed the Geneva Conventions and that the United States was bound by them in the war in Iraq.[94] That the Geneva Conventions were blatantly violated at Abu Ghraib attests to the tendency for torture sanctioned for one purpose to be used for different purposes.

United States Army Regulations (AR 190-8), in accord with the Geneva Conventions, provide for treatment of enemy prisoners of war and state that "All persons taken into custody by U.S. forces will be provided with the protections of the GPW until some other legal status is determined by competent authority." The regulations prohibit "inhumane treatment," specifically "murder, torture, corporal punishment . . . sensory deprivation . . . and all cruel and degrading treatment."[95] The United States has had a long record of officially requiring humane treatment of prisoners taken in wartime, from the early years of the Republic, to the Lieber Code of the Civil War, to World War II, Korea, and Vietnam.

The fact that the United States officially adhered to the principle of treating POWs humanely throughout its history up to the Bush administration does not mean that U.S. troops never committed atrocities or that torture never occurred. During wartime it is impossible to eliminate all acts of barbarism. The difference is that it was official U.S. policy throughout all previous U.S. wars that prisoners be treated humanely, even if the spirit of the law was not always honored. In past U.S. wars, soldiers who tortured and mistreated enemy captives did so in spite of official policy; after 9/11 they acted in conformance to Bush administration policy.[96]

UNITED STATES LAW

Even if it is posited that the Geneva Conventions do not apply, the U.S. criminal code prohibits torture. After 9/11 one of the main concerns of the Bush administration was that U.S. soldiers could be prosecuted under the U.S. War Crimes Act (18 U.S.C. Sec. 2441), which defines war crimes as "a grave breach" of the Geneva Conventions, or conduct "which constitutes a violation of Common Article 3" of the Geneva Conventions.[97]

In 1994 the United States passed legislation to implement the U.N. Convention Against Torture by passing the torture act (18 U.S.C. 2340), which provides for criminal sanctions, including the death penalty, for perpetrators of torture. Section 2340A states, "Whoever outside the United States commits or attempts to commit torture shall be . . ." punished, including if "the alleged offender is present in the United States, irrespective of the nationality of the victim or alleged offender." The law defines torture as "an act committed by a person acting under the color of law specifically intended to inflict severe physical or mental pain or suffering (other than pain or suffering incidental to lawful sanctions) upon another person within his custody or physical control."

In January of 2002, Alberto Gonzales argued that the suspension of the Geneva Conventions would preclude prosecution of U.S. personnel and that the suspension "substantially reduces the threat of domestic criminal prosecution under the War Crimes Act (18 U.S.C. 2241) . . . A determination that the GPW is not applicable to the Taliban would mean that Section 2441 would not apply to actions taken with respect to the Taliban."[98] This argument by Gonzales indicated that the administration expected that the actions that it would authorize in treating detainees would likely be liable to criminal prosecution under the U.S. War Crimes Act unless some legal protection were provided. That legal protection was the suspension of the Geneva Conventions by President Bush.

INTERNATIONAL LAW

Lawyers for the administration asserted that the president is not bound by international law and that he is not bound by treaties.[99] However, several international laws arguably bind the United States. The treatment of prisoners is constrained by the United Nations Convention Against Torture and Other Cruel, Inhuman or Degrading Treatment or Punishment.[100] The Convention Against Torture (CAT) defines torture as "any act by which severe pain or suffering, whether physical or mental, is intentionally inflicted on a person for such purposes as obtaining from him or a third person information or a confession."[101] The U.N. Torture Convention provides that "no exceptional circumstances whatsoever, whether a state of war or a threat of war, internal political instability or any other public emergency, may be invoked as a justification of torture."[102] The United States implemented the Convention Against Torture by passing 18 U.S.C. 2340.

With respect to prisoners, customary international law may bind the United States, regardless of whether the Geneva Conventions are considered to apply or not. According to another U.S. Army Field Manual on the law of land warfare, "Unwritten or customary law is firmly established by the custom of nations and well defined by recognized authorities on international law. . . . The unwritten or customary law of war is binding upon all nations."[103]

Sources of customary international law include: Protocol I, Article 75, of the Geneva Conventions, Common Article 3 of the Geneva Conventions, and the U.N. Convention Against Torture. Protocol I, Article 75, of the Geneva Conventions, signed in 1977 but not ratified by the United States, is considered to be part of customary international law. Protocol I provides that some acts "shall remain prohibited at any time and in any place whatsoever, whether committed by civilian or by military agents." These acts include (among others): "murder," "torture of all kinds," and "outrages upon personal dignity, in particular humiliating and degrading treatment."[104] Goldman and Tittemore argue that "The core provisions of Article 75 should also be considered to constitute a part of customary international law binding on the United States."[105] They conclude that, based on the U.N. Convention against Torture and Article 75 of Protocol I (as part of customary international law), it is "beyond question that the United States is subject to an absolute and nonderogable obligation under international human rights and humanitarian law to ensure that unprivileged combatants under its power are not subjected to torture or other cruel, inhuman or degrading treatment or punishment."[106]

Common Article 3, discussed above, is also considered part of customary international law. It provides that in conflicts "not of an international character," its provisions "shall be bound to apply as a minimum" to "persons taking no active part in the hostilities." "International" in this context means wars between sovereign nations, in contrast to other types of conflicts such as the one between the United States and al Qaeda.[107] In *Hamdan*, Justice Stevens wrote that the principles articulated in Article 75 are "indisputably part of the customary international law."[108] The *Law of War Handbook* of the Department of the Army states that Common Article 3 "serves as a minimum yardstick of protection in *all* conflicts, not just internal armed conflicts" (emphasis added).[109] According to Jennifer Elsea, of the Congressional Research Service, "Common Article 3 is now widely considered to have attained the status of customary international law."[110]

Thus even if the Geneva Conventions are deemed not to apply to captured persons suspected of terrorism, and U.S. law is not applicable, customary international law binds the United States to treat detainees humanely. Even the Office of Legal Counsel, when it revised the Bybee memo of 2002, has admitted that the United States might be bound by customary international law.[111]

In summary, with regard to the treatment of detainees, the United States is bound by the

—Geneva Conventions Common Article 3, which prohibits "violence to life and person, in particular murder of all kinds, mutilation, cruel treatment and torture," and "outrages upon personal dignity, in particular, humiliating and degrading treatment";

—U.N. Convention Against Torture, which provides that: "no exceptional circumstances whatsoever, whether a state of war or a threat of war, internal political instability or any other public emergency, may be invoked as a justification of torture"; and

—U.S. War Crimes Act (18 U.S.C. Sec. 2441), which defines war crimes as "a grave breach" of the Geneva Conventions, or conduct that "constitutes a violation of Common Article 3" of the Geneva Conventions.

OLC MEMO ON TORTURE

After purporting to establish that suspending the Geneva Conventions would insulate U.S. personnel from prosecution, the administration sought to protect U.S. personnel from prosecution by defining torture very narrowly, so that U.S. personnel had leeway to engage in a wide range of harsh practices that would not legally be defined as torture. In making this argument, the administration used the definition of torture contained in U.S. law (18 U.S.C. 2340). Assistant Attorney General Jay S. Bybee, head of the Office of Legal Counsel (OLC), signed a legal memorandum (hereinafter the Bybee memo) dealing with what would constitute torture under Title 18, Sections 2340 and 2340A of the U.S. Code.[112]

Part I of the Bybee memo construes the definition of torture narrowly and elevates the threshold of "severe pain" necessary to amount to torture. "We conclude that for an act to constitute torture, it must inflict pain that is . . . equivalent in intensity to the pain accompanying serious physical injury, such as organ failure, impairment of bodily function, or even death."[113] This narrow definition would allow a wide range of brutal actions that do not meet the exacting requirements specified in the memo. The memo specifically excludes from torture "cruel, inhuman, or degrading treatment or punishment," some examples of which are specified, such as wall standing, hooding, noise, sleep deprivation, and deprivation of food and drink. But the memo did specify that some practices would be torture, such as severe beatings with clubs, threats of imminent death, threats of removing extremities, burning, electric shocks to genitalia, rape or sexual assault.[114]

According to the memo, for the law to apply, the torturer must have the "specific intent to inflict severe pain" and it must be his "precise objective" (p. 3). "Thus, even if the defendant knows that severe pain will result from his actions, if causing such harm is not his objective, he lacks the requisite specific intent *even though the defendant did not act in good faith*" (emphasis added). Thus one could inflict pain that amounted to torture, but not be guilty of torture if the main objective was, for instance, to extract information rather than to cause pain. This reasoning borders on sophistry.

Finally the memo argues that any U.S. person accused of torture who was acting pursuant to the orders of the commander in chief could defend himself against the charge by arguing, among other things, "the right to self-defense," since "the nation itself is under attack."[115] This overly broad defense of torture could be used in virtually any military or combat situation.

In June of 2004, Alberto Gonzales tried to minimize the importance or the legal status of administration memos about torture, saying they were "unnecessary, over-broad discussions" and "not relied upon" by policymakers.[116] But the previous year he placed strong emphasis on the legal importance of Office of Legal Counsel opinions. "OLC's interpretation of this legal issue [Geneva Conventions applicability to al Qaeda] is definitive. The Attorney General is charged by statute with interpreting the law for the Executive Branch. This interpretive authority extends to both domestic and international law. He has, in turn, delegated this role to OLC."[117]

When Jack Goldsmith became head of the Office of Legal Counsel in October of 2003, he concluded that the legal arguments in the Bybee memo were seriously flawed, and "in effect gave interrogators a blank check." He characterized the reasoning of the memo as "legally flawed, tendentious in substance and tone, and overbroad and thus largely unnecessary."[118] He decided that the Bybee memo was so flawed that he had to withdraw the opinion. This extraordinary action was particularly sensitive because the memo "had been vetted in the highest circles of government."[119] "Highest circles" in this context must mean Vice President Cheney and President Bush, thus tying the very narrow definition of torture and its "blank check" directly to President Bush. The task of withdrawing and replacing the memo fell to OLC lawyer Daniel Levin; after six months of work, the replacement memo was issued on December 30, 2004, several weeks before the Senate hearings on the nomination of Alberto Gonzales to be Attorney General.[120]

The Levin memo began with a ringing denunciation of torture: "Torture is abhorrent both to American law and values and to international norms. This universal repudiation of torture is reflected in our criminal law, . . . international agreements, . . . and the longstanding policy of the United States repeatedly and recently reaffirmed by the President."[121] The White House, however, insisted that Levin include a footnote undermining much of the substance of the memo.[122] In footnote 8, Levin stated: "While we have identified various disagreements with the August 2002 Memorandum, we have reviewed this Office's prior opinions addressing the issues involving treatment of detainees and do not believe that any of their conclusions would be different under the standards set forth in this memorandum." Goldsmith concluded that "in other words, no approved interrogation technique would be affected by this more careful and nuanced analysis."[123]

John Yoo, who claimed to have written the "Bybee memo" (at least part of it), condemned the Levin memo as "second guess[ing]" his work with "the benefit of 20/20 hindsight." He also concluded that "the differences in the opinions were for appearances' sake. In the real world of interrogation policy nothing had changed. The new opinion just reread the statute to deliberately blur the interpretation of torture as a short-term political maneuver in response to public criticism."[124] Thus the White House, despite the memo's rhetoric condemning torture, prevented the memo from having any legal effect on interrogation practices. Whatever was legal under the reasoning of the Bybee memo was considered by the administration to be legal after the Bybee memo was withdrawn.

After Gonzales became attorney general in 2005, he replaced OLC Director Daniel Levin (author of the memo retracting the Bybee memo) with Stephen G. Bradbury. Bradbury authored several new secret memoranda approving the use of aggressive interrogation techniques. A February memorandum approved as legal the combination of techniques that included head slapping, extremely cold temperatures, and waterboarding. When Congress was considering the McCain amendment that would forbid "cruel, inhuman and degrading" treatment, another secret memorandum was issued in May 2005 that decided that none of the interrogation techniques currently being used would violate that standard, thus providing a preemptive legal judgment that current interrogation practices would not violate the (yet to be passed) Detainee Treatment Act (DTA).[125] U.S interrogation practices would thus not have to change when the DTA was passed. Deputy Attorney General James Comey objected to the first secret memo, but he was overruled by Gonzales, and he left the administration in the summer of 2005.[126]

COMMANDER-IN-CHIEF AUTHORITY

Section 5 of the memo argued that the president's commander-in-chief authority can overcome any law. "The President enjoys complete discretion in the exercise of his Commander-in-Chief authority and in conducting operations against hostile forces."[127] Thus "any effort to apply Section 2340A (anti-torture act) in a manner that interferes with the President's direction of such core war matters as the detention and interrogation of enemy combatants thus would be unconstitutional."[128] Although the memo mentions al Qaeda in this connection, the arguments are broad enough to apply to any "military campaign."[129] It argues further that any effort by Congress to limit the interrogation of enemy combatants would be unconstitutional.[130]

Despite Article I, Section 8, of the Constitution, which provides that Congress shall have the power "To make Rules for the Government and

Regulation of the land and naval Forces," the Bush administration denied that the president could be bound by public law with respect to torture.[131] According to John Yoo, Congress cannot "tie the President's hands in regard to torture as an interrogation technique. . . . It's the core of the Commander-in-Chief function. They can't prevent the President from ordering torture."[132] According to this argument, Congress cannot regulate presidential actions when he is acting as commander in chief, and any law, such as the torture law "must be construed as not applying to interrogations undertaken pursuant to his Commander-in-Chief authority."[133] This reasoning leads to the conclusion that Congress cannot pass a (constitutional) law that forbids torture by any member of the executive branch, as long as the president claims that he is ordering the torture under his commander-in-chief authority.

The use of the commander-in-chief clause to defend against a charge of torture directly connects the president with the acts of torture. A contractor, CIA agent, or soldier cannot invoke the commander-in-chief authority; only the president can. The Bush administration arguments that the president is not bound by the law thus make a direct connection between the actions of possible torturers and the president by arguing that it is the president who is not bound by the law. If the Bush administration did not intend to approve interrogation techniques that many consider torture, why would these arguments about his constitutional authority have been necessary or made so vehemently by his administration?

The Article II, Section 3, provision of the Constitution that the president "shall take care that the Laws be faithfully executed," would thus be negated by the commander-in-chief clause, as would the Article I, Section 8, provision that Congress has the authority to "make Rules concerning Captures on Land and Water."[134] The administration thus argued that the president, when acting as commander in chief, is above the law because no congressional enactment (whether signed by a president or not) can impinge on the president's authority with respect to the interrogation of enemy combatants. The argument of this book is that the commander-in-chief clause does not override the "take care" clause or the authority of Congress to "make rules concerning captures." This argument rests on the plain words of the Constitution and the principle that the rule of law binds the president. That is, the president is not above the law.

THE McCAIN AMENDMENT:
THE DETAINEE TREATMENT ACT OF 2005

Senator John McCain (R-AZ) endured five years as a prisoner of war in Vietnam and suffered severe torture. Thus his publicly expressed outrage at reports of torture perpetrated by U.S. soldiers and civilians at Guantánamo, Abu Ghraib, and in Afghanistan carried a large measure of legitimacy.[135] McCain introduced an amendment to the Department of Defense Appropriations Act for 2006 that would ban torture by U.S. personnel, regardless of geographic location. Section 1003 of the Detainee Treatment Act (DTA) of 2005 provides that "no individual in the custody or under the physical control of the United States Government, regardless of nationality or physical location, shall be subject to cruel, inhuman, or degrading treatment or punishment."[136]

President Bush threatened to veto the bill if it were passed, and Vice President Cheney led administration efforts in Congress to defeat the bill.[137] Cheney first tried to get the bill dropped entirely, then to exempt the CIA from its provisions. Their efforts, however, were unavailing, and the measure was passed with veto-proof majorities in both Houses, 90 to 9 in the Senate, and 308 to 122 in the House. In a compromise, McCain refused to change his wording, but he did agree to add provisions that would allow civilian U.S. personnel to use the same type of legal defense that is accorded to uniformed military personnel.[138] (The habeas corpus aspects of the DTA were discussed in chapter 5). In 2007 Congress considered a bill that would require the CIA to limit its interrogation methods to those sanctioned in the Army Field Manual. President Bush vetoed this bill when it came to his desk in 2008.[139]

In a signing statement after signing the DTA bill into law, President Bush used language that called into question whether he considered himself or the executive branch bound by the law. A signing statement is a statement by the president when a bill is signed indicating how the president interprets the bill. It is intended to provide evidence of presidential intent corresponding to the weight given by federal courts to congressional intent in interpreting the law (signing statements will be discussed in chapter 8).[140] When President Bush signed the bill, he issued a signing statement that declared: "The executive branch shall construe Title X in Division A of the Act, relating to detainees, in a manner consistent with the constitutional authority of the President to supervise the unitary executive branch and as Commander in Chief and consistent with the constitutional limitations on the judicial power."[141] Previous memoranda (quoted above) of the Bush administration interpreted executive power in expansive ways that argued that the president is not subject to the law when acting in his commander-in-chief capacity.[142] That President Bush did not consider himself bound by this law is therefore a reasonable conclusion.

As mentioned above, President Bush's memorandum excluding al Qaeda from the Geneva Accords declared that detainees would be treated humanely "to the extent appropriate and consistent with military necessity."[143] This presidential directive led to (or allowed) the abuses that occurred at Guantánamo and Abu Ghraib. Thus if President Bush's reservation about the McCain amendment is interpreted in a similar fashion, he may have thought that he had the constitutional authority to ignore the law as well as to use "military necessity" as a justification.[144]

The Military Commissions Act of 2006

In order to overcome the roadblock that the Supreme Court threw in the way of administration policy with its *Hamdan* decision, President Bush sought legislation that would authorize the creation of military commissions and spell out limits on the rights of detainees. *Hamdan* ruled that Common Article 3 bound President Bush and thus implied that interrogation techniques used by U.S. personnel were not in accord with Common Article 3 of the Geneva Conventions. The Military Commissions Act of 2006 (MCA) allowed the president to interpret Common Article 3 through an executive order that specified which interrogation techniques the CIA would be allowed to use.

In arguing for passage of the MCA, President Bush argued that the types of harsh interrogation methods that he termed "the program" used by the CIA to interrogate detainees were essential to the war on terror. He threatened that he would shut down the program of harsh interrogations unless Congress passed a law authorizing them. "The professionals will not step up unless there's clarity in the law. So Congress has got a decision to make: Do you want the program to go forward or not? I strongly recommend that this program go forward in order for us to be able to protect America."[145] He said that the administration's proposal would provide "intelligence professionals with the tools they need."[146] The allowed interrogation techniques were not specified in the law, but were said to include prolonged sleep deprivation, stress positions, and extremely loud noises, but administration sources said that "waterboarding" would not be used in the future.[147] Members of Congress, including John McCain, also said that waterboarding was not allowed by the Military Commissions Act.[148] Waterboarding was not allowed under the revised rules of interrogation for the Armed Forces. In McCain's words: "It [waterboarding] is not a complicated procedure. It is torture."[149]

There was no unanimity in the Bush administration over the use of harsh interrogation techniques. In June 2005 Gordon England, the acting deputy secretary of defense, and Philip Zelikow, counselor to the State Department, wrote a nine-page memo urging the administration to adhere to the minimum standards of treatment of detainees in the Geneva Conventions.[150] On September 13, 2006, former secretary of state Colin Powell wrote a public letter to Senator McCain urging him to oppose the MCA and its redefinition of Common Article 3 because "the world is beginning to doubt the moral basis of our fight against terrorism," and because "it would put our own troops at risk."[151] It is very unusual for a former secretary of state to argue publicly against a bill that the president who appointed him is advocating.

Forty retired generals and high-level DOD officials wrote a letter to Senators Warner and Levin urging them to resist the proposed MCA language intended to "redefine Common Article 3 [CA3] of the Geneva Conventions." They said that the United States has abided by CA3 "in every conflict since the Conventions were adopted, . . . even to enemies that systematically violated the Conventions themselves." "If degradation, humiliation, physical and mental brutalization of prisoners is decriminalized, . . . we will forfeit all credible objections should such barbaric practices be inflicted upon American prisoners."[152] Former chairman of the Joint Chiefs of Staff Hugh Shelton in a letter to John McCain said that approving those sections of the MCA reinterpreting Common Article 3 would be an "egregious mistake" that would send a "terrible signal" to other nations, and that it would invite "reciprocal action" by other nations.[153] The consensus of so many distinguished general officers of the armed forces as well as civilian officials and diplomats that passing the MCA would abrogate our obligations under Common Article 3 and undermine protections for U.S. troops is striking.

Nevertheless after several weeks of contentious debate between the two political parties, the MCA was passed by both houses of Congress. President Bush signed the Military Commissions Act of 2006 (PL 109-366) into law on October 17, 2006. The Bush administration succeeded in having its version of the bill passed. It provided a lawful way for the president to establish military commissions, as described in chapter 5. The MCA forbids the use of testimony obtained through "torture," and it explicitly outlaws the more extreme forms of torture. But it also opened the door for the administration to continue the harsh interrogation methods that it argued did not amount to torture. The law required the president to issue an executive order that interprets U.S. obligations under Common Article 3 of Geneva.

Formerly, 18 USC 2241 defined as a war crime any "grave breach" of the Geneva Conventions. In order to allow the Bush administration to get around compliance with Common Article 3 of the conventions, the MCA repealed references to the Geneva Conventions and replaced them with a list of egregious actions and any action that would "amount to cruel, inhuman, or degrading treatment prohibited by section 1003 of the Detainee Treatment Act of 2005" (Sec. 948r). Left out of the MCA was "outrageous and humiliating" treatment, which was prohibited in Common Article 3, which forbade "violence to life and person, in particular murder of all kinds, mutilation, cruel treatment and torture" and "outrages upon personal dignity, in particular humiliating and degrading treatment."[154] According to the MCA "outrageous and humiliating" treatment would not constitute a war crime. Under the administration's interpretation, the new law would forbid only techniques that "shock the conscience."

The MCA satisfied President Bush that "the program" of "enhanced" interrogations could legally continue. The allowable techniques were not specified in the law but were left to interpretation by President Bush in his executive order, and the law required the president to issue an executive order that interprets U.S. obligations under Common Article 3 of the Geneva Conventions. The techniques that the administration had been using that probably violated Common Article 3 of the Geneva

Conventions included techniques such as painful stress positions, sensory deprivation, sleep deprivation, or extremely loud music. These techniques could amount to torture, depending on the intensity and duration of their use. Proponents of the act in Congress said that waterboarding was outlawed. But the terms of the law were not explicit on these techniques, and Vice President Cheney implied that waterboarding would still be used.

The administration worked hard in order to get the top military lawyers of the Judge Advocate General Corps to state that they did not oppose the Military Commissions Act. The lawyers thought that the definition of allowable interrogation techniques under the MCA was broader than those allowed under Common Article 3 of the Geneva Conventions. After several hours of persuasion by the Pentagon General Counsel William J. Haynes II, the lawyers agreed to sign a letter that stated: "We do not object" to several sections of the act.[155]

The vice president was interviewed in the White House by a reporter who asked, "Would you agree that a dunk in water [of a suspected terrorist] is a no-brainer if it can save lives?" Cheney replied: "It's a no-brainer for me. . . . We don't torture . . . but the fact is, you can have a fairly robust interrogation program without torture, and we need to be able to do *that*. And thanks to the leadership of the President now, and the action of the Congress, we have that authority, and we are able to continue [with the] Program" (emphasis added). Asked in another question about "dunking a terrorist in water," Cheney replied, "I do agree. And I think the terrorist threat, for example, with respect to our ability to interrogate high value detainees like Khalid Sheikh Mohammed, *that's* been a very important tool that we've had to be able to secure the nation" (emphasis added). The antecedent to the word "that" and "that's" in the vice president's statements is clearly "dunking a terrorist in water," indicating that the Bush administration did not consider waterboarding to be torture.[156] The administration was making important semantic distinctions in what it considered to be the definition of torture, a line of reasoning that follows the arguments laid out in the Bybee memo of August 2002. The Bush administration later admitted that waterboarding had been used on three detainees.

The executive order issued by President Bush authorized by the MCA on July 20, 2007, said that MCA "reinforced" the president's authority "to interpret the meaning and application of the Geneva Conventions," including Common Article 3.[157] The order excluded the most egregious forms of torture, including actions covered in Title 18, sections 2241 and 2340, actions of violence that are "considered comparable to murder, torture, mutilation, and cruel or inhuman treatment," and "willful and outrageous acts of personal abuse *done for the purpose of* humiliating or degrading" persons (emphasis added). Using the reasoning of the Bybee memo, if the acts of personal abuse were done for the purpose of extracting information, they would be presumably allowed.

According to the executive order, the interrogation practices are to be used with an alien detainee who is determined be "a member" or supporter of al Qaeda or "associated organizations," and who is "likely to be in possession of information that: could assist in detecting . . . attacks within the United States . . . or [upon] other personnel, citizens, or facilities, or against allies or other countries cooperating in the War on terror . . . or their armed forces or other personnel, citizens, or facilities," *or* who "could assist in locating the senior leadership of al Qaeda, the Taliban, or associated forces." This formulation is quite broad. The person does not have to be suspected of being a member of al Qaeda, but merely to be suspected of supporting an "associated organization" and "likely" to have information that might help mitigate a terrorist attack in a "cooperating country" in the war on terror. It called for the "professional operation of the program," with "appropriate training for interrogators." Thus harsh interrogation, which most of the world might consider torture, is to be entrusted to CIA personnel specially trained in these techniques: the professionalization of torture.

The executive order allowed the CIA to continue the harsh interrogation methods, excluding only those techniques covered in the exceptions listed above, though the specific techniques allowable were not listed in the executive order or announced by the administration. The MCA and executive order amounted to congressional authorization of an unspecified range of techniques about which members of Congress presumably did not know. Thus the Bush administration convinced Congress to pass a law about interrogation techniques that did not specify which interrogation techniques would be allowed. Congress thus passed a law that was a secret to them as well as to the American people. (The problem of "secret laws" will be addressed in the conclusion.) The Justice

Department prepared a legal opinion certifying that the techniques authorized by the executive order were within President Bush's discretion in interpreting Common Article 3 of Geneva.[158]

Critics of the MCA and the president's executive order argued that they seemed to allow many of the methods that many would consider torture, including painful stress positions, sleep deprivation, ear-splitting music, and waterboarding. They argued that these techniques are cruel treatment and thus outlawed by Common Article 3 regardless of the administration's interpretation of the MCA and Common Article 3.[159] Former commandant of the Marine Corps P. X. Kelley and national security law scholar Robert F. Turner condemned the president's interpretation of the MCA and observed that it was not in accord with Common Article 3 of Geneva. They argued that World War II and the war in Vietnam did not lead the United States to "compromise our honor or abandon our commitment to the rule of law" and that the war on terror should not cause the United States to do so. They concluded that

> our troops deserve those protections, and we betray their interests when we gratuitously "interpret" key provisions of the conventions in a manner likely to undermine their effectiveness. Policymakers should also keep in mind that violations of Common Article 3 are "war crimes" for which everyone involved—potentially up to and including the president of the United States—may be tried in any of the other 193 countries that are parties to the conventions.[160]

At the symbolic level, the Military Commissions Act and President Bush's executive order sent the message to the world that the United States would continue to use harsh interrogation techniques (including waterboarding) that most countries considered to be in violation of Common Article 3 of the Geneva Conventions. Sir Andrew Collins of Britain observed about a U.S. report on Guantánamo: "America's idea of what is torture is not the same as ours and does not appear to coincide with that of most civilized nations."[161]

Conclusion

President Bush used his power as president very effectively in pursuing a policy direction that would allow U.S. personnel to use harsh interrogation methods to obtain intelligence in the war on terror. His aides marshaled legal arguments to support his position, despite serious objections from his secretary of state, Colin Powell, some general officers in the military, and professional military lawyers in the Judge Advocate General Corps. His leadership on interrogation issues was reinforced by Vice President Cheney and his staff down through the chain of command: from Defense Secretary Rumsfeld, to base and field commanders, to the military officers conducting the war in Iraq, to those in charge of interrogations, to the noncommissioned officers and enlisted personnel who carried out most of the harsh interrogations. His policy direction was also carried out by CIA personnel who often had control of the highest-ranking al Qaeda personnel.

In asserting his power as president and commander in chief of the armed forces, President Bush achieved his goal of allowing extremely harsh methods of interrogation to be used against detainees. His battle for harsh interrogation methods came, however, at a high cost to the United States. His arguments have been challenged by a range of legal opinions, including criticism by his own appointees. His policies and leadership contributed to the terrible excesses of abuse and torture publicized in the photographs of Abu Ghraib and documented by multiple military and nongovernmental investigations.

These abuses have done great harm to the reputation of the United States throughout the world and have probably added many to the ranks of terrorists who want to inflict harm upon the United States. While some tactical intelligence may have been gained from the harsh interrogation techniques, any benefit accrued has been far outweighed by the opprobrium of the international community and the damage to the professionalism of the United States Army.

John D. Hutson, Judge Advocate General for the Navy from 1972 to 2000, said of the legal memoranda prepared to defend President Bush's interpretation of the law:

> The January, 2002 memo from Judge Gonzales . . . is a short-sighted, narrow minded, and overly legalistic analysis. It's too clever by half, and frankly, just plain wrong. Wrong legally, morally, practically, and diplomatically. . . . The Bybee and Yoo memoranda are chilling. They read as though they were written in another country,

one that does not honor the Rule of Law or advocate on behalf of human rights. They contain an air of desperation.[162]

The administration argued that the use of harsh techniques was carefully limited to a few very important cases, but Charles Krulak, former commandant of the Marine Corps, argued that, once allowed by policy, torture is difficult to restrain. In commenting on "a policy of official cruelty," he said:

> As has happened with every other nation that has tried to engage in a little bit of torture—only for the toughest cases, only when nothing else works—the abuse spread like wildfire, and every captured prisoner became the key to defusing a potential ticking time bomb. Our soldiers in Iraq confront real "ticking time bomb" situations every day, in the form of improvised explosive devices, and any degree of "flexibility" about torture at the top drops down the chain of command like a stone—the rare exception fast becoming the rule.[163]

President Bush exceeded his authority as president and commander in chief by asserting his unilateral authority to ignore the Geneva Conventions as well as the U.S. criminal code. He abused his power by sending strong signals down the chain of command that set the conditions for torture to occur, despite his repeated statements that "We do not torture." And he seriously harmed the international reputation of the United States of America. It will take decades, if not generations, for the United States to recover its reputation as a country that respects the rule of law.

CHAPTER SEVEN

THE POWER TO SURVEIL

"They that can give up essential liberty to obtain a little temporary safety deserve neither liberty nor safety."
—Attributed to Benjamin Franklin

"Now, by the way, any time you hear the United States government talking about wiretap, it requires—a wiretap requires a court order. Nothing has changed, by the way. When we're talking about chasing down terrorists, we're talking about getting a court order before we do so."
—President George W. Bush, April 24, 2004

The importance of limited government to U.S. values and governance is rooted in the dictum that we have a government of laws and not of men and that no one is above the law. The sensitivity of United States culture and values to privacy and the fear of unwarranted government intrusion are expressed in the Bill of Rights. Thus the disclosure that President Bush had issued a secret order to the National Security Agency (NSA) to listen in on the communications of U.S. citizens without the warrants required by law provoked concern within the legal community, if not among the general public.

This chapter will examine the purpose of the Foreign Intelligence Surveillance Act (FISA) and President Bush's defense of his decision to violate it. It will also examine the possibility that President Bush was intentionally misleading in his statements respecting the need for a warrant for wiretapping. It will conclude that presidents ought to respect the rule of law and that the Constitution does not give the president the authority to ignore the law.[1]

NSA Warrantless Wiretapping Disclosed

In December 2005 the *New York Times* revealed that the Bush administration had been secretly monitoring telephone calls and e-mails between suspected foreign terrorists and people within the domestic United States.[2] The legal right of the executive branch to conduct electronic surveillance on foreign intelligence targets was not in dispute, but the right of the government secretly to eavesdrop or wiretap suspects within the United States is limited by the Fourth Amendment and law. The Fourth Amendment states: "The right of the people to be secure in their persons, houses, papers, and effects, against unreasonable searches and seizures, shall not be violated, and no Warrants shall issue, but upon probable cause, supported by Oath or affirmation, and particularly describing the place to be searched, and the persons or things to be seized."

In *Katz* v. *United States* the Supreme Court applied the Fourth Amendment to wiretaps (electronic surveillance) and required probable cause and a warrant.[3] Thus in criminal investigations, before executive branch investigators can wiretap a person, a warrant has to be sought from a judge who authorizes the intrusion of privacy as being reasonable because of credible evidence that the person is involved in criminal activity. The purpose of requiring a warrant is to provide a check on executive power in the sensitive area of personal privacy and because of the potential for abuse by law enforcement officials. Requiring a warrant is part of the checks and balances built into the Constitution to prevent the exercise of arbitrary power. In the only case in which the Supreme Court dealt with national security and wiretaps, it said, "These Fourth Amendment freedoms cannot properly be guaranteed if domestic security surveillance may be conducted solely within the discretion of the Executive Branch."[4] Requiring the executive branch to secure a warrant from a judicial official ensures that government officials of two different branches agree on the reasonableness of the search.

After the Terrorist Surveillance Program was made public, President Bush confirmed that he had ordered the National Security Agency to undertake surveillance of communications between foreign sources suspected of connections with al Qaeda and people in the United States. He said that the very fact that his actions had become public constituted a threat to national security and that those who were responsible for the disclosure would be sought out and punished. He added, "And the activities conducted under this authorization have helped detect and prevent possible terrorist attacks in the United States and abroad."[5] In a briefing to the press, Attorney General Alberto Gonzales said that the president's authorization of the surveillance was legal and that the program was "very, very important to protect the national security of this country."[6]

The problem with President Bush's order that NSA undertake the wiretaps was that it was against the law—the Foreign Intelligence Surveillance Act, as will be explained below. It is important to posit at the beginning that there is no argument that al Qaeda presented a serious threat to the United States. Nor is there any doubt that it is the responsibility of the president to protect the national security of the United States. Also the president can legally order surveillance or interception of communications outside of the United States. The problem with President Bush's actions in this case is that the communications in question involved at least one person in the United States, which was against the FISA law.

The issue in question is not about what measures are necessary in order for the United States to ensure the safety of Americans. It is not even directly about how to balance civil rights of Americans in times of war. The appropriate place to make these balances is in the legislative process with both the president and Congress participating, as established by the Constitution. If Congress has not acted on the issue, the president may make reasonable decisions about how to balance the two values. What is in question in the NSA eavesdropping case is whether the president has the unilateral authority to ignore the explicit dictates of the law and can undertake secret surveillance within the United States.

The fundamental values at stake are the rule of law and constitutionalism itself, not the wisdom or necessity of specific acts of surveillance. In order to make this argument, I will first posit that the threat from terrorists is real and the president has the right and duty to counter that threat. Second, it may be wise and desirable to conduct the type of surveillance that President Bush ordered the NSA to undertake. Third, it may be desirable to change the law to allow such surveillance (which eventually happened in 2007, though President Bush did not abandon his constitutional claim). In addition, what is at issue is not the president's right to intercept communications of foreign operatives. What is at issue is the president's claim that he has the constitutional authority, despite the law, to conduct without warrants surveillance of persons within the United States who may be the recipient of communications from possible terrorists outside the United States.

In a news conference in 2005 concerning his recently disclosed Terrorist Surveillance Program, President Bush claimed that he had the authority to order surveillance of Americans without warrants: "As President and Commander in Chief, I have the constitutional responsibility and the constitutional authority to protect our country. Article II of the Constitution gives me that responsibility and the authority necessary to fulfill it."[7] The reason that this assumption is problematical is that the Fourth Amendment protects citizens against unreasonable searches and seizures without a warrant, the *Katz* Supreme Court decision included electronic surveillance within the umbrella of the Fourth Amendment protections, and the Foreign Intelligence Surveillance Act forbids electronic surveillance of U.S. citizens within the United States without a warrant, as provided in that statute.[8] President Bush's claim that he had the constitutional authority to undertake such surveillance amounted to a claim that the executive has the authority to ignore the law, if he determines that it is in the interest of national security to do so.

It is not as if President Bush did not have the means to undertake the NSA spying within the law. He could have sought warrants by the special FISA courts set up for that very purpose. If speed was of importance, NSA could have carried out the surveillance and come back to the FISA court within seventy-two hours for retrospective authorization, as provided for by the law. Or if the law, as written, was too narrow to allow the kind of surveillance deemed necessary (for example, data mining), the president could have asked Congress to change the law (which he eventually did in 2007). But President Bush did none of these things; instead he secretly ordered NSA to conduct the surveillance, and when his actions were disclosed, he asserted that the commander-in-chief clause of Article II of the Constitution gave him the authority to ignore FISA and that Congress had authorized his NSA orders by passing the Authorization to Use Military Force (AUMF) in 2002.

This brings us back to the fundamental issue of constitutionalism itself, which is at stake here. In our system of limited government, the

Constitution sets limits on what the government can do, and it lays out procedures for making laws and amending the Constitution. Article I provides that "all legislative Powers herein granted shall be vested in a Congress of the United States." Article II provides that the president "shall take Care that the Laws be faithfully executed." In making the claim to the constitutional authority to ignore FISA, the president argued that his constitutional commander-in-chief powers trump his duty to execute the laws faithfully.

The Foreign Intelligence Surveillance Act

In the 1970s after the revelation of a number of abuses by the Johnson and Nixon administrations in warrantless wiretapping, a Senate Select Committee headed by Senator Church reported on some of the abuses and said that every president since Franklin Roosevelt claimed to have the authority to order wiretaps without warrants.[9] In addition,

> Since the 1930's, intelligence agencies have frequently wiretapped and bugged American citizens without the benefit of judicial warrant. . . . Past subjects of these surveillances have included a United States Congressman, Congressional staff member, journalists and newsmen, and numerous individuals and groups who engaged in no criminal activity and who posed no genuine threat to the national security, such as two White House domestic affairs advisers and an anti-Vietnam War protest group. The collection of this type of information has, in turn, raised the danger of its use for partisan political and other improper ends by senior administration officials.[10]

Some of the programs of wiretapping and keeping secret files on hundreds of thousands of Americans over the previous several decades included programs of NSA (Operations SHAMROCK and MINARET), the FBI (COINTELPRO), the CIA (Operation CHAOS), and the military (Operation CONUS).[11] The operation of some of these programs illustrates how easily a surveillance program created for purposes of national security can be expanded to include U.S. persons not directly connected to national security. It is significant that Article II of impeachment prepared to charge President Nixon cited his electronic surveillance of communications for purposes unrelated to national security.

Congress responded to these abuses by amending Title III of the Omnibus Crime Control and Safe Streets Act of 1968, which controls electronic surveillance by the government. Title III sets procedures for seeking warrants for electronic surveillance and prohibits non-warranted surveillance. Title III of the Act had provided an exception for certain national security surveillance undertaken under the "constitutional power of the President to take such measures as he deems necessary to protect the Nation against actual or potential attack [and] to obtain foreign intelligence information deemed essential to the security of the United States."[12] But in 1978 that section of Title III was repealed by the Foreign Intelligence Surveillance Act.[13] Title III was amended to allow surveillance for foreign intelligence acquisition only as long as it was carried out pursuant to the Foreign Intelligence Surveillance Act of 1978, and the amended Act specified that "the Foreign Intelligence Surveillance Act of 1978 shall be the *exclusive means* by which electronic surveillance, as defined in section 101 of such Act, and the interception of domestic wire, oral, and electronic communications may be conducted" (emphasis added).[14]

The Foreign Intelligence Surveillance Act set up a special court for the consideration of warrants for electronic surveillance, if probable cause is shown that the suspect is likely to be an agent of a foreign power. The act covered any wire, radio, or other communication that is "sent by or intended to be received by a particular, known United States Person who is in the United States."[15] In requiring a warrant from the special FISA court, the law provided for three exceptions:

1) if the attorney general determines that the communication is among foreign powers or their agents and "there is no substantial likelihood that the surveillance will acquire the contents of any communication of which a United States person is a party";

2) if the attorney general determines that there is insufficient time to obtain a warrant, but in such a case a FISA judge shall be notified within seventy-two hours (changed from twenty-four hours on December 28, 2001); and

3) if Congress has declared war, surveillance can be conducted without a warrant for fifteen days after the declaration.[16]

It is worth noting that FISA provides a strong presumption in favor of the president. A FISA court judge "must" issue a warrant under a set of relatively liberal circumstances.[17]

In confirming the *New York Times* report of the secret surveillance program, President Bush said that warrantless spying on domestic persons suspected of being in contact with terrorists was "a vital tool in our war against the terrorists,"[18] and that revealing the program damaged U.S. security. "It was a shameful act for someone to disclose this very important program in a time of war. The fact that we're discussing this program is helping the enemy."[19]

No doubt President Bush was acting in the sincere belief that he was doing so in the nation's best interest. The problem is that the decision about what means are appropriate for defending the United States is not his alone to make. The FISA statute, passed by Congress and signed by the president in 1978, provides that warrants must be sought before wiretapping persons in the United States. Overriding the law at his own discretion is not the president's prerogative.[20]

The Administration's Arguments

Given the seemingly plain language of the law, how did President Bush justify his actions? The administration made several arguments in claiming that the president's actions were legal and within his constitutional authority. First, it was argued that the program was essential for national security; second, that it was authorized by Congress; and third, that the president had the inherent constitutional authority to ignore the law.

First, the administration argued that the surveillance was essential to the national security. This may have been true, but President Bush had perfectly reasonable alternatives, if this was the case. President Bush could have followed the process set out by law; that is, he could have required NSA to get warrants from the special FISA court. The administration argued that getting a FISA warrant was too cumbersome and slow and thus it had to set up a program for the National Security Agency to conduct the surveillance without warrants and in secret. The record of the FISA court, however, does not seem to indicate that the administration had any trouble obtaining warrants. Between 1978 and 1995 there were an average of about 500 warrant applications a year.

But in 2003 there were 1,228, and in 2004 there were 1,727.[21] From the time of its creation in 1978 to the end of 2005, the special FISA court issued a total of 18,748 warrants—it refused only five.[22] This is about as close to a rubber stamp as one could wish. As for the problem of speed, if the need was immediate, NSA could act immediately and come back to the court for authorization within seventy-two hours.

The administration also argued that the Terrorist Surveillance Program (TSP) was thoroughly and regularly reviewed by executive branch officials. Vice President Cheney explained: "It's [TSP is] reviewed every 45 days by the president himself, by the attorney general of the U.S, by the president's council, by the director of CIA."[23] That the surveillance program was regularly examined by officials within the executive branch, however, does not reassure Americans who believe in the separation of powers system of checks and balances. The president holds authority over members of the executive branch and can thus control their decisions, especially within the expansive view of executive authority that the Bush administration asserted under its theory of the "unitary executive branch" (discussed in the next chapter). The reasoning behind this skepticism about unitary executive control was expressed by the Supreme Court in 1971:

> The Fourth Amendment does not contemplate the executive officers of Government as neutral and disinterested magistrates. Their duty and responsibility are to enforce the laws, to investigate and to prosecute [reference deleted]. But those charged with this investigative and prosecutorial duty should not be the sole judges of when to utilize constitutionally sensitive means in pursuing their tasks. The historical judgment, which the Fourth Amendment accepts, is that unreviewed executive discretion may yield too readily to pressures to obtain incriminating evidence and overlook potential invasions of privacy and protected speech [footnote deleted]. . . . The Fourth Amendment contemplates a prior judicial judgment [footnote deleted][,] not the risk that executive discretion may be reasonably exercised. This judicial role accords with our basic constitutional doctrine that individual freedoms will best be preserved through a separation of powers and division of functions among the different branches and levels of Government [reference deleted].[24]

It is this oversight by another branch of government that the Bush administration rejected in the case of its secret surveillance as well as on the issues of habeas corpus and the torture of detainees in the war on terror.

LEGISLATIVE AUTHORITY

The administration also argued that it had consulted with Congress about the program. President Bush said, "Not only has it been reviewed by Justice Department officials, it's been reviewed by members of the United States Congress."[25] But the briefing was to the leadership, the chairs and the ranking members of the Senate and House intelligence committees (the "gang of eight"). According to a former lawyer for the CIA, "They [briefings] are provided only to the leadership of . . . the committees, with no staff present. The eight are prohibited from saying anything about the briefing to anyone, including other intelligence panel members. . . . It is virtually impossible for individual members of Congress, particularly members of the minority party, to take any effective action."[26]

President Bush's claim to have consulted Congress was also challenged by Senator Jay Rockefeller, who had been briefed on July 17, 2003. Since the few members of Congress who were briefed were sworn to secrecy and told that they could not inform their colleagues or staff about the program, he privately communicated with the vice president. He handwrote a letter to Vice President Cheney, copied the note, and put a sealed copy in his safe as evidence that he had expressed his concern, since he had no alternative route to question what he saw as constitutional issues of privacy and executive power. He wrote to Vice President Cheney, "Clearly, the activities we discussed raise profound oversight issues."[27] In addition, as Louis Fisher points out, just because some members of Congress were informed does not make the president's actions legal.[28]

Shortly after 9/11 Congress passed the Authorization to Use Military Force (AUMF), which declared that the president could "use all necessary and appropriate force against those nations, organization, or persons he determined planned, authorized, committed, or aided the terrorist attacks that occurred on September 11, 2001, or harbored such organizations or persons, in order to prevent any future acts of international terrorism against the United States by such nations, organizations or person[s]."[29] The administration argued that the AUMF provided the statutory authorization for the warrantless wiretapping. Section 109 of FISA made it unlawful to wiretap without a warrant "except as authorized by statute." According to the Bush administration, the AUMF provided that authorization: "By expressly and broadly excepting from its prohibition electronic surveillance undertaken 'as authorized by statute' section 109 of FISA permits an exception to the 'procedures' of FISA. . . . The AUMF satisfies section 109's requirement for statutory authorization of electronic surveillance."[30] The act, however, made no mention of domestic surveillance in its wording. In arguing that the very specific FISA law was in effect repealed and nullified by the very general Authorization for the Use of Force, the administration was making a dubious argument. The Supreme Court has ruled that when Congress passes general statutes, they do not overrule previously passed, very specific laws.[31]

The argument of the administration that the AUMF overcomes FISA would entail the implication that Congress intended to repeal the section of FISA that declared FISA to be "the exclusive means by which electronic surveillance . . . may be conducted." However, as Louis Fisher points out, amending legislation must be explicit; "amendments are not made by implication." There is no evidence that members of Congress intended to repeal the FISA law when they passed the AUMF in 2001. In addition, if national security in a time of war automatically allowed the president to pursue domestic surveillance without a warrant, the section of FISA that provides for warrantless surveillance for the first fifteen days after a declaration of war would be superfluous and without meaning. Normal statutory construction leans against finding parts of laws to be without meaning.

The administration also argued that just as *Hamdi* v. *Rumsfeld*[32] decided that detention of enemy combatants on the field of battle was a necessary "incident of war" in order to keep them from returning to the battlefield, so was warrantless surveillance a necessary incident of war. "History conclusively demonstrates that warrantless communications intelligence targeted at the enemy in time of armed conflict is a traditional and fundamental incident of the use of military force authorized by the AUMF. [This practice] includes warrantless electronic surveillance to intercept enemy communications both *at home* and abroad" (emphasis added).[33] The argument was that, if the AUMF granted the president the discretion to capture prisoners, it must also be read to authorize domestic warrantless surveillance, since gathering intelligence is also a necessary incident of war.

However, when Congress was considering the authorization for the president to use force, the administration tried to insert in the language of the resolution a provision that would have allowed the "necessary and appropriate force" to be applied "in the United States" as well as against the "nations, organizations, or persons" who were involved in the 9/11 attacks. This language was rejected by the Senate. Why would the administration have tried to include the domestic language if the language as it stood gave them the authority to wiretap U.S. citizens domestically?[34]

Since Congress explicitly provided for warrantless wiretaps for fifteen days subsequent to a declaration of war, how could a resolution on the use of force, which carries less legal or constitutional weight than a declaration of war, authorize wiretaps with no limitation? As explained by Justice Frankfurter in his concurring opinion in the Steel Seizure case:

> It is one thing to draw an intention of Congress from general language and to say that Congress would have explicitly written what is inferred, where Congress has not addressed itself to a specific situation. It is quite impossible, however, when Congress did specifically address itself to a problem, as Congress did to that of seizure, to find secreted in the interstices of legislation the very grant of power which Congress consciously withheld. To find authority so explicitly withheld is . . . to disrespect the whole legislative process and the constitutional division of authority between President and Congress.[35]

In *Hamdan* v. *Rumsfeld* the Court decided that the AUMF did not give the president the right to establish military commissions because Congress had already provided the process for setting up military commissions in legislating the Uniform Code of Military Justice.[36] Thus Congress can clearly legislate about how some of the necessary incidents of war are carried out, and the specific provisions of the law cannot be easily overridden by more general laws subsequently passed.

If the administration thought that FISA as it existed did not allow the executive branch the flexibility necessary to protect the nation, it could have gone to Congress and asked for changes in the law. After all,

Congress had amended the FISA law several times since 9/11, and the administration had a Republican Congress that was willing to support most of its actions with respect to national security. Attorney General Gonzales, in explaining why the administration did not seek to amend FISA to allow for the warrantless wiretaps said, "We have had discussions with Congress in the past—certain member of Congress—as to whether or not FISA could be amended to allow us to adequately deal with this kind of threat, and we were advised that that would be difficult, if not impossible."[37] But it is contradictory to argue that Congress likely would not have granted the needed authority for warrantless wiretaps if it were asked and that, at the same time, that Congress had approved presidential authority for warrantless wiretaps in passing the AUMF.[38]

It was also disclosed that Justice Department lawyers drafted legislative changes to the USA PATRIOT Act that would have provided a legal defense for government officials who wiretapped persons in the United States without warrants as long as they had "lawful authorization" from the president. There would be no need for such legislation if the president clearly had legislative authority to authorize such wiretaps.[39]

INHERENT PRESIDENTIAL POWER

The administration argued that even if the AUMF did not give the president the authority to tap domestic communications without warrants, the inherent power that the president has, because Article II and the commander-in-chief clause of the Constitution allow him to overcome the law. Attorney General Alberto Gonzales, in a 2005 press briefing on NSA, said, "The President has the inherent authority under the Constitution, as Commander in Chief, to engage in this kind of activity."[40] Several circuit court cases have held that the president has the inherent power to wiretap without a warrant when dealing with an agent of a foreign power. All of those cases, however, were heard before passage of the FISA statute.[41]

Both sides to this issue brought up the Steel Seizure Case of 1952, *Youngstown Sheet and Tube* v. *Sawyer*.[42] In this case the Supreme Court decided that President Truman did not have the authority to seize steel mills despite the need for steel for the Korean War because Congress had provided in law for how the government must deal with strikes.

Even though "theater of war" be an expanding concept, we cannot with faithfulness to our constitutional system hold that the Commander in Chief of the Armed Forces has the ultimate power as such to take possession of private property in order to keep labor disputes from stopping production. This is a job for the Nation's lawmakers, not for its military authorities.[43]

In his oft-cited concurring opinion, Justice Robert Jackson argued that a claim for inherent presidential power is strongest "When the President acts pursuant to an express or implied authorization of Congress." A president's claim to power is less compelling "in absence of either a congressional grant or denial of authority." In this "zone of twilight" both the president and Congress "may have concurrent authority" or the allocation of power may be uncertain. But "when the President takes measures incompatible with the expressed or implied will of Congress, his power is at its lowest ebb. . . . Presidential claim to a power at once so conclusive and preclusive must be scrutinized with caution, for what is at stake is the equilibrium established by our constitutional system."[44]

Critics of the Bush administration argued that, since Congress has legislated in the Foreign Intelligence Surveillance Act, a warrant is required for eavesdropping on persons in the United States. The presumption implied in Jackson's reasoning must be that the president's claim to inherent power is dubious; he was acting directly contrary to the legislative intent of Congress. The president's lawyers, however, argued that the "AUMF places the President at the zenith of his powers in authorizing the NSA activities" because he had acted in accord with the will of Congress.[45]

The statement in the FISA Act that its provisions were the "exclusive means" of legally conducting electronic surveillance of Americans on U.S. soil explicitly states that the president does not have inherent power to ignore the law at his own discretion. The administration argued that FISA was an unconstitutional infringement on the president's constitutional authority. "In fact, if this difficult constitutional question had to be addressed, FISA would be unconstitutional as applied in this narrow context."[46] Clearly the Congress that passed the law and the president who signed it thought that the law was a constitutional exercise of the "necessary and proper" clause of Article I. Both Presidents Carter and

Ford supported FISA legislation and assumed that Congress could regulate wiretapping within the United States.

One problem with claims of inherent power of the president is that they are difficult to specify. Express powers are those that are stated in the Constitution or specified in law. Implied powers are those that are reasonable and necessary for the president to carry out express powers. But arguments for inherent powers are based on the nature of the executive and the vesting clause, have not been clearly defined, and are inherently weak claims.[47] Congress clearly has the authority to constrain the president's action through law, especially with regard to individual rights within the United States.

The Senate Judiciary Committee Report on the passage of FISA said, "Even if the President has an 'inherent' constitutional power to authorize warrantless surveillance for foreign intelligence purposes, Congress has the power to regulate the exercise of this authority by legislating a reasonable warrant procedure governing foreign intelligence surveillance."[48] Bazan and Elsea concluded that, even if the president has some inherent authority to surveillance in order to protect national security, that does not by itself mean that Congress cannot legislate to affect that authority.[49] After all, Congress has many constitutional powers regarding national security as well as domestic surveillance and the conditions under which warrants are necessary. The requirement of a warrant (with the two exceptions specified in the FISA law) was not onerous or difficult to meet, as all presidents between 1978 and 2001 found.

The administration also argued that the president has inherent power to wiretap because of his commander-in-chief role. "The NSA activities are supported by the President's well-recognized inherent constitutional authority as Commander in Chief and sole organ for the Nation in foreign affairs to conduct warrantless surveillance of enemy forces."[50] But the Constitution also requires that the president "take care that the laws be faithfully executed." Certainly the president's war powers are shared by Congress, which according to the Constitution, has the power to declare war, raise and support armies and navies, make rules for the regulation of the land and naval forces, and make rules concerning captures on land and water. Thus any powers that might be inherent in the president's constitutional responsibilities with respect to war are not exclusive and are constitutionally shared with Congress. As Justice O'Connor said in *Hamdi,* "Whatever power the United States Constitution envisions for the Executive in its exchanges with other nations or with enemy organizations in times of conflict, it most assuredly envisions a role for all three branches when individual liberties are at stake."[51] Thus Congress can legislate in ways that circumscribe the shared war power.[52] In addition, Attorney General Gonzales's statement that the administration did not seek changes in the FISA law because it did not think that such changes would be passed by Congress indicates that the administration *did* think that Congress could legislate in this area.[53]

THREATENED RESIGNATION IN THE JUSTICE DEPARTMENT

One of the most important indications that the Terrorist Surveillance Program violated the law was that the Office of Legal Counsel (OLC) in the Justice Department came to the conclusion that the White House was acting in violation of the law.[54] The OLC was led by strong Bush supporters who were conservative, yet they concluded that President Bush was violating the law. A crisis arose on March 10, 2004, when, after an extensive review by OLC, the acting attorney general, James B. Comey, refused to approve an extension of the Terrorist Surveillance Program. President Bush decided to try to bypass Comey and go to John Ashcroft who was in the hospital in intensive care recovering from gallbladder surgery the previous day. Even though Mrs. Ashcroft had indicated that her husband should not have visitors, the president called her at her husband's bedside and either told or convinced her to allow a visit by Chief of Staff Andrew Card and White House Counsel Alberto Gonzales. Gonzales carried the executive order for the program, and they intended to have Mr. Ashcroft sign it in order to reauthorize the program.

As Comey was driving home about 8:00 P.M. on March 10, 2004, Ashcroft's special assistant called him to warn him that the White House staffers were on their way to see Ashcroft. Comey rushed to the hospital room to inform Ashcroft of their impending arrival. He also called FBI Director Robert Mueller, who came to the hospital and told Mr. Ashcroft's FBI security detail not to force Comey from the room if Card and Gonzales ordered him to leave. When Card and Gonzales arrived in the room, Ashcroft told them that "he was in no condition to decide issues, and that Comey was the Acting AG."[55]

Nevertheless Gonzales and Card asked Ashcroft to sign the reauthorization. Ashcroft was very sick and sedated, but according to Comey, "He lifted his head off the pillow and in very strong terms expressed his view of the matter, rich in both substance and fact, which stunned me." Reflecting his disgust at the attempt later, Comey said (in testimony before Congress in May 2007), "I was angry. I had just witnessed an effort to take advantage of a very sick man . . . I thought he [Ashcroft] conducted himself in a way that demonstrated a strength I had never seen before, but I still thought it [the visit by White House staffers] was improper."[56] OLC Director Jack Goldsmith, who was also in the hospital room, said that the White House officials' behavior "seemed inappropriate and baffling" to him and that Ashcroft "looked very weak, very tired and ashen."[57]

After Ashcroft's refusal to sign the document, Card and Gonzales returned to the White House, and Card called Comey to an 11:00 P.M. meeting at the White House. Comey said he would come, but he told Card, "After what I just witnessed, I will not meet with you without a witness, and I intend that witness to be the solicitor general of the United States."[58] The solicitor general, Theodore B. Olson, went with Comey to the meeting at the White House, and the issues in question were discussed. President Bush decided to continue the program without the agreement of the attorney general or his deputy.[59] After the meeting, Comey prepared a letter of resignation for the next day and later told Congress that more than eight top officials at the Justice Department were prepared to resign along with him (including FBI Director Mueller). He delayed turning in his resignation so that John Ashcroft could write a letter of resignation also.[60]

The next day, March 11, Comey spoke with President Bush for fifteen minutes in the Oval Office, as did FBI Director Mueller. Bush told Comey that he would continue the program but that he would incorporate the concerns of the Justice Department about the program. Comey said that several weeks later he approved the reauthorization of the program with the assurance that it would take into account the legal concerns of the Justice Department. Comey later told Congress that the series of events was "the most difficult of my professional career."[61] Comey did not disclose what President Bush said that made him change his stand on the legality of the program.

The Office of Legal Counsel, which formally reported to Attorney General Ashcroft, had at times bypassed him and worked directly with the White House on terrorism issues. Ashcroft was upset by this and also complained that he was not able to receive the advice he needed from his staff about the TSP because the White House had not granted him access to sufficient information for him to make an informed judgment.[62] When Jack Goldsmith was its director, however, OLC sometimes made it more difficult for the White House to have its way. Goldmith said that he spent "hundreds of very difficult hours at OLC, in the face of extraordinary White House resistance, trying to clean up the legal mess that then-White House Counsel Gonzales, David Addington, John Yoo, and others had created in designing the foundations of the Terrorist Surveillance Program." During one White House encounter over the legality of the TSP, David Addington (who designed the legal justification for the TSP), told Goldsmith, "We're one bomb away from getting rid of that obnoxious [FISA] court." Goldsmith concluded that the administration "dealt with FISA the way they dealt with other laws they didn't like: they blew through them in secret based on flimsy legal opinions that they guarded closely so no one could question the legal basis for the operations."[63]

Addington kept his legal opinions so secret that he denied NSA lawyers and the NSA inspector general the permission even to see the legal justification for the TSP, much less comment on it. The Terrorist Surveillance Program, however, necessarily involved the cooperation of many telecommunications executives as well as technicians who had to provide the NSA with access to their communications processing equipment.[64] It is interesting that the corporate executives and technicians were granted security clearances in order to work with NSA, but that the Justice Department lawyers looking into the issue were denied clearances by President Bush. It is also striking that the administration denied members of Congress access to the legal justifications for the program that involved the cooperation of private company executives and technicians. The Bush administration evidently considered these private sector employees more trustworthy than John Ashcroft, NSA lawyers, the NSA inspector general, or members of the United States Congress.[65]

One industry executive, Joseph Nacchio of Quest Communications, refused to comply with NSA requests that it be given access to the private communications records of its customers. Nacchio asked if the NSA had a warrant to examine the files, and when told that there was no warrant and that one had not been applied for, he refused NSA access to the records. This request by NSA came at a meeting on February 27, 2001, well before the tragedy of 9/11. Thus it would seem that the Bush administration was seeking to monitor the communications of U.S. citizens without warrants well before 9/11, which was usually given as the justification for the need for surveillance without warrants.

The significance of this series of events is profound. John Ashcroft was a stalwart supporter of President Bush and had taken a hard line in promoting passage of the PATRIOT Act of 2001. He was often criticized by civil liberties groups for being willing to trade off too much in civil liberties, freedom, and privacy in order to give the government authority to hunt for terrorists within the United States. James Comey was a conservative lawyer appointed to be Ashcroft's deputy. Jack Goldsmith had been a Bush appointee in the Pentagon before heading OLC, and he agreed wholeheartedly with most of the policy goals of President Bush. That these three conservatives were so adamantly opposed to the way the NSA was conducting the Terrorist Surveillance Program indicates that there were serious legal problems with it. (What those problems were specifically was not revealed because the administration had classified the information.)

That President Bush decided to incorporate some changes in the program only after the top levels of the Justice Department threatened to resign shows how strongly he felt about his authority to ignore the law. The fact that more than eight top officials in the Justice Department, including Bush appointees who had been his strong supporters, were willing to resign, indicates the depth of the legal problems with the president's program. President Bush's decision to intervene so personally and assertively in the matter and to order the program to go on after DOJ authorization was refused and before their concerns were met demonstrated the extent of his belief that his executive power allowed him to supersede the laws of the United States. President Bush's actions in this case brought into serious question his commitment to the rule of law.

President Bush's Assertions about the Need for Warrants

The NSA surveillance revelations also raised the issue of whether President Bush misled the nation in reassuring questioners about government surveillance and civil liberties. In remarks made in Buffalo, New York, on April 20, 2004, President Bush said:

> Now, by the way, any time you hear the United States government talking about wiretap, it requires—a wiretap requires a court order. Nothing has changed, by the way. When we're talking about chasing down terrorists, we're talking about getting a court order before we do so. It's important for our fellow citizens to understand, when you think PATRIOT Act, constitutional guarantees are in place when it comes to doing what is necessary to protect our homeland, because we value the Constitution.[66]

Again, discussing the PATRIOT Act, President Bush said, "For years, law enforcement used so-called roving wire taps to investigate organized crime. You see, what that meant is if you got a wiretap by court order—and, by the way, everything you hear about requires [a] court order, requires there to be *permission from a FISA court,* for example" (emphasis added).[67]

Later, on June 9, 2005, in Columbus, Ohio, President Bush argued for the renewal of the PATRIOT Act: "The judicial branch has a strong oversight role. Law enforcement officers need a federal judge's permission to wiretap a foreign terrorist's phone, a federal judge's permission to track his calls, or a federal judge's permission to search his property. Officers must meet strict standards to use any of these tools. And these standards are fully consistent with the Constitution of the [United States]."[68]

What interpretation of these statements would make them truthful? The president clearly was aware of his secret order and that the NSA was continuing to carry on surveillance of communications between U.S. citizens and foreign-based persons. He emphasized that he had reauthorized the program more than thirty times, approximately once every forty-five days. When asked about his previous remarks, the president said, "I was talking about roving wiretaps, I believe, involved in the PATRIOT Act. This is different from the NSA program."[69]

The president's defense of his reassurances was that his remarks were intended to refer only to the specific provisions of the PATRIOT Act implied that he had a mental reservation in uttering his statement. This explanation implied that his words had a special meaning for him that was not apparent to others. Thus, according to his argument, the words—"any time you hear the United States government talking about wiretap, it requires—a wiretap requires a court order. Nothing has changed"—did not mean what they appear to mean. The words "any time," given the president's possible mental reservation, must have been limited to only the PATRIOT Act. To interpret his words in this manner, however, flies in the face of the plain meaning of his words. In Hershey, Pennsylvania, the president referred to the necessity of gaining permission from a FISA court. Thus his remarks evidently referred to FISA and its restrictions rather than to merely the PATRIOT Act.[70]

Vice President Cheney told an interviewer that the Terrorist Surveillance Program was "reviewed every forty-five days by the president himself, by the attorney general of the U.S., by the president's council, by the director of CIA." When the interviewer said, "The Constitution calls for a court, a co-equal branch of government, as a check on the power of the executive, to give a say-so before an American or someone in America is surveilled, or searched, or spied upon," Cheney replied, "This has been done."[71]

The question here is not whether there was a serious threat from terrorism or whether the government ought to be able to wiretap U.S. citizens without a warrant under certain circumstances. It may indeed be good policy to allow the government to conduct such surveillance, but the constitutional process for making such decisions entails legislative procedure and judicial interpretation of the law. President Bush however claimed that, despite the laws enacted by Congress and duly signed by the president, he had inherent authority to ignore the law and set up a secret surveillance program that could act without warrants. The question is one of his assertion of inherent presidential authority versus the other two branches; the wisdom of surveillance policy is a separate issue.

On December 6, 2005, President Bush made a special plea to New York Times publisher Arthur Sulzberger and its executive editor, Bill Keller, not to publish the story on the secret NSA program. He argued that its exposure would hurt national security. As he said later, "the fact that we are discussing this program is helping the enemy."[72]

That terrorists would not understand that their electronic communications might be intercepted by the United States is difficult to imagine. After all, government interception of all foreign communications is perfectly legal; only for persons in the United States are warrants required.

And in the case of domestic targets, the FISA court approved more than 18,000 and rejected only five requests. The president's argument would have us believe that if the terrorists suddenly discovered that the NSA could act without a warrant that it would change their behavior because the 5 in 18,000 chance that the warrant would be refused was eliminated. It strains credulity to believe that terrorists would be aware of, much less change their behavior because of, the increased likelihood (of 5 in 18,000) that their communications to persons in the U.S. might be monitored.

Vice President Cheney argued that the secret NSA program might have enabled the executive branch to prevent the 9/11 attacks. He said that if the program had been operating "before 9/11, we might have been able to pick up on two of the hijackers who flew a jet into the Pentagon."[73] If that is true, the administration was unconscionably neglecting its obligation to protect the American people. If wiretapping of Americans would have prevented such attacks, the administration should have completed the necessary paperwork to obtain the warrants; or it should have undertaken the surveillance and within seventy-two hours applied for a retroactive warrant (as provided in FISA); or it should have sought changes in the law. Mr. Cheney's argument seems to imply that before 9/11 the Bush administration put the American people in serious jeopardy of terrorist attacks such as 9/11 merely because it did not want to comply with FISA or ask for a change in the law. Alternatively, when he implied that the TSP was not undertaken until after 9/11, Vice President Cheney may have been misrepresenting the time of the actual beginning of the operation of the TSP. As noted above, Joseph Nacchio of Quest Communications was approached by NSA in February 2001 for access to private phone records of their customers, and he refused. Thus it seems highly likely that NSA gained permission of other, more cooperative, phone companies well before 9/11. If this was the case, NSA had been wiretapping domestic communications well before 9/11, and the TSP did not prevent 9/11.

President Bush's assurances that NSA career professionals used strict criteria to decide whom to wiretap, that Justice Department lawyers had vetted the program, and that he personally reviewed the program every forty-five days are beside the constitutional point.[74] The framers set up a system of separation of powers in order to assure that governmental power would not be abused. They passed the Bill of Rights to assure the anti-Federalists that citizens would be protected from the potential abuse of power by governmental officials. Arguments that citizens should trust the executive branch to act with restraint when it decides to ignore the law fly in the face of the Constitution and the wisdom of the framers.

Congress passed FISA in order to provide a judicial check on executive power; if the executive wanted to wiretap U.S. citizens, it was required to obtain a judicial warrant. President Bush's claim to constitutional authority to ignore this law thus presents a direct challenge to the system of limited government and rule of law.

The Administration Changes Tactics

In January 2005, two weeks before an appeals court in Cincinnati was going to hear a case on the legality of the Terrorist Surveillance Program and just before a Senate Committee hearing on the nomination of Alberto Gonzales for attorney general, the government announced that it had come to an agreement with the FISA court for a process that would allow more "speed and agility" in the handling of requests for warrants. The judge on the FISA court was not named; the decision was made in secret; there were no adversarial procedures; and apparently no possibility for appeal of the decision.[75] The administration said that, because of asserted security concerns, they would not explain how the new process operated.

In February Attorney General Gonzales wrote a letter to clarify his testimony to the Senate Judiciary Committee. In his testimony he had said that the Terrorist Surveillance Program had been authorized by President Bush, "and that is all that he has authorized." In a letter revising his testimony, he said, "I did not and could not address . . . any other classified intelligence activities." It seems reasonable to infer that there may have been other secret surveillance programs that the president had authorized. Such programs may or may not have been within the law. The reason for the letter may have been that Gonzales did not want to be caught misleading Congress if another secret surveillance program were disclosed in the future.[76]

The administration continued to maintain that the president had the constitutional authority to ignore the FISA law, even though it asserted that the revised process conformed to the law. On May 1, 2007, the newly appointed director of National Intelligence, Michael McConnell, said that the president had the authority to order NSA surveillance of individuals in the United States without warrants. When he was asked by a senator whether he could assure Congress that the FISA law would be obeyed, he replied, "Sir, the president's authority under Article II is in the Constitution. So if the president chose to exercise Article II authority, that would be the president's call."[77]

Early in 2006 the Office of Professional Responsibility (OPR) of the Justice Department began an investigation into the legal advice given to the White House and NSA about the legality of the Terrorist Surveillance Program. But when the office indicated that it was going to interview several attorneys and it was probable that the actions of Attorney General Gonzales would be examined, President Bush personally intervened in order to deny security clearances to the members of OPR. Security clearances were essential in order for the investigation to proceed, and as a result of the denial, the investigation was shut down. This was the first time in the thirty-year history of OPR that its members had ever been denied the security clearances necessary to do their job, and a personal intervention at this level by the president is unusual.

Many other officials in the Justice Department had been given security clearances, and the five members of the civilian privacy board appointed by the White House also had clearances. For instance, the large contingent of lawyers who were investigating the initial leak of the existence of the program to the *New York Times* all had been issued clearances. On May 10, 2006, H. Marshall Jarrett, the director of OPR, wrote to Congress that "our repeated requests for access to classified information about the NSA program have not been granted. As a result, this office . . . has been precluded from performing its duties."[78] President Bush stopped the investigation into a matter (illegal NSA wiretapping) that might have implicated the attorney general or President Bush himself in ignoring the law. In November 2007, after Michael Mukasey was confirmed as attorney general, President Bush granted the necessary clearances to Mr. Jarrett's staff.[79]

In August 2007 President Bush signed a law that provided a framework for the administration to undertake warrantless surveillance of phone calls and e-mails between people in the United States and overseas, as long as the "target" is "reasonably believed" to be overseas. The new law essentially made legal the surveillance that the administration had been carrying out since 2001. The role of the FISA court was circumscribed to reviewing the procedures that the executive branch carried out after the fact. The surveillance was broadened from terrorist targets to "foreign intelligence," providing a much broader scope to the administration's power. The new authority was to expire in six months, when it would have to be reauthorized.[80]

Regardless of the wisdom of the balance struck between security and privacy by the new law, the Bush administration was finally forced to return to the constitutional process in seeking approval of its surveillance program. Even though the new law legalized President Bush's future surveillance, the administration had been breaking the FISA law. The principle that presidents must obey the law was not obviated by the change in the FISA law. The Constitution thus worked in the sense that President Bush was at last convinced to go to Congress to get what he wanted rather than merely claim the inherent authority to ignore the law. His claim to inherent power was not vindicated; whether that would affect his behavior in other areas of national security surveillance could not be known as long as any other programs remained secret.

Conclusion

Surveillance of communications between suspected terrorists and U.S. persons may indeed help protect the national security, but there is no good reason that the surveillance could not have been undertaken within the law, or under an amended FISA law. The actions of President Bush undermined the rule of law. That President Bush undertook the Terrorist Surveillance Program secretly makes this case particularly troubling. If the president breaks the law in secret, it is impossible for the separation of powers system to operate as was intended.

The intention of the FISA statute was to strike a balance between legitimate and necessary national security needs and the protection of individual rights as guaranteed by the Constitution. The law required the executive branch to obtain a warrant from the judicial branch before it could monitor communications of persons in the United States. In rejecting the balance required in law, President Bush short-circuited the constitutional policy process and arrogated to himself the right to strike that balance according to his own judgment. And by implementing this decision, he undermined the constitutional balance.

Even if one were to posit that President Bush was entirely trustworthy, was acting from sincere motives, and would in no case abuse his power, the constitutional argument against his assertion of authority would not be overcome. Justice Brandeis noted, "Experience should teach us to be most on our guard to protect liberty when the government's purposes are beneficent."[81] Because the framers knew that executives would tend to aggrandize power, they designed a means to control that power. James Madison argued in *Federalist* No. 51 that a "dependence on the people is, no doubt, the primary control on the government; but experience has taught mankind the necessity of auxiliary precautions." These "auxiliary precautions" were designed when the framers set up the separation of powers system in which "ambition must be made to counteract ambition."

Thus even if it were posited that President Bush would not abuse his claimed power, the authority that he claimed to be able to ignore the law would constitute a dangerous precedent that future presidents might use to abuse their power. As Madison pointed out in *Federalist* No. 10, "Enlightened statesmen will not always be at the helm." That President Bush finally went to Congress for a change in the law was important. But he did so out of prudence rather than conceding the principle that the Constitution required it.

A constitution must be designed so that if a future executive tries to abuse his or her power, the other two branches will be able to check that excess. That is why it is crucial for presidents to obey the law. Future presidents may not be "enlightened statesmen" and might be willing to use the claimed surveillance power to harass political enemies and undermine the political process. To find such an example we need look no further from the present than the 1970s, during which President Nixon abused his presidential authority by wiretapping his political enemies and undermining the political process by interfering with the opposing party's campaign in the 1972 run-up to the presidency.

For the Constitution of the United States to endure, governmental officials must act with restraint and admit that they do not have exclusive power where the Constitution has specified that it be shared. In its resolution concerning unwarranted surveillance, the American Bar Association called on President Bush "to abide by the limitations which the Constitution imposes on a president under our system of checks and balances and respect the essential roles of the Congress and the judicial branch in ensuring that our national security is protected in a manner consistent with constitutional guarantees."[82]

CHAPTER EIGHT

THE POWER TO IGNORE THE LAW: SIGNING STATEMENTS

"Our Nation is built upon the rule of law. . . . The strength of our legal system requires the ongoing commitment of every citizen."
—President Bush on Law Day 2007

"The executive branch shall construe Title X [of the Detainee Treatment Act of 2005] relating to detainees, in a manner consistent with the constitutional authority of the President to supervise the unitary executive branch."
—President Bush in his signing statement accompanying the anti-torture law

In 2005 Senator John McCain introduced an amendment to a military authorization act that would outlaw any torture by United States personnel anywhere in the world.[1] When signing the bill into law, President Bush issued a signing statement that read in part: "The executive branch shall construe Title X [of the Detainee Treatment Act] relating to detainees, in a manner consistent with the constitutional authority of the President to supervise the unitary executive branch."[2] By issuing this signing statement, President Bush raised the possibility that he would not execute the law, using the justification that it might interfere with his prerogatives as commander in chief.

On March 9, 2006, President Bush signed a reauthorization of the PATRIOT Act (H.R. 3199), which was soon to expire. Legislators worried about civil liberties were concerned that the FBI was conducting searches of homes and private records without warrants and called for more congressional oversight. In order to end a filibuster that delayed a vote on the bill, the administration agreed to provisions that would require it to report to oversight committees about its use of the law's search provisions. These guarantees convinced some members of Congress to drop their objections and to allow the bill to come to the floor for a vote and be passed. President Bush signed the bill into law with much fanfare in the East Room of the White House. Yet after signing the bill, the president issued a signing statement declaring, "The executive branch shall construe the provisions of H.R. 3199 that call for furnishing information to entities outside the executive branch [that is, Congress] . . . in a manner consistent with the President's constitutional authority to . . . withhold information the disclosure of which could impair foreign relations, national security, the deliberative processes of the Executive, or the performance of the Executive's constitutional duties."[3]

In 2008 Congress passed the National Defense Authorization Act of Fiscal Year 2008; Section 1222 of the act provided that "no funds appropriated pursuant to an authorization of appropriations in this Act may be obligated or expended . . . to establish any military installation or base for the purpose of providing for the permanent stationing of United States Armed Forces in Iraq." When President Bush signed the law, he issued a signing statement that said, "Provisions of the Act, including sections 841, 846, 1079, and 1222 purport to impose requirements that could inhibit the President's ability to carry out his constitutional obligations to take care that the laws be faithfully executed. . . . The executive branch shall construe such provisions in a manner consistent with the constitutional authority of the President."[4] Thus President Bush left open the possibility that U.S. troops would be stationed in Iraq in permanent bases and signaled his conviction that Congress could not control expenditures from the treasury through law.

In these signing statements President Bush directly challenged the ability of Congress to constrain executive actions, the nature of the rule of law in the United States, and the meaning of the separation of powers system. In hundreds of other objections to laws contained in signing statements, President Bush challenged the authority of Congress and the law to force him to do anything he deemed an unconstitutional infringement on his authority as president. This chapter examines the history and uses of signing statements in the United States. It then analyzes the way in which signing statements have been justified by presidents and arguments criticizing those justifications. Finally, it concludes that, although some signing statements are unobjectionable, President Bush's systematic and expansive use of signing statements constitutes a direct threat to the separation of powers system in the United States.

The struggle of Parliament in England to wrest the power of making law from the absolute right of the king lasted centuries. One of the key turning points in that struggle was the elimination of the right of the king to suspend laws. Even after kings had lost the exclusive power to make all laws, the crown still had the authority not only to issue an absolute veto—to nullify an act of Parliament—but it also had the power to suspend the law for specific purposes when it suited the royal interests. If a law were nullified, it would not go into effect; with the suspension power, kings could merely suspend the effect of the law for themselves or others at their own convenience. The framers of the U.S. Constitution explicitly and unanimously rejected granting the president an absolute veto or the "power to suspend any legislative act."[5]

One of the powers that Parliament had been able to win in the several centuries after Magna Carta was sealed was the authority to approve new taxes for the king. Thus if the king wanted to conduct a war, new revenues would probably be necessary and he had to go to Parliament for authority to raise taxes. This gave Parliament important leverage, and it would sometimes insist that the king accede to some of its demands before it would grant him the right to collect the revenues. One stratagem that kings employed to get additional funds but evade their part of the bargain was to approve of the law, but then use the royal power to suspend the law when it suited them. Thus the king did not have to veto the law requiring royal concessions, which might provoke Parliament not to give its consent to additional revenues; but he could approve the law, then suspend the law when it came to acting on his promises.[6] President Bush threatened to use the same gambit when he signed a law but issued a signing statement implying that he might not execute it.

Although by the fifteenth century the right of Parliament to pass binding laws was established in theory, it seldom exercised this power against the will of the monarch during the sixteenth century. In the seventeenth century, the Stuart monarchy tried to reassert the divine right of kings, part of which was the power to suspend the laws. Even after the Civil

War and the restoration of the monarchy, Charles II attempted to use the power of suspension, and James II continued to assert the suspension power in the 1680s. When the suspension power was challenged in court during the 1688 trial of seven bishops who were accused of seditious libel, Justice Powell said that if the suspension power "be once allowed of, there will need no parliament; all the legislature will be in the king, which is a thing worth considering."[7] The jury returned a verdict of acquittal of the bishops, and the suspending power was finally abolished. When the English Bill of Rights was written in 1689, it included a provision abolishing the suspending authority of the crown: "The pretended power of suspending of laws, or the execution of laws, by regal authority, without consent of Parliament, is illegal."[8]

This battle, which was hard-won by Parliament after centuries of struggle against the prerogatives of the crown, was, in effect, reasserted by President George W. Bush in his many sweeping challenges to provisions of laws that he claimed impinged on his constitutional powers. This chapter will examine those claims and their constitutional implications.

As argued in chapter 3, the framers of the Constitution adapted from English legal history individual rights as against the crown, and they reaffirmed the progress that Parliament had made in establishing legislative supremacy in domestic policy. Part of that supremacy was the outlawing of the authority of the king to suspend the laws. In his *Commentaries on the Laws of England,* written in the mid-eighteenth century, Blackstone confirmed this limit on the royal power:

> An act of parliament, thus made, is the exercise of the highest authority that this kingdom acknowledges upon earth. . . . And it cannot be altered, amended, dispensed with, suspended, or repealed, but in the same forms, and by the same authority of parliament. . . . It is true, it was formerly held, that the king might, in many cases, dispense with penal statutes: but now, by statute . . . it is declared that the suspending or dispensing with laws by regal authority, without consent of parliament, is illegal.[9]

It is these principles—that the legislature makes the law, and the executive must obey the law—that are at issue in considering presidential signing statements.

The Nature of Signing Statements

Presidents since James Monroe have occasionally issued statements upon the signing of bills into law, though it was unusual for the first 150 years of the republic. Most of these signing statements were rhetorical and meant to show presidential support for the legislation or occasionally to record publicly presidential reservations about a law. Rhetorical signing statements began to increase with the Truman administration, but the most controversial use of signing statements has been to register reservations about the constitutionality of the law in question. The use of signing statements for this purpose began to be taken seriously during the Carter and Ford presidencies. During the Reagan presidency, however, signing statements were used in a systematic way to argue that presidential opinions about legislative intent should be considered by courts (when the language of the statue is unclear), just as congressional committee reports have been used. The Reagan administration also used signing statements to assert that the president might not be obligated to execute laws.

Signing statements can be defined as

official pronouncements issued by the President contemporaneously to the signing of a bill into law that, in addition to commenting on the law generally, have been used to forward the President's interpretation of the statutory language; to assert constitutional objections to the provisions contained therein; and, concordantly, to announce the threat that provisions of the law will be administered in a manner that comports with the Administration's conception of the President's constitutional prerogatives.[10]

This broad definition covers the most important intentions of presidents who have used signing statements. The purpose of making presidential comments on the law is benign; there is no reason the president should not make public and official comments on a bill that are signed into law. Noting constitutional objections to the law, however, raises troubling questions, if the implication is that the president may choose not to execute laws to which he has constitutional objections.

Signing statements were issued occasionally during the first century and a half of the republic, but in the latter half of the twentieth century, they increased in usage and importance. One widely reported source of

Presidential Signing Statements

President	Constitutional	Interpretive	Rhetorical	Total
Hoover	1	0	11	12
Roosevelt	0	3	48	51
Truman	3	7	108	118
Eisenhower	9	7	129	145
Kennedy	1	0	79	80
Johnson	11	2	289	302
Nixon	6	2	181	169
Ford	10	0	120	130
Carter	24	8	215	247
Reagan	71	23	94	276
G. H. W. Bush	146	30	38	214
Clinton	105	21	265	391
G. W. Bush				159*

Source: Christopher S. Kelley, "'Faithfully Executing' and 'Taking Care'—The Unitary Executive and the Presidential Signing Statement," paper presented at the American Political Science Association annual convention, 2002. The totals of 159 and 1,167 come from Christopher Kelley's website (www.users.muohio.edu/kelleycs/).
*Total Bush challenges to laws as of February 13, 2008. In signing statements for the 159 laws, President Bush made a total of 1,167 challenges to provisions in the laws.

the frequency of signing statements has been compiled by scholar Christopher Kelley (see table).

Curtis Bradley and Eric Posner have compiled a different count of signing statements (as of June 2006) that is not far from Kelley's overall count, and generally agrees with the trends. They argue that Bush's use of signing statements that challenge statutory provisions is high but not "outside the historical norm," though they admit that Bush "has clearly departed from the norm by frequently issuing challenges to numerous statutory provisions within a single signing statement," more than 800 as of June 2006.[11] Their conclusions about signing statements will be taken up later in the chapter. The next section will describe the development of signing statements since they have become controversial, that is, from the Reagan administration to the George W. Bush administration.

THE REAGAN ADMINISTRATION

During the Reagan administration in the 1980s, executive branch lawyers made a concerted effort to enhance the authority of the presidency. President Reagan issued a total of 276 signing statements, and seventy-one of those raised constitutional questions. This was a sharp increase of constitutional objections from the twenty-four that President Carter issued, and it ushered in the era of more active use of signing statements to challenge the constitutionality of laws.[12]

The Reagan administration began its systematic campaign to use signing statements in a strategic manner for several purposes: to get signing statements institutionalized and accepted within the executive branch, to get them seen as legitimate sources of legislative intent, to allow the president to use them to instruct executive branch subordinates, and to raise challenges to the constitutionality of parts of statutes to which the president objected.[13] In 1985 the director of the Office of Legal Counsel, Ralph Tarr, wrote that signing statements were "presently underutilized and could become far more important as a tool of Presidential management of the agencies" and "a device for preserving issues of importance in the ongoing struggle for power with Congress."[14]

Another initiator of the signing statement strategy, Samuel Alito, worried that "our new type of signing statement will not be warmly welcomed by Congress," in part because of "the potential increase of presidential power." Alito thus recommended that initiation of the strategy begin carefully. "As an introductory step, our interpretive statements should be of moderate size and scope. . . . We should concentrate on points of true ambiguity, rather than issuing interpretations that may seem to conflict with those of Congress."[15] First steps in the strategy included getting signing statements published as official documents of the government, having OLC memoranda and opinions cite them regularly, and having articles defending them published in highly visible law reviews. The intent was clear: to increase presidential power; but they had to begin slowly so as not to alarm other participants in the legislative process.

Steven Calabresi and Daniel Lev brag that the use of signing statements during the administrations of Presidents Reagan and George H. W. Bush caused a "quiet revolution in the scope of the President's constitutionally prescribed 'lawmaking' powers."[16] Calabresi, in their article, points out that he was the staffer to Edwin Meese "who originally suggested the idea of the signing statement initiative."[17] Calabresi's emphasis on the "quiet" part of the revolution was part of the strategy to condition Congress, the courts, and the public to see signing statements as a legitimate part of the legislative process. Similarly, the phrase "unitary executive" was used by the Bush administration strategically to lay the groundwork for future expansions of executive power. These were self-conscious attempts to establish a record of usage (for signing statements and the phrase "unitary executive") so as in the future to be able to point back to this usage and declare that ipso facto they are part of the precedent of constitutional usage that should be accepted as part of an evolving constitution.

Part of the intent of the Reagan administration was to establish signing statements as part of the legislative record so that the president's views, when the courts determined legislative intent, would be considered along with the congressional record. This effort was led by Edwin Meese when he arranged with West Publishing Company to publish signing statements in the "Legislative History" section of *The United States Congressional Code and Administrative News* (USCCAN), which provides information about the background for the development of a law that might be relevant to the future interpretation by courts of any ambiguous language. Attorney General Meese explained that the purpose of the administration's action was "to make sure that the President's own understanding of what's in a bill . . . is given consideration at the time of statutory construction later on by a court."[18]

Such a purpose seems reasonable on its face, because it merely calls to the attention of the courts the president's perspective on the law. But in addition to merely registering the president's views on a law, the administration also argued that the courts should rely on signing statements to interpret ambiguous laws. Samuel Alito, then in the Office of Legal Counsel of the Justice Department, argued that one of the primary objectives of signing statements was to "ensure that Presidential signing statements assume their rightful place in the interpretation of legislation."[19] This controversial use of signing statements will be evaluated below.

Another intent of the Reagan administration's use of signing statements raised more serious constitutional questions. Edwin Meese, though no longer part of the government, announced in 2001 that a signing statement would indicate "those provisions of the law that might not be enforced."[20] This use of signing statements presents a serious constitutional issue. If a president can decide not to execute the law, he can avoid vetoing a law, thus precluding a possible congressional override.

He can also exercise, in effect, an item veto by isolating any part of a law that he claims impinges on his constitutional prerogatives and ignore it. Although there may be limited circumstances in which a president may legitimately decide not to carry out the law, this troubling interpretation of signing statements will be discussed below.

George H. W. Bush

President Bush (41) was concerned with asserting presidential prerogatives against Congress. He issued 214 signing statements and raised constitutional issues in 146 of them. President Bush was particularly concerned with protecting the appointment power of the president, and when a law mandated that some appointments to a commission had to be drawn from a congressionally established pool, he issued a signing statement stating that the offending provision would be treated as being "without legal force or effect."[21] President Bush subsequently worked with Congress to formulate changes to the law that would satisfy both President Bush and Congress. This seems to be a reasonable use of a signing statement—that is, to use it to call objections to the attention of Congress and then work to remedy the problem to the satisfaction of both branches.

William J. Clinton

Although he was not as assertive or as outspoken about claiming constitutional executive authority vis-à-vis Congress, President Clinton also used signing statements to claim that Congress had overstepped its authority in some laws. He issued 391 signing statements, most of which did not raise constitutional issues, although 105 of them did. President Clinton's assistant attorney general, Walter Dellinger, wrote an opinion that stated, "There are circumstances in which the President may appropriately decline to enforce a statute that he views as unconstitutional." But the opinion went on to say, "As a general matter, if the President believes that the Court would sustain a particular provision as constitutional, the President should execute the statute notwithstanding his own beliefs about the constitutional issue."[22] Here Dellinger seems to be limiting the legitimate use of signing statements to instances in which the constitutional issue seems straightforward. In one case President Clinton ordered the secretary of energy to implement a congressionally mandated organization of a unit in the Department of Energy in a way that undercut congressional intent to insulate the unit from the control of the secretary of energy.[23] If this was intended to bring the issue to the courts in order to determine the constitutionality of the law, it may have been legitimate. But as an absolute veto or item veto of a law, it was illegitimate.

GEORGE W. BUSH

In testimony before the Senate Judiciary Committee on June 27, 2006, Deputy Assistant Attorney General Michelle Boardman defended President Bush's record on signing statements, arguing that "President Bush's signing statements are indistinguishable from those issued by past Presidents."[24] At a superficial level Boardman was correct. President Bush issued signing statements regarding 159 laws (as of February 2008), fewer than the 391 of President Clinton. But most of them, 127, made constitutional claims, as opposed to the 105 of President Clinton. More important, however, was the fact that in those 159 signing statements, President Bush objected to more than 1,167 provisions of laws.[25] This is almost twice as many as all previous presidents of the United States combined. All previous presidents issued a total of fewer than 600 constitutional challenges to laws in their signing statements.[26]

Throughout her testimony Boardman quoted Walter Dellinger of the Clinton administration to show parallels between Clinton's and Bush's signing statements. This argument seems to imply that objections to signing statements are a partisan issue and that showing that a Democratic president had issued signing statements would justify President Bush's doing so also. But this point is irrelevant; the question is an institutional and constitutional issue. That Clinton issued some signing statements does not make it legitimate or constitutional.

In addition to the sheer volume of challenges to laws, President Bush used signing statements in a systematic and strategic way in order to lay the groundwork for claiming more presidential power. Any provision in a law that might conceivably relate to executive authority was subject to a signing statement objection, often of a general and vague type, rather than a specific objection accompanied by legal reasoning. Although this aspect of the signing statements was not that different from those of some previous presidents, according to T. J. Halstead, a Congressional Research Service scholar, there was a "qualitative difference" in the Bush statements because many of the objections rested on the theory of "the unitary executive branch."[27] This phrase had not been commonly used previously in constitutional law or analyses of the separation of powers. The Bush administration intended for the phrase to indicate that the president constitutionally controls the whole executive branch of government and that Congress cannot legitimately try to affect the execution of the laws (discussed later in this chapter).

One plausible interpretation of President Bush's systematic use of signing statements was that by repeated assertions of presidential prerogative, he hoped to condition Congress and the attentive public to accept the Bush administration's expansive conception of executive authority under the Constitution. As Halstead put it, the Bush administration tried "to systematically object to any perceived congressional encroachment, however slight, with the aim of inuring the other branches of government and the public to the validity of such objections and the attendant conception of presidential authority that presumably follow from sustained exposure and acquiescence to such claims of power."[28]

A more sinister reading of President Bush's motives might conclude that the administration wanted to lay the groundwork for the selective refusal to carry out certain provisions of laws, openly or secretly. When a failure to execute the law faithfully was discovered, the administration could then point to the signing statement and claim that it issued a warning that it might not execute the law and no one had objected; thus it was free to ignore the law. Other ways in which President Bush used signing statements will be discussed in more detail below.[29]

GAO STUDY

In 2007 Government Accountability Office (GAO) analysts undertook an examination of President Bush's compliance with laws, provisions of which he had objected to in signing statements. GAO examined only the appropriations bills passed in 2006 and counted 160 objections in the twelve appropriations laws passed by Congress. It found that President Bush had registered objections to each bill except the Legislative Appropriations Act for 2006. They examined nineteen of the provisions of law objected to and found that ten of the provisions were executed as the law required; six provisions were not executed as enacted; and three provisions were not triggered (thus the question of compliance did not arise).

Two of the cases of noncompliance occurred when the administration did not seek the required approval of actions from Congress. One involved a failure to report or submit plans to Congress as required in legislative veto provisions. In one case the Defense Department did not submit separate budget justifications for contingency plans in Afghanistan and Iraq. One was a seventeen-day delay in responding to Congress. And one was a failure to relocate border checkpoints as directed in law.[30] In these six cases of noncompliance, we might conclude that three were not problematical (legislative veto and seventeen-day delay), two were refusals to report to Congress, and one was a failure to carry out a mandate in the law. In its refusal to relocate checkpoints in the Tucson sector every seven days, the Customs and Border Patrol (CBP) said that the appropriations act was "advisory" and not consistent with its "mission requirements."

This refusal to carry out the law raises the question of who determines the mission of an agency of the United States government. Most often, the authorizing legislation states explicitly the purpose of agencies and programs created by law, and the president is constitutionally bound to execute the law. In themselves, these instances did not constitute egregious violations of the law. But within the broader pattern of 160 objections to the twelve appropriations acts in one year and more than 1,000 other objections to laws, they raise important constitutional questions. Many of them were arguably not merely failures to execute the law, but were formal claims of constitutional authority to ignore the law. The belief that he could selectively enforce the law pursuant to his signing statements may be part of the reason that President Bush did not issue any vetoes for the first five-and-a-half years of his administration, a record unmatched since Thomas Jefferson.

Bradley and Posner in a working paper have written one of the most sophisticated defenses of signing statements. They argue that there are many parallels between the signing statements of President Clinton and those of George W. Bush, and they illustrate Bush statements with similar objections that Clinton had made. They conclude that the "theories" articulated by Clinton do not differ significantly from those of President

Bush. (That President Clinton issued similar signing statements does not justify this executive branch practice.) They further argue that nothing is wrong with signing statements in themselves, and that critics of President Bush are really objecting to his interpretation of the Constitution. They make an important point here because there are several legitimate uses of signing statements that most critics of President Bush's use of them would admit. They also point out that merely stating a constitutional objection to a provision of law is not the same as actively violating it.

The point of critics, however, is that President Bush is systematically using signing statements to stake out an expansive interpretation of executive power that he and succeeding presidents may use in the future. Bradley and Posner are correct that the objections of critics are heavily influenced by the broader historical context and actions taken by the Bush administration. Thus if one looks at Bush's signing statements along-side the expansive claims to executive power asserted in a number of OLC memoranda (quoted in preceding chapters), one could reasonably conclude that the president's actions are consistent with the assertions of presidential authority contained in those OLC memoranda.

The other major concern of critics of President Bush is the record of secrecy around administration actions and the unwillingness to disclose the legal defenses of those actions. As has been shown previously, President Bush has secretly undertaken surveillance of persons in the United States. It was only by chance that the existence of the Terrorist Surveillance Program was disclosed. After disclosure, the administration prevented even Justice Department or NSA officials from reading the legal justifications of the program. Similarly, the Bush administration wrote secret memoranda and withheld them from administration officials who ordinarily comment on such memos until they were signed. The February and May 2005 memoranda authorizing harsh interrogation techniques that many consider torture remained secret.

Thus if one looks at the record of actions of the Bush administration that are justified by very expansive claims of executive authority, the signing statements take on a different significance than if one were merely abstractly examining the use of signing statements. Bradley and Posner also argue that Congress possesses potent tools with which to counter any overreaching of the executive.[31] But in those tools they include the authority to "require reports and audits" and "interrogate executive officials." But these traditional tools of Congress are the very ones that President Bush refuses to honor. His signing statements systematically reject the authority of Congress to require reporting by the executive branch. Furthermore, requirements of testimony of executive branch officials before Congress were regularly rejected by claims of executive privilege. Court examination of executive branch actions was rejected with the state secrets privilege. But Bradley and Posner are correct in pointing out that most critics of President Bush's use of signing statements are concerned more with how President Bush is using them to expand executive power (for himself and all future presidents) than in the instrument of signing statements themselves.

The Purposes of Signing Statements

During the Clinton administration, Assistant Attorney General Walter Dellinger wrote an opinion defending most of the uses of signing statements. Dellinger argued that signing statements were appropriate in order
    —to explain to the public the likely effects of the law,
    —to direct subordinates about how to administer the law,
    —to inform Congress that the president believes the law to be unconstitutional and that "it will not be given effect by the Executive Branch," and
    —to create a legislative history that the courts could use to interpret the law.[32]
Dellinger, however, said that he doubted that this last purpose would be a legal use of signing statements.

Calabresi and Lev, defending the Reagan and Bush (43) administrations' use of signing statements, argued that signing statements are legitimately used for three purposes:
    —to record the legislative intent of the president when signing a bill,
    —to preserve for the courts the president's interpretation of "ambiguous statutory language," and
    —to bind legally his subordinates in the executive branch to carry out the law according to presidential preferences, "under the theory of the unitary executive."[33]

The use of signing statements for hortatory, ceremonial, or informational purposes is legitimate and not controversial. Presidents ought to be able to say what they want about laws, and presidential signing statements

can legitimately be used as vehicles for these benign purposes. When presidents go further, however, in their claims for the authority of signing statements, their use of this vehicle becomes more problematic. The next sections of this chapter will consider the use of signing statements
   —as official parts of the legislative record,
   —as directions to executive branch subordinates, and
   —as declarations that the president might not execute the law because it unconstitutionally infringes on the president's constitutional authority.

The chapter will then conclude that, although there are legitimate uses of signing statements, their systematic use to expand presidential authority or to justify the refusal of the president to execute the laws faithfully presents a threat to the separation of powers system and the constitutional balance among the three branches.

LEGISLATIVE INTENT:
HOW SHOULD COURTS WEIGH SIGNING STATEMENTS?

When the president signs a bill that has been passed by both houses of Congress, it becomes law. At times there may be some disagreement about the meaning of the language in the law, or the words of the law may seem ambiguous. In such a case one party may challenge the interpretation of the law by the executive branch in court, and if it accepts the case, the court may determine the authoritative interpretation. In interpreting ambiguous language, courts often rely on the legislative history of the act in order to determine congressional intent.

Former Reagan administration lawyers Steven G. Calabresi and Daniel Lev argue that signing statements are part of the legislative process, and as such they should be used by courts in determining legislative intent when presented with ambiguous language in the law itself. They reason that Article I of the Constitution, which establishes the legislative process, requires that the president must sign a bill in order for it to become law. Thus, they argue, the president is an essential part of the legislative process. Because of the provisions of Article I, the president is "an indispensable party to the enactment of any law that is not passed over his veto or allowed to become law after ten days without his signature."[34] (This formulation would seem to preclude signing statements regarding laws passed over the president's veto.)

They reason that the Constitution requires that the president and the two houses of Congress participate in the making of laws. Thus the president is "one of the three parties to the contract that becomes a law," and his participation constitutes one third of the lawmaking power. Just as committee reports may be considered part of the legislative record when courts need to determine legislative intent, so ought presidential signing statements to be considered part of the legislative record. In their judgment, signing statements are "precisely analogous to Senate and House Committee reports." They conclude that signing statements ought to be used by courts to determine legislative intent "to the same degree—no more and no less—that they use committee reports." They argue further that signing statements are even more accurate indicators of legislative intent because the president can determine the views expressed in his one third of decisionmaking, whereas committee reports will necessarily include compromises to accommodate the concerns of the multiple members of committees.[35]

Calabresi and Lev also argue that courts ought to defer to presidential interpretation of the laws because the Supreme Court case *Chevron USA v. Natural Resources Defense Council* created a "new" doctrine of deference to the executive when it "announced a new rule" that "agency interpretations of ambiguous statutory language ought to be entitled to deference by the Article III federal courts if the agency interpretation is a reasonable one."[36] They then argue that because of the theory of the unitary executive, the president is the ultimate authority for any administrative action whatsoever and that the president has the authority to interpret laws in any way that he chooses. Thus the deference that *Chevron* granted to administrative agencies belongs to the president, and signing statements should be given deference by the courts because the president issued them. The *Chevron* decision, however, emphasized the complex technical nature of the agency decisions in question. The implication of this is that deference to executive branch decisions is due in part to the technical expertise of the agency and its experienced personnel as well as the policymaking authority of the executive branch.

Interestingly, Walter Dellinger, assistant attorney general during the Clinton administration, argued that the use of signing statements was legitimate for directing executive branch subordinates and announcing a dispute about the constitutionality of laws, but that the use of signing statements by courts to interpret ambiguous provisions in laws would probably not pass court scrutiny. Dellinger pointed out that the Supreme Court has judged that "post-passage remarks of legislators, however explicit, cannot serve to change the legislative intent of Congress expressed before the act's passage."[37] By parallel reasoning, post-enactment statements by the president should not be considered by the courts in interpreting a statute, since the president's views were presumably fully considered before legislators voted on the bills.

In contrast to Calabresi and Lev's arguments, Garber and Wimmer argue that signing statements should not be considered to provide any part of legislative intent. They argue that the president is *not* part of the legislative process because the president's options (whether to sign, veto, or allow a bill to become law) can be exercised only after the precise words of the bill have been fixed. (Before passage by Congress, of course, presidents can try to influence the final wording of a bill.) They argue that a signing statement is issued after the final wording of the bill has been fixed, and thus "The danger inherent in such a document is that its author will graft ambiguities and exceptions onto an act that was not so encumbered during the legislative process, thus making law in violation of Article I of the Constitution."[38] Garber and Wimmer conclude that, "Once the ten day period during which he can sign or veto a bill expires, his participation comes to an end." But by using signing statements, a president can try to "extend his participation in the lawmaking process beyond constitutional limits. Such over-involvement constitutes an unauthorized intrusion into Congress' lawmaking function."[39]

Both of the above contrasting arguments seem plausible and logical arguments about the extent of the president's legitimate participation in the legislative process. But the latter argument by Garber and Wimmer is more compelling because of the first words of the Constitution (after the Preamble): "All legislative powers herein granted shall be vested in a Congress of the United States, which shall consist of a Senate and House of Representatives." The Constitution thus explicitly places "*All*" (emphasis added) legislative powers in Congress; it does not say "some" or "most" or even merely "the" legislative powers. It explicitly gives the president only the limited options of recommending measures to Congress and of whether or not to sign or veto a bill or let it become law. After the bill becomes law, Article II requires that "he [the president] shall take Care that the Laws be faithfully executed." Thus the arguments of Calabresi and Lev are difficult to reconcile with the plain text of the Constitution.

The question of whether presidential signing statements should be allowed to influence judicial interpretation of the laws may be arguable, but judicial cognizance of them does not present a direct threat to the constitutional balance. Signing statements may be used by presidents to express their opinions about bills that have become law, but signing statements are not legitimately part of the legislative record. Presidents can say what they want and their opinions can be published, but ultimately judges must decide what factors to take into account when they interpret ambiguous laws. Whether signing statements may be used to direct subordinates in the executive branch is problematical and will be considered next.

CAN SIGNING STATEMENTS BE USED TO COMMAND SUBORDINATES?

In a formal opinion, the Office of Legal Counsel of the Bush administration argued that the president has complete control over members of the executive branch. "In order to fulfill those [constitutional] responsibilities, the President must be able to rely upon the faithful service of subordinate officials. To the extent that Congress or the courts interfere with the President's right to control or receive effective service from his subordinates within the Executive Branch, those other branches limit the ability of the President to perform his constitutional function."[40] The question here is whether public law can be considered "interference" with the executive branch.

The use of presidential signing statements to instruct subordinate executive branch officials presents potential constitutional problems. The president is the head of the executive branch, and in general, executive branch officials are bound to follow the chief executive's direction. In cases where a subordinate is ordered to do something illegal, the person can legitimately refuse the order. But if the official is ordered to refuse to execute the law as it stands because the president has determined that the law infringes upon his own interpretation of his constitutional authority, subordinates will almost always follow the president's direction, rather than question the president's constitutional judgment.

This situation raises serious constitutional questions if the president is trying to defeat the purpose of a law.

During the Clinton administration Assistant Attorney General Walter Dellinger wrote an opinion defending the use of signing statements in most cases. Dellinger argued that signing statements were appropriate for directing subordinates in the executive branch.

A second, and also generally uncontroversial, function of Presidential signing statements is to guide and direct Executive officials in interpreting or administering a statute. The President has the constitutional authority to supervise and control the activity of subordinate officials within the Executive Branch. . . . In the exercise of that authority he may direct such officials how to interpret and apply the statutes they administer. . . . Signing statements have frequently expressed the President's intention to construe or administer a statute in a particular manner (often to save the statute from unconstitutionality), and such statements have the effect of binding the statutory interpretation of other Executive Branch officials.[41]

Dellinger sees the use of signing statements to direct subordinates in the executive branch or to announce that the law will not be enforced as non-problematical. It is probable that Dellinger made this judgment because he did not foresee its future use to challenge the very nature of legislation and the Article II provision that "the president shall take care that the laws be faithfully executed."

Calabresi and Lev also claimed that signing statements can be used to give binding authoritative orders to executive branch subordinates of the president. "Signing statements allow the President to provide authoritative guidance to his subordinates in the executive branch as to how they should carry out and execute the law." Signing statements thus can serve as "binding directives or orders from the President to his millions of delegates in the executive branch."[42]

The problem in such instances is that if the president issues a signing statement that nullifies the intent of the law, he may use the statement to instruct or allow his subordinates in the executive branch not to execute the law. This evidently occurred when the Customs and Border Patrol did not relocate checkpoints in the Tucson sector every seven days, as required by law. As mentioned above, President Bush issued a signing statement accompanying the Detainee Treatment Act of 2005 stating that he would enforce the law consistently with his commander-in-chief authority. Since his administration previously had asserted that the commander-in-chief authority could overcome any law, it is reasonable to assume that President Bush felt that his subordinates were entitled to ignore the law and use whatever harsh interrogation procedures he preferred (short of his definition of torture), regardless of the law. This could amount to instructing interrogators in the military or CIA that the law was not binding on them.

Since President Bush had intended that the interrogation methods used on al Qaeda suspects remain secret and had argued that they could not be challenged or disclosed in court, there was no assurance that he would not use secret orders to command executive branch subordinates to ignore other laws that he deemed infringed on his constitutional prerogatives. This is exactly what happened with the NSA surveillance of persons in the United States; President Bush gave a secret order, and when the Terrorist Surveillance Program was made public, he claimed the constitutional authority to be able to carry out the program, despite the clear language of the FISA law.

This use of signing statements is worrisome because the president is head of the executive branch, and all of his subordinates have the presumptive duty to follow his legitimate orders. Only in extreme circumstances, for instance if an executive branch official feels that the president is ordering an illegal or unconstitutional act, should the official refuse to carry out the directive. Thus in the case of signing statements, if the president gives an order that is on its face reasonable, even though it may be in violation of the law, the executive branch official can quite reasonably decide not to second-guess the president's interpretation of his constitutional power. In addition, doing so could be dangerous to a government official's career. For this reason the threat implied in signing statements, as used by President Bush, is dangerous to the rule of law.

In cases similar to Bush's NSA order, he could either prospectively or retrospectively issue a signing statement and then order his executive branch subordinates to ignore the part of the law to which he objects and thereby escape all accountability. (Since the Bush administration has made important decisions by secret memos, for example about interrogation techniques, can the president issue secret signing statements?)

This undermines the whole point of the separation of powers structure of the Constitution. This interpretation of signing statements allows the president to choose which laws to obey and which to ignore. It also allows him to avoid the constitutional check of issuing a veto and submitting to the possibility of having it overridden.

CAN SIGNING STATEMENTS BE USED TO NULLIFY THE LAW?

The framers' deliberations over the veto power shed light on the use of presidential signing statements to nullify laws. The framers had chafed under the use of the absolute veto that royal governors had used to defeat laws passed by the colonial assemblies. They also resented the uses to which King George III put his authority to nullify laws. The first in the list of grievances against King George in the Declaration of Independence reads: "He has refused his Assent to laws, the most wholesome and necessary for the public Good." After independence, none of the states granted its executive an absolute veto (except South Carolina, which abolished it after two years), and only two of the states provided for a qualified veto.[43]

During the Constitutional Convention the framers overwhelmingly rejected three proposals for an absolute veto.[44] They also unanimously rejected a proposal to give the executive the power to suspend the law for a limited amount of time.[45] If the framers had intended for the president to be able to suspend the law or not to execute laws faithfully, the qualified veto they did give the president would have been superfluous. Why have a veto if the president could decide by himself which parts of laws to execute and which parts not to execute? That the designers of our Constitution gave the executive a qualified veto is a strong argument that they did not intend that the president have the authority not to carry out the law.[46]

Although recent presidents, and particularly President Bush, have asserted the right to refuse to carry out laws that they deem to be unconstitutional, the framers intended that the qualified veto power be the remedy for legislation that seems to impinge on the executive department. Elbridge Gerry said, "The primary object of the revisionary check on the President is not to protect the general interest, but to defend his own department."[47] In *Federalist* No. 73 Alexander Hamilton argued that "the primary inducement to conferring the power in question upon the Executive, is to enable him to defend himself." The idea that the president could choose not to execute the laws was never considered at the Convention.[48] Convention delegate William Paterson, in his decision as acting circuit court judge, held that the law at issue in the case

> imparts no dispensing power to the president. Does the constitution give it? Far from it, for it explicitly directs that he shall "take care that the laws be faithfully executed.". . . The president of the United States cannot control the statute, nor dispense with its execution, and still less can he authorize a person to do what the law forbids. If he could, it would render the execution of the laws dependent on his will and pleasure; which is a doctrine that has not been set up, and will not meet with any supporters in our government.[49]

In her statement to the Senate Judiciary Committee, Michelle Boardman argued that President Bush had the authority to refuse to execute the law retrospectively when he was charged with "executing a statute, passed by a previous Congress and signed by a prior President, a provision of which he finds unconstitutional under intervening Supreme Court precedent."[50] She might be referring here, though she does not mention it, to President Bush's assertion that he had the constitutional authority to ignore the FISA statute and order NSA to monitor communications to or from people within the United States. As noted before, President Bush did this secretly rather than after notifying Congress or the public (he did inform several members of Congress, but forbade them to disclose his program to colleagues or staff members). Boardman's interpretation would allow presidents to nullify any laws passed prior to their administrations whenever they claimed that their own constitutional authority allowed them to do so.

The idea of presidential signing statements begins with the reasonable presumption that each coordinate branch of government should have a role in interpreting the Constitution and its own constitutional powers. As James Madison said in *Federalist* No. 49: "The several departments being perfectly co-ordinate by the terms of their common commission, none of them, it is evident, can pretend to an exclusive or superior right of settling the boundaries between their respective powers." Thus, within the checks and balances of the Constitution, no single branch has the exclusive right to determine what the Constitution says or what public policy shall be.[51] Although the Supreme Court may have the final word in interpreting a law, the president can try to convince Congress to pass another law that passes constitutional muster to accomplish similar ends. This is what happened in the Military Commissions Act, discussed in chapter 6. Each branch has a role in interpreting the Constitution, but each is subject to constitutional checks and balances exercised by the other two branches.

Justifications for Signing Statements

If a president judges a bill or law to be an infringement on his constitutional authority, that president can legitimately take a number of actions:
—work with Congress before passage to remove the offending provision,
—veto the bill,
—issue a signing statement explaining his or her position,
—recommend that Congress repeal the law, or
—seek a judicial decision that would authoritatively settle the matter.[52]
All of these options fall short of refusing to execute the law. The following sections will consider some of the justifications that President Bush gave for his signing statements about appointments, the legislative veto, and reporting requirements.

THE APPOINTMENT POWER

Presidents might plausibly argue that they are not required to carry out some laws that are on their face unconstitutional. For instance, President Bush, as did President Clinton, objected to some laws that he asserted infringed on the appointment power of the president granted in Article II of the Constitution. In justifying these actions, administration lawyers cite *Myers* v. *U.S.* [53] In *Myers* the Supreme Court took up a case in which President Wilson had refused to abide by a law forbidding him from firing the postmaster general without congressional approval. The Supreme Court agreed with the president and struck down the law as an unconstitutional infringement on presidential authority over executive branch personnel.

Although the Court held the law to be unconstitutional, it did not affirm any claim that the president had the authority not to carry out laws he deemed to be unconstitutional. The important point here is that it was the Supreme Court that decided the issue, not the president's unilateral opinion. On the other hand, in *Humphrey's Executor v. U.S.*[54] the Court ruled that President Roosevelt did not have the authority to fire without cause an appointee who was serving a fixed term on the Federal Trade Commission as provided by law. President Bush has objected to laws that require certain qualifications for nominees for office.[55] Although Congress cannot push its requirements too far, Congress has often stipulated in law requirements for nominees for positions in the executive branch.[56]

In one instance, President George H. W. Bush did approach the question of the appointment power in a way that showed respect for Congress as a co-equal branch of the government. President Bush objected to a provision of a law that required the president to choose the nominees for some appointive positions from a list of candidates specified by Congress. President Bush argued that this was an infringement on the president's appointment power and that he would consider the provision to be "without legal force or effect." He then instructed the attorney general "to prepare remedial legislation for submission to the Congress during its next session, so that the act [could] be brought into compliance with the Constitution's requirements."[57] This act of the president was aboveboard and public, showed a willingness to work with Congress to change the law in a way that satisfied both branches, indicated the specific grounds for his objection, and admitted that Congress had a legitimate say in the matter. This action seems to be a reasonable way for a president to deal with a provision in law that the president thinks impinges on his constitutional authority.

THE LEGISLATIVE VETO

A "legislative veto" occurs when a law delegates authority to the executive branch to administer a program, but requires that the implementing agency come back to Congress in order to get permission to exercise specific instances of that discretion. For instance, an appropriations law may grant discretion to move funds from one program account to another but require the agency to check with a congressional committee before it makes the transfer. This form of "legislative veto" was struck down by the Supreme Court in *INS v. Chadha*.[58] The court reasoned that in order to be binding, a congressional mandate must be presented to the president for his signature or veto before it can bind the executive branch. President Bush objected to a number of laws that contain some form of legislative veto because of this presentment issue.[59]

Because of *Chadha*, legislative vetoes, as such, carry no legal obligation, and members of Congress realize this. But Congress may continue to insert such provisions to convey to agencies that if they do not consult with certain committees, they may suffer some sanction in their next budget request. So the president is justified in refusing to comply with these admittedly unconstitutional provisions in law, but they are unenforceable in any case.[60]

Congress, however, has a ready remedy to these situations; it can refuse to delegate discretion to executive expenditure of funds. Then if the executive branch wanted to transfer some funds, it would have to come back to Congress to ask for the enactment of a whole new law. This would cause delay and inefficiency, but it would accord with the president's wish to ignore unconstitutional legislative veto provisions. Thus Congress cannot legitimately complain about noncompliance with legislative vetoes, and it has the remedy easily at hand: require new legislation for every exercise of flexibility that they had delegated to the executive branch. Executive branch agencies, however, often find it in their best interests to comply with these unenforceable requirements in law.[61] As Louis Fisher has noted, legislative vetoes are not legal in effect, but they are, in effect, legal.

REPORTING REQUIREMENTS

President Bush has also objected to requirements in law that the executive branch report certain information to Congress. For instance, he has used them to indicate that he does not feel bound by all of the provisions of laws regarding: reporting to Congress pursuant to the PATRIOT Act; the torture of prisoners; whistle-blower protections for the Department of Energy; the number of U.S. troops in Colombia; the use of illegally gathered intelligence; and the publication of educational data gathered by the Department of Education.[62]

President Bush has also used signing statements to assert that he could withhold information from Congress and refuse to comply with laws requiring the executive branch to report information to Congress. For example, in a signing statement accompanying the Intelligence Authorization Act for FY2002, President Bush stated that he would construe the law "in a manner consistent with the President's constitutional authority to withhold information the disclosure of which could impair foreign relations, the national security, the deliberative processes of the Executive, or the performance of the Executive's constitutional duties."[63]

The point here is not the reasonableness of the president's goals—for example protecting national security—the problem is the assertion that the president alone has the right to make the determination of what is or is not constitutional. And if the president refuses to report his secret activities to Congress, there can be no independent check on the executive, as was the case with warrantless surveillance by the National Security Agency before it was revealed by the *New York Times* in 2005.

At times President Bush objected to requirements to provide information to Congress on the grounds of national security and sometimes on the basis of executive privilege. Although both of these grounds for objection have a basis in law or Supreme Court decisions, they are not unqualified rights of the president. Each case must be considered on its own merits. Thus his sweeping declarations that any requirement that the president report to Congress are much too broad to constitute a reasonable argument that its reporting requirements are unconstitutional. If the president wants to challenge the legal requirements, he should see that the issue is raised in Court. The federal courts have decided that some requirements that the president make a recommendation to Congress are not unconstitutional, for instance in *National Treasury Employee Union v. Nixon*.[64]

In contrast to most of the Bush administration's actions, Assistant Attorney General Walter Dellinger's formal advice to President Clinton recommended due respect for the other two branches: "A President should proceed with caution and with respect for the obligation that each of the branches shares for the maintenance of constitutional government."[65]

The Unitary Executive Theory

President Bush often cited the "unitary executive" theory in his signing statements. This section will briefly examine the unitary executive claim, the role of precedent in the legitimacy of executive actions, and the parallels between signing statements and impoundment of funds.

Christopher Kelley has divided the unitary executive claim into four premises:

1) The vesting clause of the Constitution confers on the executive broad powers, and the powers of the other two branches are limited by the Constitution. According to this way of thinking, the list of powers of Congress in Article I is constraining and the lack of specification, except for a few powers, in Article II is expansive;

2) The "take care" clause of Article II gives the president exclusive authority to remove members of the executive branch;

3) The "take care" clause also gives the president exclusive authority over executive branch personnel; and

4) The presidential oath to defend the Constitution gives the president extraordinary power when he acts to protect the national security of the United States.

Robert Spitzer has summarized the claims made in the name of the unitary executive theory in two sweeping assertions made by the Bush administration: "presidents have sole and complete control over the executive branch," and "the other branches of government may not interfere with presidential actions arising from these executive powers."[66]

Calabresi and Lev argue that the unitary executive theory holds that the vesting clause "is a grant of all the executive power in the country to the President." This implies that every member of the executive branch exercises executive power "by the implicit delegation of the President. . . . There is simply no other constitutional basis on which executive branch subordinates could otherwise act."[67] Thus they are arguing that law does not confer any authority on members of the executive branch; only the president can do that. The Office of Legal Counsel in the Bush administration argued that because the president must execute the laws, he must have sole authority over the executive branch. "But because the Constitution vests this power in him alone, it follows that he is solely responsible for supervising and directing the activities of his subordinates in carrying out executive functions."[68]

Notwithstanding these claims for the authority deemed to be vested in the president via the theory of the unitary executive, the courts and Congress can require actions by executive branch agencies. The courts often make decisions requiring specific action on the part of executive branch agencies. Congress, in addition to its authority to create executive branch agencies and provide funding for them, is authorized by Article I, Section 8, of the Constitution to "make all Laws which shall be necessary and proper for *carrying into Execution* the foregoing Powers, and all other Powers vested by this Constitution in the Government of the United States, *or in any Department or Officer thereof*" (emphasis added). The rigid claims based on the unitary executive theory that the president has sole control over the executive branch and that the other branches cannot affect this constitutional control is refuted by James Madison in *Federalist* No. 47. Madison, in citing Montesquieu on separation of powers, says that "he [Montesquieu] did not mean that these departments ought to have no *partial agency* in, or no *control* over, the acts of each other." In *Federalist* No. 66, Hamilton argues that the separation of powers "maxim . . . has been shewn to be entirely compatible with a partial intermixture of those departments for special purposes, preserving them in the main distinct and unconnected."

Hamilton explains further in *Federalist* No. 70 that "energy in the Executive is a leading character in the definition of good government." And he argues that "unity is conducive to energy," but here Hamilton is not arguing that the Constitution gives the president complete and exclusive control of the executive branch; rather he is arguing that the executive should consist of one person rather than several. He continues, "Decision, activity, secrecy, and dispatch will generally characterize the proceedings of *one man in a much more eminent degree than the proceedings of any greater number*" (emphasis added). The Constitution does not completely separate the functions of government into separate branches, but allows each branch some influence over the others.

Proponents of the unitary executive theory can argue that congressional actions affecting the executive branch are unwise or burdensome, but they cannot convincingly argue that congressional "interference" is inconsistent with the intent of the architects of the Constitution, the law of the land, Supreme Court decisions, or two centuries of interactions between Congress and the executive branch. Congressional acts certainly have at times interfered with the efficient operation of the executive branch through micromanagement. Although they may be unwise, most of them are constitutional.

Robert Spitzer argues that the unitary executive theory is corrosive to the constitutional separation of powers. Even if the Bush administration would have taken the same actions without the legal arguments laid out in administration memoranda and briefs, the lawyers justifying its actions "invented and legitimated a constitutional provenance for a contemporary legal construct that gave the unitary [commander in chief] a kind of status and dignity that it could not have otherwise claimed."[69]

Do Signing Statements Constitute Binding Precedent?

Steven Calabresi and Daniel Lev make an argument that signing statements are so established as to constitute "binding precedent." In arguing about the importance of the Reagan administration's use of signing statements, they say that the uses of signing statements before Reagan were not politically contentious, but that the Reagan administration's use of them was qualitatively and quantitatively different from previous uses.[70] They claim that the use of signing statements during the administrations of Presidents Reagan and George H. W. Bush has caused a "quiet revolution in the scope of the President's constitutionally prescribed 'lawmaking' powers."[71]

The "quiet" part of the revolution shows that signing statements were used strategically for the purpose of increasing executive power. Similarly, the phrase "unitary executive" was used by the Bush administration strategically to lay the groundwork for future expansions of executive power. While citing the long history of signing statements, Calabresi and Lev argue that President Reagan's presidency was "seminal" in its use of signing statements and that "signing statements today are an established feature of the legal landscape."[72] They assert, "Any technique which dates back to Jackson, Tyler, and Grant, and which was famously advocated by a president as great as Ronald Reagan should be deemed to be a part of the gloss which history has written on the bare bones text of Article II." They are no fans of original intent, and in making their argument for the importance of precedent, they quote Youngstown: "It is an inadmissibly narrow conception of American constitutional law to confine it to the words of the Constitution and to disregard the gloss which life has written upon them."[73] These actions of the Reagan administration, as reported by Calabresi and Lev, were self-conscious attempts to establish a record of the use of signing statements and the phrase "unitary executive" strategically, so as in the future to be able to claim that the signing statements establish precedents that are part of the record of constitutional interpretation.

On the one hand they are saying that signing statements were used by many presidents and thus should be blessed by usage, tradition, and precedent. On the other hand they claim that the Reagan administration's use of signing statements was qualitatively and quantitatively different from previous use and so different in fact that it amounted to a "quiet revolution" in the "seminal" use of presidential power. After their arguments that Reagan's use of signing statements was new, they can legitimately claim that an important part their precedent goes back only to Reagan, not Jackson.

A previous president's actions do not necessarily make similar future actions constitutional. As the court stated in *Powell* v. *McCormack,* "That an unconstitutional action has been taken before surely does not render that same action any less unconstitutional at a later date."[74] In Mario Cuomo's pithy words, "The Constitution cannot be amended by persistent evasion."[75] Nevertheless, precedent does play an important role in the molding of the Constitution. For instance in *Bowsher* v. *Syner,* one footnote read: "Eleven Presidents, from Mr. Wilson through Mr. Reagan, who have been presented with this issue [legislative veto] have gone on record at some point to challenge congressional vetoes as unconstitutional."[76] Legitimate or not, official presidential actions can become important precedents. That is why the Bush administration is trying so hard to establish precedents in its signing statements and why it is so important that President Bush's sweeping claims do not stand unchallenged.

Parallel with Impoundment

There is a distinct similarity between President Bush's signing statements and President Nixon's refusal to spend funds for programs of which he disapproved. In both cases the presidents were asserting the constitutional authority to ignore the law and accomplish, in effect, a line-item or absolute veto. When presidents assert the authority to accomplish through the administrative process what a president could not achieve in the legislative process and attempt to nullify the will of Congress as expressed in legislation, they are failing to execute the law faithfully. Thus they are at their weakest with respect to the constitutionality of their claims, as Justice Jackson argued in his concurrence in the *Steel Seizure* case.

In the early 1970s President Nixon refused to release funds that Congress (controlled by the Democrats) had provided in legislation for certain projects. Past presidents had exercised discretion in the expenditure of funds, either in a reasonable administrative sense (for example when the project had been accomplished with fewer funds than had been provided) or after consulting with Congress. Nixon, however, used impoundment in unprecedented ways, and perhaps more important, he declared that, as president, he had the constitutional authority to impound (refuse to spend) money provided by Congress for purposes of which the president disapproved.[77] No other president had ever made that claim, and the claim of course was a direct challenge to the legislative authority of Congress.

Federal courts heard more than seventy impoundment cases, and not one of them affirmed Nixon's claim to constitutional authority to impound funds, though some refused to take a case because they judged it not to be justiciable. The parallel with President Bush's signing statements is evident: in both cases the presidents attempted to achieve their policy preferences, not through the legislative process but by selectively refusing to execute certain provisions of the law. In the case of impoundment, the Supreme Court decisively declared that the president did not have the constitutional authority to nullify legislation unilaterally by refusing to spend funds provided in law.[78] In the case of signing statements, President Bush asserted that he would not feel bound to enforce those parts of laws of which he disapproved.

There is a close similarity between the Supreme Court impoundment cases and the Detainee Treatment Act of 2005. In the Nixon case, the president vetoed the Clean Water Act, arguing that it was too costly. Congress then overrode his veto. Nixon then declared that he would spend only half of the funds. This amounted to an absolute (in spite of the congressional override) line-item veto (because he would spend only part of the funds provided in law). President Bush's assertions were an even broader assault on Article I than were President Nixon's.

When the Detainee Treatment Act was being considered in Congress, President Bush and Vice President Cheney actively lobbied Congress not to pass the bill, and President Bush threatened to veto it. When it became clear that Congress had the votes to override a veto by the president, President Bush signed the bill into law, but announced in his signing statement that he would not feel bound by its provisions with respect to the treatment of detainees. Thus he announced that he could accomplish administratively what he had failed to do through the constitutional legislative process. Although Nixon's claim was repudiated by the Supreme Court, President Bush's has not yet been litigated.

Conclusion

Some people minimize the import of signing statements by looking at the language literally and arguing that few of them state directly and unequivocally that President Bush intends to break the law. Why should we get upset about a mere hypothetical situation? Others take comfort in the fact that signing statements have not yet had a large impact on court decisions. A Congressional Research Service scholar has stated, "Ultimately, it does not appear that the courts have relied on signing statements in any appreciably substantive fashion."[79] Similarly, GAO also found that "federal courts infrequently cite or refer to signing statements in their published opinions."[80]

But reassurances about the lack of much judicial notice so far miss the whole strategy of the Reagan and Bush administrations. Their declared intent was to establish signing statements as legitimate. They knew it would take a long time, and their campaign has been going on since 1985. Their efforts have been successful in gaining executive branch legitimacy, particularly in the Reagan and Bush 43 administrations, but also in the Clinton and G. H. W. Bush administrations. In addition Samuel Alito was appointed to the Supreme Court by President Bush; if a signing statement case arises, he will presumably be sympathetic to the arguments that he made when he was in the Reagan administration's Department of Justice. The signing statement strategy was long-term, and counting the cases that have cited them before 2007 is not an accurate indicator of their future impact.

Clearly the Bush and Reagan administrations used signing statements in a strategic way to expand what is considered legitimate discretion for the president in general and in national security policy specifically. In addition the pattern of behavior of the latter Bush administration demonstrates that its claims are not idle. President Bush secretly violated provisions of FISA and claimed the constitutional authority to do so. President Bush may have also secretly set aside other laws. Signing statements provide a convenient cover if secret lawbreaking is discovered and made public. The president can say that the authority to break the law is inherent in his office and point to the signing statement to show that he publicly said so when the law was passed.

President Bush has asserted the authority to set aside treaties (which the Constitution calls "the Supreme Law of the Land") and to encourage harsh interrogation of detainees, which most of the world considers to be torture. He also argued that he could hold detainees, citizens and noncitizens, indefinitely without charge, and he claimed that the courts have no jurisdiction to examine his actions through writs of habeas corpus. Therefore signing statements cannot be considered idle threats or harmless declarations. The Bush administration used them with the clear purpose of expanding executive power at the expense of Congress and the courts and to accomplish goals it could not achieve through the legislative process. Signing statements must be taken seriously if the constitutional roles of the other two branches of government are to be protected.

Some people argue that signing statements cannot convey any authority of the president that is not already present in the Constitution. But as a truism this distorts the reality of American constitutional law and development. For instance, presidents now have much more power in the area of national security than the framers intended or foresaw. The reason is that presidents over the decades have asserted more authority, and Congress has not confronted them effectively, often because members feared political retribution, but also because a good portion of Congress is always from the president's own party. These copartisans, even if they have doubts about institutional prerogatives, are always under great pressure to give the president of their party what he or she wants.

Defenders of President Bush's use of signing statements said that there was nothing to worry about, because President Bush would only use his claimed authority when necessary. But this misses the constitutional point that precedents can be used by future presidents. Some supporters argue that signing statements are legitimate, and even most critics would agree that some uses of them are legitimate. That is not the point. The point is what many of them purport to do: to allow a president to ignore the law at some future time in an unspecified way. The real problem with signing statements, as noted above, is not their mere existence as vehicles to express presidential opinions, but rather their use as threats to fail to execute the laws faithfully. The vehicle itself is legitimate, but the uses to which it was often put by President Bush are suspect.

To the extent that the president publicly specifies which section of a law he is challenging and states the grounds for his objection and welcomes litigation of the issue before the courts, he mitigates the illegitimacy of his actions. However when a president makes repeated, general, and vague objections to many parts of most newly enacted laws, his actions carry much less legitimacy because his challenges might be acted upon in secret at some future time. If the president's actions are secret, there is little chance for a case to be brought before the courts and little possibility that Congress will be able to object to the president's interpretation of the law.

The argument of this book is based on the premise that the Constitution does not give the president the right to decide not to execute the laws, except in some very limited circumstances. If there is a dispute about the interpretation of a law, the interaction of the three branches in the constitutional process—including the politics of passage, the choice to veto, and the right to challenge laws in court—provides legitimate ways to deal with differences in interpretation of the law; each of these options has a long record of use in U.S. history. But the assertion by the executive that it alone has the authority to interpret the law and that it will enforce the law at its own discretion is a dangerous claim.

The implications of President Bush's sweeping claims to presidential authority are profound and undermine the very meaning of the rule of law. Despite the Constitution's granting lawmaking power to Congress, if the president maintains that presidential executive authority and the commander-in-chief clause can overcome virtually any law that constrains the executive, then the executive is claiming unilateral control of the laws. If the executive claims that it is not subject to the law as it is written but can pick and choose which provisions to enforce, it is essentially claiming the unitary power to say what the law is. The "All legislative Powers" clause of Article I and the "take care" clause of Article II can thus be effectively nullified.

A government of laws under the Constitution depends on the good faith adherence to the provisions of the Constitution and the balance it sets up among the three branches of government. The main threat to this balance in the twentieth century was the executive branch's asserting increasingly broad constitutional prerogatives, especially with respect to national security policy and war making, but also with respect to the power of the purse. The commander-in-chief authority, as asserted during the war on terror, has been stretched beyond its capacity to justify presidential prerogative. The balance needs to be restored by a decent respect for comity among the branches. Otherwise these presidential actions invite an overreaction by Congress that may not be desirable, but which may be seen as necessary in order to rein in an executive that does not honor the balance among the branches established by the Constitution.

CHAPTER NINE

CONCLUSION: CONSTITUTIONALISM AND THE RULE OF LAW

"Where-ever law ends, tyranny begins."
—John Locke, *Second Treatise of Government*

In a government of laws, existence of the government will be imperiled if it fails to observe the law scrupulously. Our government is the potent, the omnipresent teacher. . . . If the government becomes a lawbreaker, it breeds contempt for law."
—Justice Louis Brandeis

The rule of law is central to any civilized nation, and the Constitution of the United States limits governmental power in general, and specifically the concentration of power in any one branch of government. President George W. Bush's actions that have been analyzed in this book have challenged the foundation of the rule of law. He has expanded the constitutional authority of the president in extraordinary ways and has tried to undo the constraints that the Constitution places on executive power. This conclusion will first take up the rule of law and how it has been challenged by President Bush. Next, it argues that secret laws and policies raise serious concerns in a democratic republic. It then addresses the idea of constitutionalism and the danger of letting these precedents stand. Finally, it will specify the ways in which President Bush has violated the separation of powers principle.

The aggrandizing actions of the Bush administration were not entirely successful. The courts declared that they had jurisdiction over habeas corpus cases in spite of the administration's arguments that they did not.

And President Bush found it in his interest to ask Congress for the authority to take some actions he had previously based on his own claims of executive power. In the cases on habeas corpus, the courts asserted that they had jurisdiction over appeals from both citizens (*Hamdi*) and noncitizens (*Rasul*). But the rulings were quite limited; the Court did not order the administration to do anything, nor did it declare illegal the incarceration of the detainees.[1] The *Hamdan* decision ruled merely that the existing commissions were not in accord with law, and the administration was able to get the Military Commissions Act (MCA) passed, which gave it the legislative authority to continue with commissions that had similar procedures. In addition, the administration was able to get Congress to strip the courts of jurisdiction over habeas appeals. That Congress was willing to give President Bush the authority he sought with respect to alien enemy combatants is not reassuring to those who consider habeas corpus to be a fundamental principle of due process of law.

In the case of torture, the Army finally prevailed in revising its field manual on interrogation and returning its doctrine to the traditional interpretation of the Geneva Conventions. President Bush, using the MCA as justification, continued to claim that the CIA could employ the type of enhanced interrogation techniques regarded by many people as torture. In the case of the Foreign Intelligence Surveillance Act (FISA), the administration was able to force through a Democratic Congress changes in the law that allowed it to continue legally many of the surveillance practices that were previously forbidden unless a warrant was obtained.

It could be argued that the constitutional system worked in reining in a president who had made extraordinary claims to executive power. But President Bush went to Congress for purposes of political prudence rather than because he was convinced that Congress or the courts had the legitimate, constitutional right to limit his discretion. One might argue that the political motives of the president in this case are made moot by the fact of congressional action. But two problems remain: neither he nor his administration admitted that, in principle, his constitutional authority was limited in the national security policy arena, nor did they withdraw any of their legal arguments claiming extraordinary power through the commander-in-chief clause. Second, Bush withheld key information (for example interrogation techniques and the scope of NSA surveillance) that would have allowed Congress to judge whether, in fact, he was abiding by the very laws it had enacted at his behest. The seeming victories for the principle of limited government, the rule of law, and the separation of powers system were both tenuous and limited.

President Bush was not the first president to take an expansive approach to his constitutional authority; he built on previous presidential excesses: FDR interned thousands of citizens of Japanese descent; Truman went to war in Korea without a declaration of war; Johnson escalated in Vietnam based on the dubious Gulf of Tonkin incident; Nixon wiretapped without warrants, among other Watergate horrors; Reagan's administration broke the law in the Iran-Contra affair; and Clinton used U.S. forces in several instances without admitting that Congress had a say.[2] As has been argued in this book, President Bush claimed executive power in ways that went beyond his predecessors: he denied habeas corpus to citizens and noncitizens alike; he suspended the Geneva Agreements, which led to torture; he violated the FISA law in secret; he used signing statements significantly more expansively than had any of his predecessors; and in each of these cases he claimed that his constitutional authority as president allowed him to act independently of the other two branches of government and to avoid oversight by them.

Future presidents, especially during times of threats to national security, could easily reassert President Bush's claims to executive prerogative, build on his precedents, and ignore the Constitution and the rule of law. Only when members of each branch admit that their own powers are circumscribed by constitutional limits will the United States be able to protect the individual freedoms that have been won over the past three or four centuries and the limits to executive power that the framers built into the Constitution.

The Rule of Law

Establishing and enforcing justice in human societies has always been a challenge, especially when one party to a dispute or conflict possesses superior physical means of force (for example police, military, and so forth). The solution, developed over centuries, has been to try to bind all parties in a web of customs, conventions, rules, and laws that set out a process of settling disputes and convincing all parties to agree to conform to the outcome of the process. In modern, developed countries, that web is the formal establishment of a legal system and laws of the land. In the polity, these laws must be accepted by all major factions as the legitimate means of settling important differences of judgment and interest. That is, when there is a serious disagreement, the rules set in law will prevail in settling the issue rather than the will or preference of any individual, regardless of the power or status of that person.

If all parties agree in advance to such a set of laws and procedures, it becomes more difficult for the relatively powerful to evade the legitimate jurisdiction of the rule of law. If the rule of law is sufficiently accepted throughout the polity, the powerful will accept the legitimacy of the laws and will endure unacceptable consequences if they violate the laws. In addition, those on whom the powerful rely to enforce their will may not carry out orders perceived to violate the law. In this way the powerful may be rendered less powerful to the extent that they feel bound by the rule of law and their subordinates refuse to carry out orders perceived to violate the rule of law.

In most societies, and certainly in modern polities, the executive controls military and police forces and thus commands physical force in the society. In centuries past, executives (monarchs) have used the control of physical force to impose their own will, and indeed in the twentieth century, powerful dictators have used physical force to commit terrible atrocities with their control of armies and police forces. Thus in order to limit the exercise of arbitrary power by these executives, systems of laws and constitutions have been established to constrain executive power.

Scholars have formulated several versions of the rule of law, but they all converge on the fundamental tenets that no one is above the law and the law must be applied to all equally. Bo Li distinguishes rule *of* law from rule *by* law. In the latter, law is used in the service of the state, and those who control the government use the law as an instrument of domination. In contrast, the rule *of* law entails the autonomy of the law in the sense that it exists apart from the incumbent rulers of the government and applies to the rulers as well as the ruled. Those who control the government are not above the law.[3] A dictatorship could have an elaborate system of laws, but they would be established and disregarded at the pleasure of the tyrant; such a system would not embody the full concept of rule of law.

The counterpoint to the rule of law is rule by individuals according to their personal preferences. This might take the form of one monarch or it might be a democratic polity in which the will of the majority rules, and those elected by the majority are not limited by the law. They would be free to disenfranchise the political minority or keep them from gaining political power in other ways. The problem with a benevolent monarch or unlimited democracy is, as Aristotle pointed out, the former carries the danger of degenerating into a dictatorship and the latter carries the danger of degenerating into mob rule and the tyranny of the majority. The essence of the idea of the rule of law was articulated pithily by Thomas Paine: "In America THE LAW IS KING. For as in absolute governments the King is law, so in free countries the law OUGHT to be King; and there ought to be no other." Where law is king, discretion of the executive is limited by law.[4]

The principle of rule of law was a key issue in the revolt of the American colonies against British rule. Colonists felt that they were suffering under the type of arbitrary rule that had long ago been abolished in England.[5] That is, they felt that they were being denied their rights as Englishmen. As John Marshall declared in the early years of the republic, "The government of the United States has been emphatically termed a government of laws, and not of men."[6] One of the foremost scholars of the rule of law, A. V. Dicey, analyzed the rule of law a century ago. His formulation of the rule of law entails two parts:

—No man is punishable or can be lawfully made to suffer in body or goods except for a distinct breach of law established in the ordinary legal manner before the ordinary courts of the land.

—No man is above the law. . . . Every man, whatever be his rank or condition, is subject to the ordinary law of the realm and amenable to the jurisdiction of the ordinary tribunals . . . from the Prime Minister down to a constable or a collector of taxes.[7]

Dicey argued that the key to the rule of law is the absence of arbitrary power.

When a president is inaugurated, Article II of the Constitution prescribes that he or she take the oath:

I do solemnly swear (or affirm) that I will faithfully execute the Office of President of the United States, and will to the best of my ability, preserve, protect and defend the Constitution of the United States.

In light of the above formulations of the rule of law, President Bush arguably violated his oath of office insofar as he has ignored the law of the land and asserted that his constitutional authority as president exempts him from obeying the law. President Bush abrogated the rule of law by taking actions not authorized by law and sometimes directly against the law:

—He created military commissions entirely within the executive branch and in doing so ignored U.S. laws that provided authority and procedures for establishing military commissions;

—He used the term "enemy combatant" to exempt the government from granting persons so labeled legal and constitutional rights;

—He denied the writ of habeas corpus to U.S. citizens as well as other detainees suspected of terrorism;

—He suspended the Geneva Conventions, which, because they were agreed to in a treaty, are the "supreme Law of the Land," according to Article VI of the Constitution;

—He authorized the interrogation of detainees using techniques that most of the world considers torture, and which violate the Geneva Conventions and U.S. law;

—He ordered the National Security Agency to monitor the communications of Americans without a warrant as required by FISA; and

—He asserted the sweeping right to ignore more than 1,000 provisions of public law because he deemed them to be in conflict with his authority as president.

In the face of a genuine crisis, such as the attacks of 9/11, President Bush might make a reasonable argument that the letter of some laws cannot be obeyed while the executive deals with the emergency. But in his violations of and claimed exemptions from the law, he argued that the emergency of 9/11 continued to exist for years after the attack and that he therefore had the authority to ignore the law. He has also asserted that the war on terror "will not end until every terrorist group of global reach has been found, stopped and defeated,"[8] that is, it will continue indefinitely. President Bush was correct that the threat of terrorism was real and continuing, but in the years since 9/11, the ordinary courts of the land have operated and dealt responsibly with some terrorists, when allowed to by the Bush administration.

Congress was in session and could have changed the laws that President Bush thought hindered the fight against terrorism, as it did in passing the PATRIOT Act and revising the FISA statute several times early in his first term. Later, political necessity forced President Bush to request changes in the law to authorize the actions he had previously undertaken. It has also become clear that some of the detainees in Guantánamo were not terrorists who presented a threat to the security of the United States. As the Supreme Court reasoned, captives on the battlefield cannot be accorded the rights that the American system provides civilians. However years after the battles, detainees were held by the Bush administration indefinitely with no opportunity to argue before an independent judge that they were not guilty of the crimes for which they were detained.

In medieval England the legal principle prevailed that "the King can do no wrong." That is, if the king was anointed by God, he could not be accused of wrongdoing, though his ministers might be impeached for doing wrong in the king's name. Regarding the United States presidency, the principle that the president is exempt from the law was asserted by President Nixon. When he was interviewed by David Frost in 1977, one particular exchange characterized his stance toward the rule of law:

> David Frost: Wiretappings, burglaries or so-called black bag jobs, mail openings and infiltration against antiwar groups and others, [actions that were] clearly illegal. . . . Can [the president] decide that it's in the best interests of the nation or something, and do something illegal?
>
> Nixon: Well, when the president does it, that means that it is not illegal.
>
> Frost: By definition?
>
> Nixon: Exactly. Exactly. If the president, for example, approves something because of the national security, or in this case because of a threat to internal peace and order of significant magnitude,

then the president's decision in that instance is one that enables those who carry it out, to carry it out without violating a law. Otherwise they're in an impossible position.[9]

In rejecting his constitutional duty to obey the law or to allow Congress or the courts to constrain his actions, President Bush was reverting to the principles of monarchical prerogative. President Bush seemed to be taking a plebiscitary approach to the presidency. That is, once a president has been elected, he or she has carte blanche to act in whatever way he or she considers to be justified. Under this approach election gives the president the right to make the fundamental decisions about U.S. policy to the exclusion of Congress or the courts. President Bush put it this way: "We had an accountability moment, and that's called the 2004 elections."[10] John Yoo argued in his book, "Our nation had a presidential and congressional election after Abu Ghraib and the leaking of the OLC [Office of Legal Counsel] memos. If the people had disagreed with administration policies, they could have made a change."[11] In other words, Yoo argued that anything the Bush administration might have done in its first term was affirmatively approved by the electorate in 2004.

A Bush appointee, acting assistant attorney general Steven Bradbury of the Office of Legal Counsel in the Justice Department, echoed Nixon's stance when he testified before the Senate. He was asked by Senator Leahy (D-Vt.) if President Bush was right or wrong in his expansive interpretation of presidential war power. Bradbury replied: "The president is always right."[12] This monarchical principle was an echo of the Minority Report of the congressional Iran-Contra committee, which was led by Richard Cheney. The Minority Report stated: "To the extent that the Constitution and laws are read narrowly, as Jefferson wished, the Chief Executive will on occasion feel duty bound to assert monarchical notions of prerogative that will permit him to exceed the law."[13] This assertion, in effect, amounted to a claim that in national security issues the president was above the law. This notion undermines the principles of limited government and separation of powers in which each branch is subject to check by the other two. Vice President Cheney in 2005 declared victory in the Bush administration's effort to increase executive power: "I think, in fact, there has been over a time a restoration, if you will, of the power and authority of the president."[14]

The Problem of Secrecy

Most people understand that it is necessary for the government to keep some secrets. For instance troop movements that would warn the enemy should they become known are legitimate secrets. Likewise covert operations by the CIA must also remain secret. Troop movements and covert operations should be taken in accord with the policies of the government, under authority provided by Congress in law and under the direction of the president. But secret policies—when the government says its policy is X, when in fact it is doing Y—are inconsistent with a democratic republic. Some secrets (and even lies) are justified when pursuing public policies; for instance, President Carter's aborted attempt to rescue the hostages in Iran should certainly have been kept secret (whether or not it was a wise decision). The policy of the United States to rescue U.S. citizens imprisoned in foreign countries is understood, and covert actions taken to pursue that policy are legitimate. In contrast, the Reagan administration's attempt to trade arms to Iran for release of (other) hostages directly contradicted the U.S. policy of not trading with terrorist states, a policy articulated by Secretary of State George Shultz. It also arguably violated the law.[15] The diversion of funds obtained from Iran to provide aid to the Contras directly violated the law in secret.

In general, citizens, and particularly members of Congress, should know the policies of the United States government. The fundamental premise of representative democracy is that citizens know about the policies of the government and thus can make informed decisions when voting. One important way of establishing governmental policy is the passing of laws. Citizens (and the legislators representing them) have a right to presume that the executive branch is obeying the law. But President Bush argued that he was not bound to follow the FISA law. After his actions were disclosed, members of Congress were not even allowed to see the legal justifications for President Bush's actions. Not only were members of Congress excluded, but also lawyers in the Department of Justice and NSA, both headed by Bush appointees, were denied access to the memoranda. For members of Congress to cast informed votes when they are not allowed to know the content of the president's program (in this case, the Terrorist Surveillance Program or its legal justification) is difficult.

The problem of secret laws was raised again when Congress was asked by the Bush administration to pass the Military Commissions Act. The secrecy issue concerned the authorization of the president to interpret Common Article 3 of the Geneva Conventions. Common Article 3 provides that detained persons be treated "humanely," and it prohibits "violence to life and person, in particular murder of all kinds, mutilation, cruel treatment and torture," and "outrages upon personal dignity, in particular, humiliating and degrading treatment." The authority (in U.S. law) to interpret these words was granted to President Bush by the MCA. Compliance with Common Article 3 had not previously been a problem in U.S. policy, but President Bush had suspended the Geneva Conventions in February 2002. This suspension led, eventually, to the many instances of abuse and torture treated earlier in this book. The Supreme Court, in the *Hamdan* decision, ruled that the president was legally bound by the Geneva Conventions. Thus President Bush needed legal justification for the types of harsh interrogations of detainees that he was authorizing, and the MCA gave him that authority.

The MCA forbade torture in its most egregious forms, but it allowed the president to issue rules specifying those techniques of "enhanced interrogation" the CIA would be allowed to use on suspected terrorists. Congressional critics of the Bush administration argued that, for instance, waterboarding constituted torture; but the administration refused to reveal what techniques were authorized by the president. In the case of the MCA, Congress was voting for a bill about an important issue—which harsh interrogation techniques were not considered torture by the president—without knowing what they were approving. In addition the Bush administration issued two memos in 2005 that gave specific guidance to members of the executive branch about what interrogation techniques were allowed. These important issues were kept secret from the public and Congress; thus Congress had no way of knowing whether the administration was obeying the Detainee Treatment Act of 2005.

The disturbing aspect of these secret laws (or interpretations of laws) is that the Bush administration interpreted the law according to its own legal standards. Those standards, as discussed above, give the president, as commander in chief, virtually unlimited authority in dealing with detainees. The legal memoranda of the administration also argued that any congressional enactment (law) that constrained the president in his treatment of detainees would be unconstitutional. With secret policies and standards, or signing statements, the chief executive is bound by the law only to the extent that he believes he is constrained by the law. Thus it is impossible in these instances for members of Congress to know what the law in operation is; and they are expected to vote on laws, the consequences of which have not been revealed to them. Such situations undercut the very ideas of the rule of law and representative democracy. These situations present two problems: first, there can be no oversight or external check on the executive in these cases. Members of Congress and the American public must trust that the executive is faithfully conforming to the law in secret.

The second, and more serious, problem is that this pattern of executive actions has the effect of robbing the legislative branch of its most important power: the power to make law. If presidents can now claim or exercise lawmaking authority by secret and novel interpretations or selectively ignoring laws, they usurp the most important power of the first branch of government. Such a course of action seriously threatens the separation of powers system because it places into the hands of the executive, in effect, the power to make as well as execute the law—the very type of governance the founders said led to tyranny.

Thinking Constitutionally

Constitutions establish the fundamental principles upon which a polity is based. They establish the institutions of government; they prescribe how positions of authority will be filled; they prescribe a process for making authoritative decisions (such as laws); and they establish how citizens relate to the government. In order for a constitution to be effective for its purposes, it must reflect the social, economic, ethnic, and religious realities of the polity. In addition, it must reflect the power structure in the country, for if a constitution is not accepted by those who hold significant power, it will be ignored and rendered ineffectual. One of the most important functions of constitutions, at least in Anglo-American legal systems, is to limit governmental power. The acceptance of the provisions of the constitution by those who hold power entails abiding by the rules about changes of personnel in the government.

If those who control physical force in a polity do not accept the limitations on their power that are specified in the constitution, they might use their control of power to keep themselves or their associates in office and govern as they please. In the United States the president controls the military as commander in chief and also national law enforcement entities, such as the FBI and the Secret Service. Congress can pass laws, but it has no power outside the executive branch to enforce those laws. The courts can make judgments, but they have no physical means of enforcing their decisions aside from executive branch compliance. For these important reasons, the president must accept the limitations on executive power specified in the Constitution and the laws of the land. President Bush's actions threatened the Constitution and the republic. President Bush refused to abide by the habeas corpus provisions of the law and the Constitution, and he enforced his actions with military and police forces by keeping detainees imprisoned and denying them habeas corpus and severely restricting their access to lawyers.

The architects of the Constitution expected that each branch would protect its own constitutional powers. During most of the twentieth century, presidents often acted aggressively to assert their own authority as against Congress. But Congress has only rarely asserted its own constitutional powers as against the president. Partly this is because Congress always contains a sizable portion of members who are of the president's party and want to see him succeed for partisan and short-term policy reasons.

Some presidents feel that it their duty to their successors to protect and expand the constitutional powers of the presidency. Seldom have presidents exhibited the willingness to abdicate their own powers to Congress, though Congress has often been willing to abdicate its power to the president.[16] The Supreme Court most often defers to the executive, in part out of prudence because it cannot enforce its decisions, and in part in recognition that the president (and Congress) has the legitimacy of being elected by the people. Presidential actions that seek to expand executive prerogative can be seen as idealistic attempts to uphold the Constitution or as cynical attempts to buttress their own personal and partisan power when they are in office.

To separate idealistic from partisan motives is difficult. Some scholars genuinely believe that the presidency is constitutionally weak and needs strengthening with more discretion and authority. Insofar as these scholars believe that their prescriptions should also apply to presidents of the other party into the future, they are thinking constitutionally (though mistakenly, in my opinion). They believe that, institutionally, Congress and the courts are inferior in judgment, regardless of partisan views, and that any executive is institutionally more likely to make wise decisions about public policy. Or they may feel that Congress, controlled by either party, and the courts often exhibit too much concern for individual rights and are thus more likely to compromise national security. These people would argue that the executive is most likely to protect national security and would argue that granting presidents more power would be better for the United States in the long run. These philosophical executivists are arguing from principles rather than from expediency. It is also possible, however, that those arguing for more executive power are concerned more with their present political and policy interests than with remaining faithful to the Constitution. This book, in contrast, argues that it is better in the long run for power to be balanced among the three branches.

Of course this argument about the separation of powers principle embedded in the Constitution does not guarantee that Congress and judges will always act with wisdom or that justice will prevail. In the history of the United States, both institutions have made unwise decisions that led to disaster. But this reality does not negate the important principle in the Constitution that governmental powers should be shared among the three branches of government. The purpose of the separation of powers system is to assure that power does not become concentrated in one set of hands—not that government will act smoothly, expeditiously, or even wisely.

Creating a constitution entails granting certain powers to certain institutions. But in reality the institutions do not exercise the powers; the individual incumbents of the positions exercise the power. Constitutions must be designed in light of the possibility that any one position may be occupied by a person who is corrupt and wants to abuse power or is sincere but deluded in thinking that he or she is right about important issues and willing to use the power of the position in ways not in accord with the limits in the Constitution. In John Marshall's words, "We must never forget that it is a constitution we are expounding."[17]

But just as constitution-makers must keep the possibility of unwise rulers' holding office in mind, so also must those who can legitimize exercises of executive power. If power is abused and seen as illegitimate—for example, President Nixon's creation of the "plumbers" to carry out illegal activities—the threat to the rule of law is mitigated. Such abuses may have bad consequences, but insofar as they are recognized as abuses and treated with opprobrium, the harm is mitigated because the incidents do not legitimize similar actions by future presidents. Furthermore the punishment of those abuses can be cited when future presidents want to extend their powers beyond the bounds of the Constitution.

If presidents do not want their own actions to be used as precedents by the other party or future presidents of whom they disapprove, they ought not to claim expanded powers for short-term gains. As argued in the preceding chapter, precedents make a difference. Justice Jackson commented on the power of precedent when he argued in his dissent in *Korematsu* that the Supreme Court should not legitimize the incarceration of Japanese Americans based on their ancestry. He argued that once a precedent is rationalized as conforming to the Constitution: "The principle then lies about like a loaded weapon ready for the hand of any authority that can bring forward a plausible claim of an urgent need. Every repetition imbeds that principle more deeply in our law and thinking and expands it to new purposes."[18]

John Locke asserted that "good princes" (wise rulers) "have been always most dangerous to the liberties of their people." Locke explained this paradox by pointing out that bad princes, with the interest of aggrandizing their own power, "would draw the actions of those good rulers into precedent, and make them the standard of their *prerogative,* as if what had been done [by wise rulers] only for the good of the people was a right in them [unwise rulers] to do, for the harm of the people, if they so pleased."[19] Thus those who defend the extraordinary constitutional actions of President Bush often point to precedents in other presidencies.

The danger of allowing one president to stretch the constitutional limits on presidential power is that future presidents will effectively claim the same power. For example,

—Lincoln's temporary suspension of habeas corpus during an emergency was used by defenders of President Bush to justify his denial of habeas indefinitely to "enemy combatants" years after the emergency of 9/11.

—FDR's creation of a military tribunal to try Nazi saboteurs was used by President Bush's defenders to justify his own unilateral creation of military tribunals to try "enemy combatants."

—The Justice Department under Presidents Reagan, Bush, and Clinton tried to legitimize some presidential signing statements, and those opinions were used to justify President Bush's much-expanded and sweeping use of signing statements.

Legitimizing violations of the Constitution or separation of powers for temporary, expedient purposes is usually unwise. These precedents have long-range repercussions and can undermine the separation of powers balance.

Separation of Powers

Even if one trusted President Bush's judgment implicitly, the authority that he claims to be able to ignore the law, if allowed to stand, would constitute a dangerous precedent that future presidents might use to abuse their power. As Joel Aberbach points out, "In the end, this is not a partisan issue, for someday the Democrats will have unified control, and even that somewhat-less-disciplined party might countenance a government of the type Bush and Cheney have apparently structured."[20] Thinking constitutionally means looking ahead and realizing that future executives will likely claim the same authority as their predecessors. Executive claims to constitutional power ratchet up; they do not swing like a pendulum, unless the other two branches protect their own constitutional authorities.

Insofar as President Bush tried to exclude Congress and the courts from their legitimate constitutional duties, he claimed the authority of all three branches of government to himself. James Madison argued in *Federalist* No. 47: "The accumulation of all powers, legislative, executive, and judiciary, in the same hands, whether of one, a few, or many, and whether hereditary, self-appointed, or elective, may justly be pronounced the very definition of tyranny." In each of the above cases of claims to constitutional authority, President Bush asserted that he alone could exercise the authority of each of the three branches:

—Geneva Conventions and torture: President Bush acted as *lawmaker* in suspending the treaty, which according to the Constitution is "the

supreme law of the Land"; *executive* in carrying out the policy by interrogating prisoners with harsh interrogation practices; and he acted as
judge by keeping the proceedings secret and asserting that any appeal
could only be to him and that the courts had no jurisdiction to hear
appeals.

—Military tribunals: President Bush acted as *lawmaker* in creating the
commissions himself, not in accord with enacted laws; *executive* in
detaining suspects in prisons; and he acted as *judge* in asserting the
authority to conduct the trials, impose sentences, and serve as the final
appeal.

—NSA warrantless wiretapping: President Bush acted as *lawmaker* by
determining that he could ignore the regularly enacted law and impose
his own rules in order to conduct surveillance in the United States; *executive* in ordering NSA to carry out his policies; and he acted as *judge* by
arguing that it was his inherent right as president to do it in secret and
prevent any review by the courts.

—Signing statements: President Bush undermined the rule of law itself
by claiming the authority to ignore those parts of the law that he said
impinged on his own prerogatives and refusing to accept the legitimacy
of either Congress or the Courts to limit his authority.

Contempt for the other branches of government was reflected in the
congressional Minority Iran-Contra Report in 1987 (headed by Richard
Cheney, then a member of Congress): "Congress has a hard time even
conceiving of itself as contributing to the problem of democratic
accountability."[21] Policymakers in the Department of Defense during the
Bush administration denigrated the rule of law as embodied in the due
process of law. They included our judicial processes along with terrorism
as both weakening the United States. They declared that "our strength as
a nation state will continue to be challenged by those who employ a
strategy of the weak, using international fora, judicial processes, and terrorism."[22] On the contrary, our judicial processes are sources of the
strength of the United States and the vitality of our Constitution; they are
essential to ensure individual liberty. Insofar as one agrees with these
expressions of contempt for Congress and the judicial process, one will
favor granting all future presidents the power that George W. Bush has
seized. But if one believes along with the framers of the Constitution that
a balance among the branches is essential to liberty, President Bush's

assertions of extraordinary presidential authority should not be left unopposed.

Aharon Barak, President of the Israel Supreme Court, declared, "Terrorism does not justify the neglect of accepted legal norms. This is how we distinguish ourselves from the terrorists themselves. They act against the law by violating and trampling it, while in its war against terrorism, a democratic state acts within the framework of the law and according to the law."[23] The threat of terrorism in the United States is real, and the president has the duty to take appropriate actions to thwart terrorists. But in doing so, the balance between security and liberty must be made, and that balancing is not the president's alone to make. Congress and the federal court system are legitimate branches of government, and the president has no constitutional right to ignore them.

The president should have enough power to accomplish reasonable policy goals, but not enough to override the other two branches unilaterally, acting merely on the basis of his own judgment. In the above cited cases of extraordinary claims to executive authority, President Bush claimed that the checks and balances in the Constitution did not bind him. The United States Constitution created a system in which the concentration of power in one branch would be countered by actions of the other two branches. The other two branches may in the future repudiate the claims that President Bush made. Nevertheless his claims have severely challenged the balance of constitutional authority. The principles of constitutionalism and the rule of law are basic to the United States polity. Insofar as President Bush, in cases such as these, refused to acknowledge the constitutional limits on his executive authority, he undermined two of the fundamental principles upon which the United States was established: the rule of law and the Constitution.

NOTES

Chapter One

Epigraph:
John Emerich Edward Dalberg, Lord Acton (1834–1902), in a letter to Bishop Mandell Creighton in 1887. Great Books on Line, Bartleby.com (www.phrases. org.uk/meanings/288200.html).

Chapter Two

Epigraphs:
Senior adviser to Bush quoted by Ron Suskind, "Without a Doubt," *New York Times Magazine* (October 17, 2004) (www.ronsuskind.com/articles/).

Keynes's quote from John Maynard Keynes, *General Theory* (1947), as reported in *The Oxford Book of Political Quotations* (Oxford University Press, 2001), p. 201.

1. See, for example, John Yoo, "The Continuation of Politics by Other Means: The Original Understanding of War Powers," *California Law Review* 84: 167–305; *War by Other Means* (New York: Atlantic Monthly Press, 2006); and *The Powers of War and Peace* (University of Chicago Press, 2005).

2. For a detailed account of the intellectual sources of the ideas of the framers, see Bernard Bailyn, *The Ideological Origins of the American Revolution* (Harvard University Press, 1967); Forrest McDonald, *The American Presidency: An Intellectual History* (University Press of Kansas, 1994), chaps. 1–10; Harvey C. Mansfield Jr., *Taming the Prince: The Ambivalence of Modern Executive Power* (New York: Free Press, 1989), chaps. 8–10; M. J. C. Vile, *Constitutionalism and the Separation of Powers* (Indianapolis, Ind.: Liberty Fund, 1998), chap. 6; Gordon S. Wood, *The Creation of the American Republic* (New York: Norton, 1972).

3. See John P. Roche, "The Founding Fathers: A Reform Caucus in Action," *American Political Science Review* 55, no. 4 (December 1961): 799–816.

4. If one were a "textualist," one would disapprove of applying the Fourth Amendment to electronic communications because the framers could not conceive

of them in the eighteenth century. If one were an "originalist," one would have to believe that the electors from Texas could not have voted for Richard Cheney as vice president, because both Bush and Cheney were "inhabitants" of the same state. See Article 2 and the Twelfth Amendment: "The Electors shall . . . vote by ballot for President and Vice President, one of whom, as least, shall not be an inhabitant of the same state with themselves." The Constitution did not say anything about legal residence, owning homes, or voting locations.

5. Niccolò Machiavelli, *The Prince,* trans., William J. Connell (New York: Bedford/St. Martin's, 2005).

6. Ibid.

7. See Mansfield, *Taming the Prince,* pp. 121–50.

8. McDonald, *American Presidency,* p. 40.

9. Machiavelli, *The Prince,* p. 87.

10. Both quotes from Machiavelli, *The Prince,* p. 87.

11. Ibid.

12. Ibid., p. 91.

13. Ibid.

14. Ibid.

15. Ibid., pp. 91, 95.

16. Thomas Hobbes, *Leviathan* (London: Penguin Books, 1985), p. 189. *Leviathan* was first published in 1651. All subsequent quotations from Hobbes come from this edition of *Leviathan.*

17. Ibid.

18. Ibid., pp. 185–86.

19. Ibid., p. 188.

20. Ibid., pp. 228–29.

21. Ibid., p. 233.

22. Ibid., p. 229.

23. John Locke, *Second Treatise of Government,* C. B. Macpherson, ed. (Cambridge: Hackett Publishing, 1980), p. 8 (ch. 2). Locke's *Second Treatise* was originally published in 1690. (Throughout this section, all of the emphases in italics are Locke's.)

24. Locke, *Second Treatise of Government,* p. 12 (ch. 2).

25. Ibid.

26. Ibid., p. 14 (ch. 3).

27. Ibid., p. 15 (ch. 3).

28. Ibid., pp. 16 (ch. 3), 46 (ch. 7).

29. Ibid., p. 46 (ch. 7).

30. Ibid., p. 52 (ch. 8).

31. Ibid., p. 66 (ch. 9).

32. Ibid., p. 68. (ch. 9).

33. Ibid., p. 69 (ch. 11).

34. Ibid., p. 71 (ch. 11).

35. Ibid., p. 73 (ch. 11).

36. Ibid., p. 78 (ch.13).

37. Locke, *Second Treatise of Government,* p. 79 (ch. 13).

38. Ibid.

39. Ibid.

40. Ibid.

41. Ibid., pp. 79, 110 (ch. 19).

42. McDonald, *American Presidency,* p. 50. See also Edward S. Corwin, *The President: Office and Powers* (New York University Press, 1957), p. 7.

43. Locke, *Second Treatise,* p. 84 (ch. 14).

44. Ibid.

45. Ibid.

46. Ibid.

47. For arguments that the executive has extensive prerogative powers, see Gordon S. Jones and John A. Marini, eds., *The Imperial Congress: Crisis in the Separation of Powers* (New York: Pharos Books, 1988), and L. Gordon Crovits and Jeremy A. Rabkin, eds., *The Fettered Presidency: Legal Constraints on the Executive Branch* (Washington: American Enterprise Institute, 1989). For more recent arguments for sweeping executive prerogative, see John Yoo, "The Continuation of Politics by Other Means; *War by Other Means;* and *Powers of War and Peace.*

48. Locke, *Second Treatise,* pp. 83–84 (ch. 14). See the discussion by Jack Rakove, "Taking the Prerogative out of the Presidency: An Originalist Perspective," *Presidential Studies Quarterly* 37, no. 1 (March 2007): 4–8.

49. Locke, *Second Treatise,* p. 76 (ch. 12).

50. Ibid., pp. 79–80 (ch. 13).

51. See Rakove, *Presidential Studies Quarterly,* p. 15 of 17.

52. Locke, *Second Treatise,* p. 85 (ch. 14).

53. For a cogent argument that the prerogative power in Locke is constrained, see Thomas S. Langston and Michael E. Lind, "John Locke and the Limits of Presidential Prerogative," *Polity* 24, no. 1 (Fall 1991): 49–68. For an analysis of Locke's concern with the dangers of prerogative, see Benjamin A. Kleinerman, "Can the Princes Really Be Tamed? Executive Prerogative, Popular Apathy, and the Constitutional Frame in Locke's *Second Treatise,*" *American Political Science Review* 101, no. 2 (May 2007), pp. 209–22.

54. There is also a difference between acting when no law addresses the issue and ignoring a law that prohibits what the president desires to do. Locke's prerogative is much more sympathetic to the former than the latter. See Langston and Lind, "John Locke and the Limits of Presidential Prerogative."

55. M. J. C. Vile, *Constitutionalism and the Separation of Powers* (Indianapolis, Ind.: Liberty Fund, 1998), p. 107. Originally published in 1967 by Oxford University Press.

56. See ibid., pp. 58–59.

57. Locke, *Second Treatise*, p. 76 (ch. 12). Locke also said, "WHERE the legislative and executive power are in distinct hands, (as they are in all moderated monarchies, and well-framed governments) there the good of the society requires, that several things should be left to the discretion of him that has the executive power: for the legislators not being able to foresee, and provide by laws, for all that may be useful to the community, the executor. . . ." Locke, *Second Treatise*, p. 83–88 (ch. 14).

58. Mansfield, *Taming the Prince*, p. 230; see also McDonald, *American Presidency*, p. 58.

59. Vile, *Constitutionalism*, p. 93.

60. All references to Montesquieu are from *The Spirit of the Laws*, by Charles de Secondat, Baron de Montesquieu, translated by Thomas Nugent, revised by J. V. Prichard. Based on a public domain edition published in 1914 by G. Bell and Sons, London. Rendered into HTML and text by Jon Roland of the Constitution Society. No page numbers in this online version. Available at www.constitution. org/cm/sol.htm.

61. According to Harvey Mansfield, Montesquieu "establishes for the first time anywhere the independence of the judiciary, creating the three powers as we know them today." Mansfield, *Taming the Prince*, p. 216. Vile, *Constitutionalism*, pp. 95–97.

62. Montesquieu, *Spirit of the Laws*, ch. 12.

63. Ibid.

64. Ibid.; Vile, *Constitutionalism*, pp. 96–99.

65. Vile, *Constitutionalism*, pp. 96–97.

66. Montesquieu, *Spirit of the Laws*, ch. 12.

Chapter Three

Epigraph:
Robert Perry, "Gonzales Questions Habeas Corpus," Consortiumnews.com, January 19, 2007 (consortiumnews.com [accessed on January 27, 2007]).

1. Quote from the *Charter of Liberties* comes from Paul Halsall (February 1996), "Medieval Sourcebook: Charter of Liberties of Henry I, 1100," found at fordham.edu/halsall/source/hcoronation.html. See also F. W. Maitland, *The Constitutional History of England* (Cambridge University Press, 1965).

2. Claire Breay, *Magna Carta: Manuscripts and Myths* (London: British Library, 2002), pp. 12–18.

3. Only four copies of Magna Carta still exist; two copies are on display to the public in the British Library, one at Salisbury and one in Lincoln Cathedral. See Breay, *Magna Carta*; Daphne I. Stroud, *Magna Carta* (Southampton: Pal Cave Publications, 1985); J. C. Holt, *Magna Carta*, 2nd ed. (Cambridge University Press, 1992, 2003).

4. Breay, *Magna Carta*, pp. 28–29.

5. The translations of these provisions from Latin are taken from Breay, *Magna Carta*, pp. 54–59.

6. Stroud, *Magna Carta*, p. 6.

7. Breay, *Magna Carta*, p. 54.

8. Ibid., p. 40.

9. Quoted from David C. Douglas, ed., *English Historical Documents* (London: Eyre and Spottiswoode, 1957), pp. 325–26.

10. Magna Carta was reissued with minor changes in 1216, 1217, and 1225.

11. Holt, *Magna Carta*, p. 4.

12. Petition of Right, 1628, found at Britannia's British History Department (www.constitution.org/eng/petright.htm).

13. See "The Long Parliament," Encyclopedia Britannica on line (www.britannica.com/ed/article-44864/UnitedKingdom). The Grand Remonstrance can be found at www.constitution.org/eeng/conpur043.htm43.

14. "The Bill of Rights, 1689," printed in W. C. Costin and J. Steven Watson, eds., *The Law and Working of the Constitution, Documents 1660–1914*, vol. 1 (London: Adam and Charles Black, 1952), pp. 67–74. The wording of the Bill has been slightly modernized by the author.

15. Michael A. R. Graves, *Early Tudor Parliaments* (London: Longman, 1990), p. 1.

16. Ibid., p. 2.

17. Clayton Roberts, *The Growth of Responsible Government in Stuart England* (Cambridge University Press, 1966), p. 7.

18. Ibid.

19. Ibid., p. 40.

20. Ibid., p. 7.

21. Ibid., p. 10.

22. Henry Hallam, *The Constitutional History of England*, 8th ed. (London: John Murray, 1855), pp. 1–5.

23. Paul Langford, *Eighteenth-Century Britain* (Oxford University Press, 1984), pp. 13–15.

24. A. H. Dodd, *The Growth of Responsible Government: From James the First to Victoria* (London: Routledge and Kegan Paul, 1956), pp. 5–6.

25. Roberts, *Growth of Responsible Government*, pp. 9–10.

26. Michael A. R. Graves, *Elizabethan Parliaments* (London: Longman, 1987), p. 6.

27. Dodd, *Growth of Responsible Government*, pp. 9–10; Graves, *Elizabethan Parliaments*, p. 75.

28. Graves, *Elizabethan Parliaments*, pp. 8–11.

29. See David Starkey, *Monarchy: From the Middle Ages to Modernity* (New York: Harper Press, 2006), pp. 84–86.

30. Quoted in Glenn Burgess, *Absolute Monarchy and the Stuart Constitution* (Yale University Press, 1996), p. 91 (original spelling retained). James also declared: "Kings are called Gods; they are appointed by God and answerable only to God." Starkey, *Monarchy*, p. 92. The following several paragraphs are based on Starkey's account, pp. 90–140.

31. Margaret Judson argues that after 1640 the theory of divine right of kings ended in terms of serious political thought. After 1642, even the Royalists based their arguments on law rather than the divine right of kings. Margaret Judson, *The Crisis of the Constitution* (Rutgers University Press, 1949, 1988), p. 386.

32. Larry W. Yackle, *Federal Courts: Habeas Corpus* (New York: Foundation Press, 2003), p. 12.

33. By this time, Judson argues, no serious theorist argued the pure case for divine right of kings and the Royalists thought the king was supreme, but limited in some important ways by law and Parliament. Judson, *Crisis of the Constitution*, pp. 388–89, 394.

34. Quoted in Starkey, *Monarchy*, p. 181.

35. Ibid., p. 196.

36. Ibid., p. 218.

37. See ibid., p. 224.

38. Roberts, *Growth of Responsible Government*, p. vii.

39. Both quotes from Starkey, *Monarchy*, pp. 249–50.

40. Ibid., p. 257.

41. Ibid.

Chapter Four

Epigraphs:

Franklin's quote is from the notes of Dr. James McHenry, a Convention delegate from Maryland. The notes were first published in *The American Historical Review*, vol. 11 (1906). The notes were included in *The Records of the Federal Convention of 1787*, Max Farrand, ed., vol. 3, Appendix A, p. 85 (1911, reprinted in 1934). Great Books on Line (Bartleby.com/73/1593.html).

John C. Yoo, "The Continuation of Politics by Other Means: The Original Understanding of War Powers," *California Law Review* 84 (March 1996): 275.

1. Quoted in Charles C. Thatch Jr., *The Creation of the Presidency, 1775–1789* (Johns Hopkins University Press, 1923, 1969), p. 101.

2. Gordon S. Wood, *The Creation of the American Republic* (New York: Norton, 1972), p. 150.

3. For an analysis of the intellectual sources of the framers' ideas about government, see Forrest McDonald, *The American Presidency: An Intellectual History* (University Press of Kansas, 1994), pp. 38–97.

4. See McDonald, *American Presidency,* pp. 99–25; much of the discussion of the colonial experience below is drawn from McDonald.

5. Ibid., p. 110.

6. Ibid., p. 111–24.

7. Ibid., p. 132.

8. Thatch, *Creation of the Presidency,* pp. 18–19.

9. Ibid., p. 35.

10. Ibid., p. 33.

11. Wood, *Creation of the American Republic,* p. 154–61, 454.

12. Jefferson, quoted in Thatch, *Creation of the Presidency,* p. 30.

13. Gerhard Casper, *Separating Powers* (Cambridge: Harvard University Press, 1997), p. 10.

14. M. J. C. Vile, *Constitutionalism and the Separation of Powers,* 2nd ed. (Indianapolis: Liberty House, 1998), p. 166.

15. Montesquieu, Book XI, based on a public domain edition published in 1914 by G. Bell and Sons, London. Rendered into HTML and text by Jon Roland of the Constitution Society. No page numbers in this online version. Available at www.constitution.org/cm/sol_11.htm#005.

16. Sir William Blackstone, *Commentaries on the Laws of England,* 7th edition (1775), pp. 154–55. Excerpted in David C. Douglas, ed., *English Historical Documents* (London: Eyre and Spottiswoode, 1957), p. 89.

17. Quoted in Vile, *Constitutionalism and the Separation of Powers,* p. 131.

18. Quoted in Casper, *Separating Powers,* p. 7.

19. Max Farrand, ed., *The Records of the Federal Convention of 1787* (Yale University Press, 1966), vol. 1, pp. 30–31.

20. Ibid., p. 65.

21. Ibid., p. 113.

22. Ibid., p. 66.

23. Ibid., p. 93.

24. Thatch, *Creation of the Presidency,* p. 92.

25. Farrand, *The Records of the Federal Convention of 1787,* (Yale University Press, 1966), vol. 2, p. 171.

26. See Shlomo Slonim, "Designing the Electoral College," in Thomas E. Cronin, ed., *Inventing the American Presidency* (University Press of Kansas, 1989), pp. 48, 49.

27. Farrand, *Records of the Federal Convention of 1787,* vol. 2, p. 397.

28. See Vile, *Constitutionalism and the Separation of Powers,* passim.

29. See Alexander Hamilton's arguments in *Federalist* No. 84 that a bill of rights was not necessary.

30. Madison to Jefferson (October 10, 1788), quoted in Thatch, *Creation of the Presidency,* pp. 24–24.

31. Wood, *Creation of the American Republic,* p. 472.

32. Farrand, *Records of the Federal Convention of 1787,* vol. 1, p. 82 (June 2).

33. *The Writings of James Madison,* April 2, 1798. Edited by Gaillard Hunt. 9 vols. New York: G. P. Putnam's Sons, 1900–10. Found at press-pubs.uchicago. edu/founders/documents/a1-8-11s8.html.

34. Farrand, *Records of the Federal Convention of 1787,* vol. 2, p. 319.

35. See Rakove, "Taking the Prerogative out of the Presidency," *Presidential Studies Quarterly* (March 2007): 85–100.

36. Both quotes are from House of Lords, Select Committee on the Constitution, Fifteenth Report, "Waging War: Parliament's Role and Responsibility," pp. 1–5; available at www.publications.parliament.uk (accessed March 29, 2007). According to the House of Lords: "The United Kingdom's constitution is a combination of statute, common law, and unwritten convention, with the result that it is flexible and constantly evolving" (p. 7).

37. William Blackstone, *Commentaries on the Laws of England,* vol. 2, facsimile of the original text published in 1889 by Callaghan and Company, Chicago, pp. 223–24.

38. Ibid., p. 258.

39. Ibid., p. 262.

40. John C. Yoo, "The Continuation of Politics by Other Means: The Original Understanding of War Powers," *California Law Review* 84 (March 1996): 276. Yoo also argues on p. 208: "In adopting elements of the British Constitution's checks and balances, the Framers reasonably could expect those elements to produce a relationship between the President and Congress similar to the one that they thought existed between Crown and Parliament."

41. Yoo, "The Continuation of Politics by Other Means," p. 275.

42. Memorandum for Alberto R. Gonzales, counsel to the President, "Standards of Conduct for Interrogation under 18 U.S.C. Sc. 2340–2340A" (August 1, 2002). Reprinted in Karen Greenberg and Joshua Dratel, *The Torture Papers: The Road to Abu Ghraib* (Cambridge University Press, 2005), p. 202.

43. This discussion is based on the analysis of David Gray Adler in "The Constitution and Presidential Warmaking: The Enduring Debate," *Political Science Quarterly* 103, no. 1 (Spring 1988): 9. See also Adler, "George Bush as Commander in Chief: Toward the Nether World of Constitutionalism," *Presidential Studies Quarterly* (September 2006): 525–40.

44. Adler, "George W. Bush as Commander in Chief," p. 527.

45. See the analysis by Adler, "George W. Bush and the Abuse of History: The Constitution and Presidential Power in Foreign Policy" (paper presented at the Midwest Political Science Convention, Chicago, April 12–14, 2007), pp. 52–53. See also David J. Barron and Martin S. Lederman, "The Commander in Chief at the Lowest Ebb—Framing the Problem, Doctrine, and Original Understanding," *Harvard Law Review* 121, no. 3 (January 2008): 689–804.

46. Yoo, "The Continuation of Politics by Other Means," p. 216.

47. Ibid., p. 226.

48. Ibid., p. 275.

49. Ibid., pp. 207–08.

50. "Examination of Jefferson's Message to Congress," in *Hamilton's Works,* vol. 3 (New York: John F. Trow, Printer), p. 746; from the University of Michigan Library, accessed on line at books.google.com.

51. James Madison, in *The Writings of James Madison,* vol. 6, p. 146, quoted by Louis Fisher in "Exercising Congress's Constitutional Power to End a War," Statement before Congress, January 30, 2007 (Law Library of Congress, p. 4).

52. Ibid., Madison, p. 174.

53. Farrand, *Records of the Federal Convention of 1787,* vol. 1, pp. 65–66, as quoted in Rakove, *Presidential Studies Quarterly* (March 2007).

54. Quoted in Rakove, "Taking the Prerogative out of the Presidency," p. 10 of 17.

55. Hamilton's long speech, Farrand, vol. 1, p. 292.

56. *The Federalist Papers,* No. 69 (New York: Mentor Books, 1961), p. 418.

57. *The Papers of Alexander Hamilton,* edited by Herald C. Syrett and others, 26 vols. (Columbia University Press, 1961), pp. 454–57. Posted on /prespubs.uchicago.edu/founders/documents.

58. Farrand, *Records of the Federal Convention of 1787,* vol. 1, pp. 64–68.

59. Farrand, ed., *Records of the Federal Convention of 1787,* vol. 2, p. 318.

60. Ibid., pp. 318–19. Note that Gerry's statement further undermines Yoo's argument that the word "declare" was intended by the Framers to denote merely the legal status of a conflict. Gerry and the other Framers in this exchange clearly understood the word "declare" to mean the decision to go to war, and they gave it to Congress.

61. Hunt, ed., "Letters of Helvidius, No. 1," in *The Writings of James Madison,* vol. 6, p. 174.

62. Rakove, "Taking the Prerogative out of the Presidency," p. 13 of 17.

63. Thatch, *Creation of the Presidency, 1775-1789,* pp. 138–39.

64. McDonald, *American Presidency,* p. 181.

65. Rakove, "Taking the Prerogative out of the Presidency," p. 14 of 17.

66. Adler, "George W. Bush and the Abuse of History," p. 29.

67. All of the quotes in this discussion of Curtis-Wright are taken from Louis Fisher, "President's Game," *Legal Times,* vol. 29, no. 49 (December 4, 2006), from *Legal Times* website. See also Adler, "George W. Bush and the Abuse of History," pp. 29–30.

68. 343 U.S. 579, 1952.

69. Quoted in Adler, "George W. Bush and the Abuse of History," p. 31. Much of this discussion is based on Adler's analysis.

70. *Youngstown Sheet and Tube* v. *Sawyer,* 343 U.S. 579, p. 646.

71. Ibid., p. 635.

72. Ibid., p. 637.

73. Justice Brandeis dissenting I *Myers* v . *U.S.* 272 U.S. 52, p. 293. That the framers wanted to solve the problems of inefficiency of the plural executive of the Continental Congress is a separate point that does not refute Brandeis's dictum. Thus Brandeis's statement should not be read to mean that the framers were not concerned with the effectiveness of the executive branch. As scholar Louis Fisher argued, part of the purpose of calling the Constitutional Convention was to overcome the problems arising from placing the executive power in committees of the Continental Congress. See Louis Fisher, "The Efficiency Side of Separation of Powers," *Journal of American Studies* 5, no. 2 (August 1971): 113–31. See also Fisher, *President and Congress* (New York: Free Press, 1972), pp. 1–28.

Chapter Five

Epigraphs:

President Bush, Prime Minister Blair Discuss War on Terror, Press Conference, July 17, 2003 (www.whitehouse.gov/news/releases/2003/07/20030717-9.html).

Quote attributed to Martin Niemöller. See www.history.ucsb.edu/faculty/marcuse/niem.htm#versions.

1. In the twentieth century the writ has also been used to argue that a suspect has not been given due process of law and thus cannot be jailed because the executive has denied the suspect fundamental rights. See Larry W. Yackle, *Federal Courts: Habeas Corpus* (New York: Foundation Press, 2003).

2. Associated Press, "No Legal Rights for Enemy Combatants, Scalia Says," *Washington Post,* March 27, 2006, p. A3.

3. See Mark Denbeaux and Joshua Denbeaux, "Report on Guantanamo Detainees: A Profile of 517 Detainees through Analysis of Department of Defense Data" (April 2005) (law.shu.edu/aaafinal.pdf). Their data will be discussed later in the chapter.

4. See Benjamin Wittes, "Detention Retention," *New Republic,* December 7, 2007.

5. Wittes argues that a full legal architecture should be set up to make a reasonable compromise between the minimal due process owed captives in a war and the full range of civil rights and due process owed to citizens in a civil court. See Benjamin Wittes, "Terrorism, the Military and the Courts," *Policy Review,* no. 143 (June & July 2007): 21–42.

6. Charles E. Wyzanski Jr., "Writ of Habeas Corpus," *Annals of the American Academy of Political and Social Science,* vol. 243 (January 1946), pp. 101–06, p. 101.

7. *Amici Curiae Brief of British and American Habeas Scholars,* in *Khaled A. F. al Odah, et al.* v. *U.S.,* Circuit Court of Appeals for the District of Columbia (January 25, 2006), p. 3 (http://law.shu.edu/aaafinal.pdf).

8. Quoted in Wyzanski, "Writ of Habeas Corpus."

9. Claire Breay, *Magna Carta* (London: British Library, 2002), p. 52. The two phrases *law of the land* and *due process of law* "are employed interchangeably in constitutional law, and mean the same thing." See William Blackstone, *Commentaries on the Laws of England,* vol. 1 (Chicago: Callaghan and Company, 1899), facsimile of the 4th ed., pp. 134–35, n. 1.

10. Larry W. Yackle, *Federal Courts: Habeas Corpus* (New York: Foundation Press, 2003), pp. 13–14.

11. Wyzanski, "Writ of Habeas Corpus," pp. 101–06, p. 101.

12. *Amici Curiae Brief of British and American Habeas Scholars,* p. 3.

13. The Petition of Right of 1628 is available at www.constitution.org/eng/petright.htm.

14. A copy of the Habeas Corpus Act can be found at: www.fordham.edu/halsall/mod/1679habeascorp.html.

15. Blackstone, *Commentaries on the Laws of England,* pp. 136–37.

16. Ibid., p. 138.

17. Ibid., p. 135.

18. Francis Paschal, "The Constitution and Habeas Corpus," *Duke Law Journal* 1, no. 4 (August 1970): 605–51, at 622–23. Eric M. Freedman, *Habeas Corpus: Rethinking the Great Writ of Liberty* (New York University Press, 2001).

19. Max Farrand, ed., *The Records of the Federal Convention of 1787* (Yale University Press, 1911, 1966), vol. 2 (August 20), p. 341.

20. Ibid., p. 438.

21. Blackstone, *Commentaries on the Laws of England,* pp. 136–37.

22. Freedman, *Habeas Corpus,* p. 14.

23. Freedman, *Habeas Corpus,* p. 14; Hamilton, *Federalist* No. 84.

24. Freedman, *Habeas Corpus,* p. 16.

25. The passage is found in Blackstone, *Commentaries on the Laws of England,* pp. 136–37.

26. Wyzanski, "Writ of Habeas Corpus," p. 103. The 1971 Detention Act (18 U.S.C. section 4001) provides that "no citizen shall be imprisoned or otherwise detained by the United States except pursuant to an Act of Congress."

27. Denbeaux and Denbeaux, "Report on Guantanamo Detainees." Of course, this assumes that fighting against U.S. forces in Afghanistan constituted a violation of the laws of war, for instance because the combatants were deceptively dressed as civilians or taking cover behind innocent civilians, and so on.

28. Ibid., p. 2 (discussed below).

29. Quoted in Louis Fisher, *Military Tribunals and Presidential Power* (University Press of Kansas, 2005), p. 41.

30. Louis Fisher, "Invoking Inherent Powers: A Primer," *Presidential Studies Quarterly* 37 (March 2007), web edition.

31. Lincoln's Attorney General, Edward Bates, argued that President Lincoln had the duty to suspend habeas corpus because of the insurrection that imperiled the Union itself and that during a "great and dangerous rebellion, like the pres-

ent," the president had to act, though his authority to suspend the writ was "temporary and exceptional." Quoted in Fisher, *Military Tribunals,* p. 43. Despite the argument by Bates in his report to the president, Lincoln himself did not make the constitutional claim put forward by Bates.

32. *Ex parte Bollman,* 8 U.S. (4 Cranch) 75 (1807).

33. Fisher, *Military Tribunals,* p. 41.

34. 17 F. Cas. 1444 (1861).

35. Fisher, *Military Tribunals,* p. 55–56.

36. 17 F. Cas. 1444 (1861).

37. *Amici Curiae Brief of British and American Habeas Scholars,* p. 13.

38. 71 U.S. 2 (1866).

39. Ibid.

40. Ibid.

41. Ibid.

42. 317 U.S. 1 (1942). This section is based on Fisher, *Military Tribunals,* pp. 91–129.

43. Fisher, *Military Tribunals,* p. 95.

44. See Ronald Rotunda, "Federalism and the Separation of Powers," *Engage* 8, no. 3 (2006): 54–62, and "The Detainee Cases of 2004 and 2006 and Their Aftermath," *Syracuse Law Review* 57, no. 1 (2006): 1–62.

45. Fisher, *Military Tribunals,* p. 125.

46. Quoted by Louis Fisher, *Presidential War Power,* 2d ed. (University Press of Kansas, 2004), p. 207.

47. Scalia dissenting in *Hamdi.*

48. "Detention, Treatment, and Trial of Certain Non-Citizens in the War against Terrorism," found at www.whitehouse.gov/news/releases/2001/11/20011113-27.html.

49. This account of the preparation of the document is taken from Barton Gellman and Jo Becker's series of articles on Vice President Cheney in the *Washington Post* beginning on June 24, 2007, p. 1. This article was entitled "A Different Understanding with the President."

50. Gellman and Becker, "A Different Understanding with the President."

51. Section 3 (e), "Detention, Treatment, and Trial of Certain Non-Citizens in the War Against Terrorism," November 13, 2001.

52. See the analysis in Howard Ball, *Bush, the Detainees, and the Constitution* (University Press of Kansas, 2007), pp. 90–124.

53. *Johnson v. Eisentrager,* 399 U.S. 763 (1950).

54. See Brief for the Respondents in Opposition, *Rasul v. Bush,* nos. 03–334 and 03–343, pp. 10–13. Posted on FindLaw.com.

55. Brief for the Respondents, quoted in Ball, *Bush, the Detainees, and the Constitution,* p. 92.

56. *Johnson v. Eisentrager,* 339 U.S. 763 (1950).

57. Ibid.

58. 542 U.S. 466 (2004).

59. *Rasul v. Bush,* 542 U.S. 466 (2004).

60. Excerpt in Richard M. Pious, *The War on Terrorism and the Rule of Law* (Los Angeles: Roxbury, 2006), p. 173.

61. *Rasul v. Bush,* 542 U.S. 466 (2004).

62. The Habeas Corpus statute, 28 U.S.C. Sec. 2241, gives federal courts the jurisdiction to hear habeas corpus appeals.

63. Brief for the Respondents, *Hamdi v. Rumsfeld,* no. 03–6696, p. 10. Posted on FindLaw.com.

64. *Hamdi v. Rumsfeld,* 542 U.S. 507 (2004).

65. Ibid.

66. Ibid.

67. Ibid. See Rotunda, "Federalism and the Separation of Powers" pp. 54–62, and "Detainee Cases of 2004 and 2006 and Their Aftermath," pp. 1–62.

68. In remarks after she had retired from the Supreme Court, Justice O'Connor said about the intimidation of federal judges, "We must be ever-vigilant against those who would strongarm the judiciary into adopting their preferred policies. It takes a lot of degeneration before a country falls into dictatorship, but we should avoid these ends by avoiding these beginnings." Her remarks were reported by Nina Totenberg of National Public Radio, according to Raw Story, "Retired Supreme Court Justice Hits Attacks on Courts and Warns of Dictatorship" (March 10, 2006), available at rawstory.com.

69. *Hamdi v. Rumsfeld,* 542 U.S. 507 (2004), Scalia dissent.

70. Pious, *War on Terrorism and the Rule of Law,* p. 153.

71. "Detention, Treatment, and Trial of Certain Non-Citizens in the War against Terrorism," found at whitehouse.gov/news/releases/2001/11/20011113-27.html.

72. See Fisher, *Military Tribunals,* p. 168.

73. Ibid., p. 173.

74. Department of Defense, Military Commission Order No. 1 (March 21, 2002), signed by Donald Rumsfeld; available at www.defenselink.mil/news/Mar2002/d20020321ord.pdf.

75. Public Law 109-148, 119 Stat. 2739.

76. 28 U.S.C. Sec. 2241 (e).

77. The Court noted that Congress explicitly rejected language that would have made the law apply to previous appeals and that Senators Graham and Kyl inserted language into the *Congressional Record* after the Senate debate and tried to make it appear that their words were spoken during the debate over the bill. *Hamdan v. Rumsfeld* (2006), no. 05-184, Slip Opinion, p.15, n. 10.

78. *Hamdan v. Rumsfeld* (2006), no. 05–184, Slip Opinion, pp. 27, 60–61.

79. Ibid., pp. 2–4.

80. Military Commission Order No. 1, March 21, 2002; found at www.defenselink.mil/news/Mar2002/d20020321ord.pdf.

81. See Michael C. Dorf, "A Federal Appeals Court Upholds . . . Jurisdiction-Stripping of MCA." Posted on FindLaw.com (writ.news.findlaw.com/dorf/2007 0228.html [accessed February 28, 2007]), p. 4 of 5.

82. *Hamdan v. Rumsfeld* (2006), no. 05–184, Slip Opinion, pp. 4, 6.

83. *Law of War Handbook* (2004), p. 144, Slip Opinion, p. 68, n. 63.

84. *Hamdan* v. *Rumsfeld* (2006), p. 7.

85. 28 U.S.C. Section 2241(e).

86. See Jennifer K. Elsea and Kenneth R. Thomas, "Enemy Combatant Detainees: Habeas Corpus Challenges in Federal Court," Congressional Research Service (April 6, 2007) (code RL33180), pp. 20–21.

87. 476 F.3d 981.

88. See Dorf, "Federal Appeals Court Upholds the Jurisdiction-Stripping Provisions of the MCA."

89. This account is based on the "Declaration of Stephen Abraham, Lieutenant Colonel, United States Army Reserve" (www.scotusblog.com/movable type/archives/Al%20Odah%20reply%206-22-07.pdf), and Susan Schmidt, "Trail of an 'Enemy Combatant': From Desert to U.S. Heartland," *Washington Post,* July 20, 2007, pp. 1, 16.

90. Schmidt, "Trail of an 'Enemy Combatant,'" pp. 1, 16.

91. "Declaration of Stephen Abraham," p. 5.

92. Schmidt, "Trail of an 'Enemy Combatant,'" pp. 1, 16.

93. Morris D. Davis, "AWOL Military Justice," *Los Angeles Times,* December 10, 2007.

94. Ibid.

95. Ben Fox, "Ex-Prosecutor to Serve as Defense Witness in Terror Case," *Washington Post,* February 22, 2008, p. A14.

96. See Scott Shane and Adam Liptak, "Shifting Power to a President," *New York Times,* September 30, 2006, p. 1.

97. See Shane and Liptak, "Shifting Power to a President," p. 1; Kate Zernike, "Senate Approves Broad New Rules to Try Detainees," *New York Times,* September 29, 2006, p. 1; Tim Grieve, "The President's Power to Imprison People Forever," *Salon,* September 26, 2006; Michael A. Fletcher, "Bush Signs Terrorism Measure," *Washington Post,* October 18, 2006, p. A4.

98. See Robert Perry, "Gonzales Questions Habeas Corpus," Consortiumnews.com, January 19, 2007 (consortiumnews.com [accessed January 27, 2007]). Also quoted in John Dean, "The Controversy over Curtailing Habeas Corpus Rights," posted on FindLaw.com (accessed January 26, 2007).

99. Denbeaux and Denbeaux, "Report on Guantanamo Detainees." The text of the U.S. offers of $4,285 and is found at the end of Report No. 1.

100. Denbeaux and Denbeaux, "Report on Guantanamo Detainees," p. 2.

101. Ibid., p. 4.

102. Joseph Felter and Jarret Brachman, "An Assessment of 516 Combatant Status Review Tribunal (CSRT) Unclassified Summaries," July 25, 2007. Combating Terrorism Center, West Point, New York.

103. Report of the International Committee of the Red Cross (ICRC) on the Treatment by the Coalition Forces of Prisoners of War and Other Protected Persons by the Geneva Conventions in Iraq during Arrest, Internment and Interrogation (February 2004), sec. 1, para. 7. Posted at www.globalsecurity.org (accessed July 12, 2004). The report is printed in Greenberg and Dratel, *The Torture Papers,* pp. 383–404.

104. Denbeaux and Denbeaux, "Second Report on Guantanamo Detainees: Inter- and Intra-Departmental Disagreements about Who Is Our Enemy." Available at law.shu.edu/news/second_report_guantanamo_detainees_3_20_final.pdf, p. 25.

105. Ibid., p. 23.

106. Quoted in Joseph Margulies, *Guantanamo and the Abuse of Presidential Power* (New York: Simon and Schuster, 2006), p. 69.

107. Tim Golden, "Administration Officials Split over Stalled Military Tribunals," *New York Times,* October 25, 2004, p. A1, and Margulies, *Guantanamo,* p. 65.

108. Greg Miller, "Many Held at Guantanamo Not Likely Terrorists," *Los Angeles Times,* December 22, 2002.

109. Ibid.

110. Ibid.

111. Jane Mayer, "Outsourcing Torture," *New Yorker,* February 14, 2007, p. 1 of 14.

112. See Louis Fisher, "The State Secrets Privilege: Relying on Reynolds," *Political Science Quarterly* 122, no. 3 (2007): 385–408. See also Carol D. Leonnig and Eric Rich, "U.S. Seeks Silence on CIA Prisons," *Washington Post,* November 4, 2006, p. 1.

113. Mayer, "Outsourcing Torture," p. 12 of 14.

114. Doug Struck, "Cases of Detained Muslims Tarnish Canadian Mounties' Noble Image," *Washington Post,* December 15, 2006, p. A30.

115. Ian Austin, "Canadians Fault U.S. for Its Role in Torture Case," *New York Times,* September 19, 2006.

116. Struck, "Cases of Detained Muslims Tarnish Canadian Mounties' Noble Image." See also Margulies, *Guantanamo,* pp. 190–91.

117. This case is based on Neil A. Lewis, "Man Mistakenly Abducted by C.I.A. Seeks Reinstatement of Suit," *New York Times,* November 29, 2006, p. A15.

118. Dana Priest, "The Wronged Man," *Washington Post,* November 29, 2006, p. C1.

119. Craig Whitlock, "Germans Charge 13 CIA Operatives," *Washington Post,* February 1, 2007, p. A1, and Mark Landler, "German Court Challenges C.I.A. over Abduction," *New York Times,* January 31, 2007.

120. CNN, "Bush: CIA Holds Terror Suspects in Secret Prisons" (September 7, 2006) (edition.cnn.com/2006/POLITICS/09/06/bush.speech/index.html).

121. Priest, "Wronged Man."

122. This whole account is based on Michael Moss, "American Recalls Torment as a U.S. Detainee in Iraq," *New York Times,* December 8, 2006, pp. A1, A12.

123. *Padilla v. Rumsfeld* (352 F.3rd 695), quoted in Pious, *War on Terrorism and the Rule of Law,* pp. 130–37.

124. Dan Eggen, "Padilla Case Raises Questions about Anti-Terror Tactics," *Washington Post,* November 19, 2006, p. A3.

125. Deborah Sontag, "Defense Calls Padilla Incompetent for Trial," *New York Times,* February 23, 2007.

126. Sontag, "A Videotape Offers a Window into a Terror Suspect's Isolation," *New York Times,* December 4, 2006, p. A1, A22.

127. Ibid.

128. Sontag, "Jailers Testify about Padilla's Confinement," *New York Times,* February 28, 2007.

129. Sontag, "Videotape Offers a Window into a Terror Suspect's Isolation."

130. Eggen, "Padilla Case Raises Questions about Anti-Terror Tactics."

131. Peter Whorisky, "Jury Convicts Jose Padilla on Terror Charges," *Washington Post,* August 17, 2007, p. A1.

132. Craig Whitlock, "82 Inmates Cleared but Still Held at Guantanamo," *Washington Post,* April 29, 2007, p. A1.

133. Ibid.

134. Ibid.

135. William Glaberson, "Court Asked to Limit Lawyers at Guantanamo," *New York Times,* April 26, 2007.

136. "Unveiled Threats," *Washington Post,* January 12, 2007, p. A18.

137. See Scott Shane, "Detainees' Access to Lawyers Is Security Risk, C.I.A. Says," *New York Times,* November 5, 2006.

138. Scalia (joined by Stevens) dissent in *Hamdi v. Rumsfeld,* 542 U.S. 507 (2004).

Chapter Six

Epigraphs:

Memorandum for Alberto R. Gonzales, counsel to the President, "Standards of Conduct for Interrogation under 18 U.S.C. Sc. 2340-2340A" (August 1, 2002). Reprinted in Karen Greenberg and Joshua L. Dratel, eds., *The Torture Papers: The Road to Abu Ghraib* (Cambridge University Press, 2005), p. 172.

President Bush meets with President Torrios of Panama, Panama City, November 7, 2005 (www.whitehouse.gov/news/releases/2005/11/20051107.html).

Lewis Carroll, *The Annotated Alice,* annotated by Martin Gardner (New York: Bramhall House, 1960), p. 269.

1. President Bush was connected to torture practices by his suspension of the Geneva Agreements, his statements that the detainees at Guantanamo were "bad people," his arguments against the Detainee Treatment Act and threat to veto it, his arguments in favor of the Military Commissions Act, his veto of the bill that would have required the CIA to conform to the Army Field Manual on interrogation, and his personal, repeated questions about the interrogation of Khalid Sheikh Mohammed. For the latter, see Ron Suskind, *The One Percent Doctrine* (New York: Simon and Schuster, 2006), p. 229.

2. "Executive Order: Interpretation of the Geneva Conventions Common Article 3 as Applied to a Program of Detention and Interrogation Operated by the Central Intelligence Agency," July 20, 2007, posted on White House website.

3. Antonio M. Taguba, *Article 15-6 Investigation of the 800th Military Police Brigade,* February 26, 2003, hereinafter, the Taguba Report, part 1, sec. 2, no. 5. The report is printed in Greenberg and Dratel, *Torture Papers,* pp. 405–65. The types of "intentional abuse of detainees by military police" documented included: punching, slapping, and kicking detainees; jumping on their naked feet; videotaping and photographing naked male and female detainees; arranging naked male detainees in a pile and then jumping on them; positioning a naked detainee on an MRE Box, with a sandbag on his head, and attaching wires to his fingers, toes, and penis to simulate electrical torture; a male MP guard having sex with a female detainee; using military working dogs (without muzzles) to intimidate and frighten detainees.

4. Taguba Report, part 1, sec. 2, no. 10.

5. Seymour Hersh, "The General's Report," *New Yorker,* June 25, 2007.

6. Eric Schmitt, "Army Report Says Flaws in Detention Didn't Cause Abuse," *New York Times,* July 23, 2004.

7. *Investigation of the Abu Ghraib Detention Facility and 205th Military Intelligence Brigade,* Major General George R. Fay, investigating officer (hereinafter the *Fay Report*). Printed in *The Abu Ghraib Investigations,* edited by Steven Strasser (New York: Public Affairs, 2004), pp. 109–71.

8. *Fay Report,* p. 110–11.

9. *AR 15–6 Investigation of the Abu Ghraib Detention Facility and 205th MI Brigade,* LTG Anthony R. Jones (hereinafter *Jones Report*). Reprinted in Greenberg and Dratel, *Torture Papers,* pp. 991–1018.

10. *Jones Report,* pp. 15–16.

11. Ibid., pp. 3, 4, 5, 17.

12. Ibid., p. 17.

13. FBI officials had complained in December 2003 that "DOD interrogators impersonating Supervisory Special Agents of the FBI" worked with detainees and that "these tactics have produced no intelligence of a threat neutralization nature to date and CITF believes that techniques have destroyed any chance of prosecuting this detainee." They feared that if the interrogation became public, "The

FBI will [be] left holding the bag before the public." The memo was released via a FOIA request and posted on the ACLU website.

14. E-mail printout: From [deleted] (DL) (FBI); Sent Saturday, May 22, 2004, 2:08 P.M.; to: Briese, M C (Div13) (FBI); Subject: Request for Guidance regarding OGC EC, dated 5/19/04. It is not clear what memo the writer was referring to, or whether the FBI official had seen such a memo or merely believed that it existed. The memo was released via a FOIA request and posted on the ACLU website.

15. From [deleted] (BS) (FBI); Sent Monday, August 02, 2004 10:46 A.M.; To [deleted] (INSD) (FBI); Subject: RE GTMO. The memo begins "As requested, here is a brief summary of what I observed at GTMO." The memo was released via a FOIA request and posted on the ACLU website.

16. *Report of the International Committee of the Red Cross (ICRC) on the Treatment by the Coalition Forces of Prisoners of War and Other Protected Persons by the Geneva Conventions in Iraq during Arrest, Internment and Interrogation* (February 2004). Posted at www.globalsecurity.org (accessed July 12, 2004). The report is printed in Greenberg and Dratel, *Torture Papers,* pp. 383–404.

17. ICRC Report, Executive Summary.

18. ICRC Report, sec. 3.1.

19. ICRC Report, sec. 1, paragraph 7.

20. The numbers are based primarily on Scott A. Allen and others, "Deaths of Detainees in the Custody of US Forces in Iraq and Afghanistan from 2002 to 2005," Medscape.com, December 5, 2006 (www.medscape.com/viewarticle/ 547787). The ACLU compiled lists of homicides of detainees, "Autopsy Reports Reveal Homicides of Detainees in U.S. Custody," which are posted on its website (action.aclu.org/torturefoia/released/102405). See also Tom Squitieri and Dave Moniz, "One Third of Detainees Who Died Were Assaulted," *USA Today,* May 31, 2004, p. 1; Bradley Graham, "Number of Army Probes of Detainee Deaths Rises to 33," *Washington Post,* May 22, 2004, p. A17; Steven Lee Myers, "Military Completed Death Certificates for 20 Prisoners Only after Months Passed," *New York Times,* May 31, 2004, p. A8. Bradley Graham, "Army Investigates Wider Iraq Offenses: Cases Include Deaths, Assaults outside Prison," *Washington Post,* June 1, 2004; editorial, "The CIA's Prisoners," *Washington Post,* July 15, 2004, p. A20. The CIA inspector general is conducting an investigation of a prisoner who died after questioning by CIA interrogators at Abu Ghraib. John Barry, Michael Hirsh, and Michael Isikoff, "The Roots of Torture," *Newsweek,* May 24, 2004, pp. 28–34.

21. Another variation on this scenario is a case, reported by Mark Bowden, in which a young boy was kidnapped, tied, and gagged and hidden by the kidnapper. When he was captured by police, he would not reveal where the boy was. The police thought the boy might still be alive and threatened to bring in an interrogator to apply torture to the man to get him to reveal the location of the boy (the man revealed the location, but the boy was dead). A reasonable person

might conclude that torture was justified in this instance. See Mark Bowden, "The Dark Art of Interrogation," *Atlantic Monthly,* October 2003 (www.the atlantic.com [accessed July 29, 2004]).

22. Jane Mayer, "Whatever It Takes," *New Yorker,* February 19 and 26, 2007, pp. 66–82.

23. Amy Argetsinger and Roxanne Roberts, "The Reliable Source," *Washington Post,* November 5, 2007, p. C3, and November 8, 2007, p. C3.

24. Mayer, "Whatever It Takes," p. 68.

25. Ibid., p. 72.

26. For an insightful analysis and refutation of the ticking time bomb scenario, see David Luban, "Liberalism, Torture, and the Ticking Bomb," *Virginia Law Review* 91, no. 6 (October 2005): 1425.

27. See the detailed analysis of interrogation methods by Bowden, "Dark Art of Interrogation."

28. For examples where torture evidently worked in preventing terrorist attacks, see John Yoo, *War by Other Means* (New York: Atlantic Monthly Press, 2006), pp. 189–91.

29. Seymour M. Hersh, "Torture at Abu Ghraib," *New Yorker,* May 10, 2004, p. 47. See also Tim Golden and Don Van Natta Jr., "U.S. Said to Overstate Value of Guantanamo Detainees," *New York Times,* June 21, 2004, p. 1.

30. Sec. 4A3, Current Doctrine. The relevant portions of the Army Field Manual 34–52 are attached to Secretary Rumsfeld's Memorandum for the Commander, U.S. Southern Command; Subject: Counter-Resistance Techniques in the War on Terrorism (S), April 16, 2003.

31. Douglas Jehl, "Questions Left by C.I.A. Chief on Torture Use," *New York Times,* March 18, 2005, p. A1.

32. John McCain, "Torture's Terrible Toll," *Newsweek,* November 25, 2005.

33. Michael Isikoff, "Forget the 'Poisons and Deadly Gases,'" *Newsweek,* July 5, 2004, p. 6; Douglas Jehl, "High Qaeda Aide Retracted Claim of Link with Iraq," *New York Times,* July 31, 2004; Dana Priest, "Al Qaeda-Iraq Link Recanted," *Washington Post,* August 1, 2004, p. A20. See also Joseph Margulies, *Guantanamo* (New York: Simon and Schuster, 2006), p. 119. The DIA concluded in February 2002 that "it is more likely this individual is intentionally misleading the debriefers. Ibn al-Shaykh has been undergoing debriefs for several weeks and may be describing scenarios to the debriefers that he knows will retain their interest." Letter from Kathleen P. Turner, Chief of the Office of Congressional Affairs, Defense Intelligence Agency, October 26, 2005; "Levin Releases Report on Pre-War Intelligence," press release (http://levin.senate.gov/newsroom/release.cfm?id=227625) [accessed March 11, 2008]).

34. Jane Mayer, "Outsourcing Torture," *New Yorker,* February 14, 2007, p. 9 of 14.

35. Vikram Dodd and Tania Branigan, "Questioned at Gunpoint, Shackled, Forced to Pose Naked, British Detainees Tell Their Stories of Guantanamo Bay,"

The Guardian, August 4, 2004. Posted on TruthOut.org (accessed August 9, 2004). Mayer, "Outsourcing Torture."

36. Department of Defense news release, June 12, 2005 (www.defenselink. mil/releases/2005/nr20050612-3661.html); Department of Defense, Interrogation Log, Detainee 063 (November 23, 2002 to January 11, 2003), at www. time.com/time2006/log/log.pdf; as cited in Retired Federal Jurists Amici Curiae Brief in Support of Petitioners' Supplemental Brief Regarding the Military Commissions Act of 2006 (November 1, 2006), U.S. Court of Appeals for the District of Columbia, *Khaled A. F. al Odah, et al. v. U.S.,* pp. 3, 12–13.

37. Josh White, "Interrogation Research Is Lacking, Report Says," *Washington Post,* January 16, 2007, p. A15; Intelligence Science Board, *Educing Information—Interrogation: Science and Art—Foundations for the Future,* National Defense Intelligence College, 2007.

38. Letter from General Petraeus to the troops, May 10, 2007, quoted in testimony of Elisa Massimino, before the Committee on the Judiciary of the House of Representatives, December 20, 2007, p. 6.

39. President Bush, Prime Minister Blair Discuss War on Terror, press conference, July 17, 2003 (www.whitehouse.gov/news/releases/2003/07/20030717-9.html).

40. Donna Miles, "Bush: Guantanamo Detainees Receiving Humane Treatment," Department of Defense, American Forces Press Service, June 20, 2005 (www.defenselink.mil/news/newsarticle.aspx?id=16359 [accessed April 2, 2005]). Although this statement was made in 2005, it represents President Bush's tone since 9/11. By 2005 it had been demonstrated that many detainees were innocent and posed no threat to the United States.

41. Fox News, "Rumsfeld: Afghan Detainees at Gitmo Bay Will Not Be Granted POW Status," January 28, 2002 (www.foxnews.com/story/0,2933, 44084,00.html).

42. News conference of Secretary of Defense Rumsfeld, January 27, 2002 (www.defenselink.mil/transcripts/2002/t01282002_t0127enr.html).

43. See Strasser, ed., *Abu Ghraib Investigations,* p. 69. James R. Schlesinger chaired a panel that resulted in publication of the *Final Report of the Independent Panel to Review Department of Defense Detention Operations* (hereinafter Schlesinger Report), reprinted in *The Abu Ghraib Investigations.* The report notes that "despite the number of visits and the intensity of interest in actionable intelligence, however, the panel found no undue pressure exerted by senior officials. Nevertheless, their eagerness for intelligence may have been perceived by interrogators as pressure."

44. R. Jeffrey Smith, "Bush Adviser Toured Abu Ghraib," *Washington Post,* June 19, 2004; CBS News Report, "Prison Officer Says He Felt Heat," June 18, 2004.

45. According to the Schlesinger Report, "Interrogators and list of techniques circulated from Guantánamo and Afghanistan to Iraq." See Strasser, ed., *Abu Ghraib Investigations,* p. 7.

46. Barry and others, "The Roots of Torture," p. 32.

47. The relevant portions of the Army Field Manual 34–52 were attached to Secretary Rumsfeld's Memorandum for the Commander, U.S. Southern Command; Subject: Counter-Resistance Techniques in the War on Terrorism (S) (April 16, 2003). In 2006 the newly revised Army Field Manual on Human Intelligence Collector Operations (FM 2-22.3, FM 34–52) was released and did not include the "robust" interrogation techniques favored by the administration.

48. DODJTF 170 (October 11, 2002) Memorandum for Commander, Joint Task Force 170; Subject: Request for Approval of Counter-Resistance Strategies, signed: Jerald Phifer, LTC, USA, Director; J2. In Greenberg and Dratel, *Torture Papers*, pp. 227–28.

49. Ibid.

50. Quoted in Jess Bravin, "Pentagon Report Set Framework for Use of Torture," *Wall Street Journal*, June 7, 2004.

51. Memorandum for Commander, United States Southern Command, Subject: Counter-Resistance Strategies (October 11, 2002); signed Michael E. Dunlavey. In Greenberg and Dratel, *Torture Papers*, p. 225.

52. Action Memo for: Secretary of Defense; From: William J. Haynes II, General Counsel; Subject: Counter-Resistance Techniques (November 27, 2002). On this memo, Secretary Rumsfeld wrote by hand, "However, I stand for 8–10 hours a day. Why is standing limited to 4 hours?" This penned comment by Rumsfeld trivializing the use of stress positions must have been intended as either a glib joke or a serious question. In either case it is unworthy of the secretary of defense. If he was serious, it demonstrates an amazing lack of familiarity with the stress techniques used by interrogators, which often involved standing in awkward and painful positions for long periods of time in the context of little food, little sleep, terror of dogs, and disorientation due to combinations of these techniques. If he did not, in fact, understand this, he was naïve. If it was a joke, it was made in poor taste for the official of the United States government who authorized the series of techniques that led to the abuses of Abu Ghraib. A photocopy of the memo is contained in Greenberg and Dratel, *Torture Papers,* p. 236.

53. Memorandum for Commander USSOUTHCOM; Subject: Counter-Resistance Techniques (January 15, 2003), signed by Secretary Rumsfeld. In Greenberg and Dratel, *The Torture Papers,* p. 239. See also Golden and Van Natta, "U.S. Said to Overstate Value of Guantánamo Detainees."

54. Memorandum for Commander USSOUTHCOM; Subject: Counter-Resistance Techniques (January 15, 2003), signed by Secretary Rumsfeld. In Greenberg and Dratel, *Torture Papers,* p. 239.

55. Memorandum for the Commander, U.S. Southern Command; Subject: Counter-Resistance Techniques in the War on Terrorism (S) (April 16, 2003), signed by Secretary Rumsfeld. Printed in Greenberg and Dratel, *Torture Papers,* p. 360–63.

56. Schlesinger Report, in Strasser, ed., *Abu Ghraib Investigations,* p. 33.

57. See Schlesinger Report, in Strasser, ed., *Abu Ghraib Investigations,* p. 72, for specification of techniques used at Guantánamo and Afghanistan.

58. According to a DOD handout to the press of June 22, 2004, category 2 techniques that were actually used at Guantánamo included isolation, deprivation of light, 20-hour interrogations and forced grooming. Those approved but not used, according to the press handout, included hooding, removal of clothing, use of dogs, and noninjurious physical contact.

59. Bravin, "Pentagon Report Set Framework for Use of Torture."

60. Golden and Van Natta, "U.S. Said to Overstate Value of Guantánamo Detainees," p. 1. See also Seymour Hersh, *Chain of Command* (New York: HarperCollins, 2004), pp. 2–3.

61. Scott Higham, Josh White, and Christian Davenport, "A Prison on the Brink," *Washington Post,* May, 9, 2004, p. A1.

62. Mark Marzzetti, Julian E. Barnes, and Edward T. Pound, "Inside the Iraq Prison Scandal," *U.S. News and World Report,* May 24, 2004, p. 22. See the elaboration of Karpinski on the Miller takeover of Abu Ghraib in her interview by Leon Wordon, "Newsmaker Interview: Brig. Gen. Janis Karpinski," *Signal Newspaper* (Santa Clara, Calif.), July 4, 2004, posted on Turthout.org, accessed July 10, 2004.

63. Schlesinger Report, in Strasser, ed., *Abu Ghraib Investigations,* p. 8. See also Marzzetti and others, "Inside the Iraq Prison Scandal," p. 22.

64. Taguba Report, "Assessment of DOD Counter-Terrorism Interrogation and Detention Operations I Iraq (MG Miller's Assessment)," no. 2. See also Marzzetti and others, "Inside the Iraq Prison Scandal," p. 22.

65. Taguba Report, "10 Coments on MG Miller's Assessment," sec. 1 and 2.

66. Taguba Report, part 1, sec. 11b.

67 Ibid., sec. 11.

68. Ibid., sec. 12.

69. R. Jeffrey Smith and Josh White, "General Granted Latitude at Prison," *Washington Post,* June 12, 2004, p. 1, A18.

70. Interview by Wordon, "Newsmaker Interview: Brig. Gen. Janis Karpinski."

71. Memorandum for Commander, U.S. Central Command; Subject: CJTF-7 Interrogation and Counter-Resistance Policy (September 14, 2003), signed by General Sanchez.

72. Memorandum for C2 and C3, Combined Joint Task Force Seven, Baghdad, Iraq 09335, Commander, 205th Military Intelligence Brigade; Subject CJTF-7 Interrogation and Counter-Resistance Policy (September 14, 2003).

73. Smith and White, "General Granted Latitude at Prison." General Sanchez has denied approving the use of dogs, sleep deprivation, or noise. Jackson Diehl, "Officers' Unheroic Example," *Washington Post,* July 19, 2004, p. A17.

74. Schlesinger Report, in Strasser, ed., *Abu Ghraib Investigations,* pp. 8–9.

75. Ibid., p. 9.

76. Taguba Report, part 3, sec. C.8.A.1.

77. This line of reasoning follows that of Karen Greenberg in "Bush's Criminal Confessions" (salon.com, December 11, 2006 [accessed March 3, 2007]).

78. Memorandum for William J. Haynes II, General Counsel, DOD; from John Yoo, RE: Application of Treaties and Laws to al Qaeda and Taliban Detainees (January 9, 2002), in Greenberg and Dratel, *Torture Papers*, pp. 38–79.

79. Memorandum for Alberto R. Gonzales, Counsel to the President, and William J. Haynes II, General Counsel of the Department of Defense, from Assistant Attorney General Jay S. Bybee, RE: *Application of Treaties and Laws to al Qaeda and Taliban Detainees* (January 22, 2002), printed in Greenberg and Dratel, *Torture Papers*, pp. 81–121.

80. Memorandum for the President (January 25, 2002) From Alberto R. Gonzales. Subject: Decision RE application of the Geneva Convention on Prisoners of War to the Conflict with al Qaeda and the Taliban (printed in Greenberg and Dratel, *Torture Papers,* pp. 118–21). According to *Newsweek,* the memo was "actually" written by David Addington, Vice President Cheney's legal aide. Daniel Klaidman, "Homesick for Texas," *Newsweek,* July 12, 2004, p. 32. Gonzales has been criticized in the press for saying that the "new paradigm" renders the Geneva limitations "quaint." But the context of his use of the word "quaint" is not as damning as excerpting the word makes it seem. The end of the sentence reads, "renders quaint some of its provisions requiring that captured enemy be afforded such things as commissary privileges, scrip (i.e., advance of monthly pay), athletic uniforms, and scientific instruments." Whether Gonzales correctly characterized the Geneva requirements is a separate issue.

81. Memorandum to: Counsel to the President and Assistant to the President for National Security Affairs, From: Colin L. Powell (January 26, 2002), Subject: Draft Decision Memorandum for the President on the Applicability of the Geneva Convention to the Conflict in Afghanistan, pp. 2, 4. The memo is printed in Greenberg and Dratel, *Torture Papers,* pp. 122–25. Many of the memoranda and oral directives included statements that detainees were to be treated "humanely" despite the more aggressive interrogation techniques to which they could be subjected. The problem was that if the detainees were in fact treated humanely, it would be more difficult to extract information from them. Thus these statements must have been considered to be pro forma, while the overall thrust of the directives was that detainees were to be subject to more aggressive interrogation techniques that were outside the Geneva Convention limits.

82. Ibid., "Comments on the Memorandum of January 25, 2002," appended to memorandum.

83. Memorandum for the Vice President and others, Subject: Humane Treatment of al Qaeda and Taliban Detainees (February 7, 2002), signed by President Bush. The memorandum is reproduced in Greenberg and Dratel, *Torture Papers,* pp. 134–35.

84. For a detailed analysis of the legal issues involved in the treatment of prisoners and the international and legal obligations of the United States regarding detainees, see Robert K. Goldman and Brian D. Tittemore, "Unprivileged Combatants and the Hostilities in Afghanistan: Their Status and Rights under International Humanitarian and Human Rights Law" (Washington: American Society of International Law Task Force Paper, 2002). See also Jennifer K. Elsea, "Lawfulness of Interrogation Techniques under the Geneva Conventions," Congressional Research Service Report to Congress (RL32567), September 8, 2004; Jennifer K. Elsea, "U.S. Treatment of Prisoners in Iraq: Selected Legal Issues," Congressional Research Service Report for Congress (RL32395), December 2, 2004; and L. C. Green, *The Contemporary Law of Armed Conflict* (Manchester University Press, 1993).

85. Schlesinger Report, in Strasser, ed., *Abu Ghraib Investigations*, p. 29.

86. "Memorandum for General Counsel of the Department of the Air Force," from Thomas J. Romig, Major General, U.S. Army, The Judge Advocate General (not dated). Quoted in Richard M. Pious, *The War on Terrorism and the Rule of Law* (Los Angeles: Roxbury, 2006), pp. 196–97.

87. John Barry and others, "Roots of Torture," pp. 28–34; Seymour M. Hersh, "The Gray Zone," *New Yorker*, May 24, 2004, p. 42.

88. See the Schlesinger Report, in Strasser, ed., *Abu Ghraib Investigations*, pp. 7, 34, 35.

89. For an argument that the president is bound by treaties, see Derek Jinks and David Sloss, "Is the President Bound by the Geneva Conventions?" *Cornell Law Review* 90 (November 2004): 97. They conclude that presidents can terminate or suspend a treaty as long as the provisions of the treaty provide for it and the president's actions are in accord with international law, though he cannot unilaterally abrogate a treaty without congressional approval.

90. See memorandum from Gordon England, Subject: Application of Common Article 3 of the Geneva Conventions to the Treatment of Detainees in the Department of Defense (July 7, 2006): "The Supreme Court has determined that Common Article 3 to the Geneva Conventions of 1949 applies as a matter of law to the conflict with Al Qaeda."

91. On POWs see Green, *Contemporary Law of Armed Conflict*, pp. 188–206, p. 197.

92. Convention (III) relative to the Treatment of Prisoners of War. Geneva, August 12, 1949. Article 17, paragraph 4, provides that "No physical or mental torture, nor any other form of coercion, may be inflicted on prisoners of war to secure from them information of any kind whatever. Prisoners of war who refuse to answer may not be threatened, insulted, or exposed to unpleasant or disadvantageous treatment of any kind."

93. Geneva Convention III, Article 4.

94. Alberto Gonzales, "The Rule of Law and the Rules of War," *New York Times*, May 15, 2004, p. A27.

95. U.S. Army Regulation 190–8, quoted in Elsea, "U.S. Treatment of Prisoners in Iraq: Selected Legal Issues," Congressional Research Service Report for Congress (RL32395), December 2, 2004, p. 10.

96. Joseph Margulies, *Guantanamo and the Abuse of Presidential Power* (New York: Simon and Schuster, 2006), pp. 71–83.

97. The law was amended by the Military Commissions Act of 2006, discussed later in this chapter.

98. Memorandum for the President (January 25, 2002) from Alberto R. Gonzales, Subject: Decision RE application of the Geneva Convention on Prisoners of War to the Conflict with al Qaeda and the Taliban.

99. Memorandum for William J. Haynes II, General Counsel, Department of Defence, from Patrick F. Philbin, Deputy Assistant Attorney General, and John C. Yoo, Deputy Assistant Attorney General, December 29, 2001, p. 1.; quoted in Louis Fisher, *Military Tribunals and Presidential Power* (University Press of Kansas, 2005), p. 196. For an argument that the United States and the president are bound by international law, see Jordan J. Paust, *Beyond the Law* (New York: Cambridge University Press, 2007), pp. 20–24.

100. General Assembly Resolution 39/46, Annex, 39 U. GAOR Sup. No. 51, U.N. Doc. A.39/51 (1984).

101. Convention against Torture and Other Cruel, Inhuman or Degrading Treatment or Punishment, December 10, 1984, S. Treaty Doc. No. 100–20, 1465 U.N.T.S. 85. See also Elsea, "Lawfulness of Interrogation Techniques," p. 9.

102. Goldman and Tittemore, "Unprivileged Combatants," p. 49.

103. U.S. Army Field Manual 27, "U.S. Law of Land Warfare," paragraph 4(b), 7(c), quoted in L. C. Green, *Contemporary Law of Armed Conflict,* p. 31.

104. Elsea, "Lawfulness of Interrogation Techniques," p. 9.

105 Goldman and Tittemore, "Unprivileged Combatants and the Hostilities in Afghanistan," p. 38.

106. Ibid., p. 49.

107. See the analysis in *Hamdan v. Rumsfeld,* Slip Opinion, pp. 66–68.

108. Ibid., p. 71.

109. Ibid., p. 68, n. 63.

110. Elsea, "Lawfulness of Interrogation Techniques," p. 8.

111. Memorandum for the Deputy Attorney General, December 30, 2004, signed by Daniel Levin; in a footnote Levin wrote: "It has been suggested that the prohibition against torture has achieved the status of *jus cogens* (*i.e.,* a peremptory norm) under international law. See, e.g., *Siderman de Blake* v. *Republic of Argentina,* 965 F.2d 699, 714 (9th Cir. 1992); *Regina* v. *Bow Street Metro.* Stipendiary Magistrate Ex Parte Pinochet Ugarte (No. 3), [2000] 1 AC 147, 198; *see also* Restatement (Third) of Foreign Relations Law of the United States § 702 reporters' n. 5."

112. Memorandum for Alberto R. Gonzales, counsel to the President, "Standards of Conduct for Interrogation under 18 U.S.C. Sc. 2340-2340A" (August 1,

2002). Reprinted in Greenberg and Dratel, *Torture Papers,* p. 172. According to *Newsweek,* the memo was written in close consultation with White House lawyers. Daniel Klaidman, "Homesick for Texas," *Newsweek,* July 12, 2004, p. 32.

113. Ibid., pp. 1, 6.

114. Ibid. pp. 15, 24, 28.

115. In the memo printed in Greenberg and Dratel, *Torture Papers,* p. 44.

116. Quoted in Dana Milbank, "The Administration vs. the Administration," *Washington Post,* June 29, 2004, p. A21.

117. Memorandum for the President, From: Alberto R. Gonzales; Subject: Decision Re Application of the Geneva Convention on Prisoners of War to the Conflict with al Qaeda and the Taliban (January 25, 2002).

118. Goldsmith, *Terror Presidency,* p. 151. Goldsmith revealed that there was a "second August 1, 2002, opinion that still remains classified." This memo approved specific interrogation techniques that were classified.

119. Goldsmith, *Terror Presidency,* p. 155.

120. Memorandum Opinion for the Deputy Attorney General, Daniel Levin, Acting Assistant Attorney General, Office of Legal Counsel, December 30, 2004, "Legal Standards Applicable Under 18 U.S.C. §§ 2340-2340A *U.S.C.* §§ *2340-2340A.*" The memo "supersedes in its entirety the August 1, 2002, opinion of this Office entitled Standards of Conduct under 18 U.S.C. §§ 2340-2340A." That statute prohibits conduct "specifically intended to inflict severe physical or mental pain or suffering." The Levin opinion concludes that "severe" pain under the statute is not limited to "excruciating or agonizing" pain or pain "equivalent in intensity to the pain accompanying serious physical injury, such as organ failure, impairment of bodily functions, or even death." The statute also prohibits certain conduct specifically intended to cause "severe physical suffering" distinct from "severe physical pain."

121. Memorandum for James B. Comey, Deputy Attorney General, December 30, 2005, Re: Legal Standards Applicable under 18 U.S.C. Sec. 2340–2340A (www.usdoj.gov/olc/18usc23402340a2.htm).

122. Jane Crawford Greenberg and Ariane de Vogue, "Bush Administration Blocked Waterboarding Critic," ABC News (abcnews.go.com/WN/DOJ/story?id=3814076&page=1 [accessed November 23, 2007]).

123. Goldsmith, *Terror Presidency,* p. 165. Footnote 8 was inserted in Levin's retraction memo at the insistence of the White House when Alberto Gonzales was still counsel to the president. See Greenberg and de Vogue, "Bush Administration Blocked Waterboarding Critic."

124. Yoo, *War by Other Means,* pp. 182–83.

125. Scott Shane, David Johnston, and James Risen, "Secret US Endorsement of Severe Interrogations," *New York Times,* October 4, 2007, p. 1. The article was based on interviews with more than twenty-four Bush administration officials who demanded anonymity. According to the article, several more secret memoranda were issued after 2005.

126. Shane, Johnston, and Risen, "Secret US Endorsement of Severe Interrogations," p. 1. In a Law Day talk at Fort Meade, home of the National Security Agency, Comey said, "We are likely to hear the words: 'If we don't do this, people will die.' . . . It takes far more than a sharp legal mind to say 'no' when it matters most . . . it takes moral character."

127. Bybee memo of August 1, 2002, p. 33.

128. Ibid., p. 31.

129. Ibid., p. 36.

130. Ibid., p. 39.

131. Article I, Section 8, also gives Congress the power "to provide for organizing, arming, and *disciplining* [emphasis added], the Militia, and for governing such Part of them as may be employed in the Service of the United States." A significant portion of U.S. troops in Iraq were from state National Guard units, especially those who were photographed abusing Iraqi prisoners.

132. Jane Mayer, "Outsourcing Torture," p. 8 of 14. John Yoo's belief in the legal right of the president to order torture was quite broad. When asked by Doug Cassel (director of the Notre Dame Law School Center for Civil and Human Rights) if it would be legal for the president to order that the testicles of a child of a suspect be crushed in order to get a suspect to talk, Yoo replied: "I think it depends on why the president thinks he needs to do that." Yoo could have replied that such an act would be morally wrong but that the president had the legal authority to do it, but he didn't. See Nat Hentoff, "Don't Ask, Don't Tell," *Village Voice,* January 27, 2006 (www.villagevoice.com/news/0605, hentoff,71946,6.html).

133. Bybee memo (August 1, 2002), p. 34.

134. Article VI of the Constitution also provides that "all Treaties made, or which shall be made, under the authority of the United States, shall be the supreme Law of the Land."

135. In a public statement, Senator McCain said that "the intelligence we collect must be reliable and acquired humanely. . . . To do differently not only offends our values as Americans, but undermines our war effort, because abuse of prisoners *harms*—not helps—us in the war on terror. . . . Mistreatment of our prisoners endangers U.S. troops who might be captured by the enemy—if not in this war, then in the next. And third, prisoner abuses exact on us a terrible toll in the war of ideas. . . ." From "Statement of Senator John McCain Amendment on (1) the Army Field Manual and (2) Cruel, Inhumane, Degrading Treatment," November 4, 2005 (www.humanrightsfirst.info/pdf/05117-etn-mccain-stat-detain-amdts-auth.pdf). See also his article, "Torture's Terrible Toll," *Newsweek,* November 22, 2005.

136. The Act defines cruel, inhuman, or degrading treatment as "the cruel, unusual, and inhumane treatment or punishment prohibited by the Fifth, Eighth, and Fourteenth Amendments to the Constitution, as defined in the United States Reservations, Declarations and Understandings to the United Nations Convention

against Torture and Other Forms of Cruel, Inhuman or Degrading Treatment of Punishment Done at New York, December 10, 1984." Source: "H.R. 2863, Department of Defense Appropriations Act, 2006 (Enrolled as Agreed to or Passed by Both House and Senate)" (thomas.loc.gov/cgi-bin/query/F?c109:7./ temp/~c109yVTxt7:e189414:).

137. Josh White, "President Relents, Backs Torture Ban," *Washington Post,* December 16, 2005, p. 1.

138. That is, if the U.S. person undertakes interrogation practices that "were officially authorized and determined to be lawful at the time that they were conducted, it shall be a defense that such officer, employee, member of the Armed Forces, or other agent did not know that the practices were unlawful and a person of ordinary sense and understanding would not know the practices were unlawful." See "H.R. 2863, Department of Defense Appropriations Act, 2006 (Enrolled as Agreed to or Passed by Both House and Senate)" (thomas.loc. gov/cgi-bin/query/F?c109:7./temp/~c109yVTxt7:e189414).

139. Dan Froomkin, "Bush Demands Freedom to Torture," White House World, washingtonpost.com, December 14, 2007 (www.washingtonpost.com/ ac2/wp-dyn/NewsSearch?sb=-1&st=froomkin). See the letter by former generals urging Congress to ignore Bush's veto threat, *Huffington Post* (www.huffington-post.com/2007/12/13/military-leaders-ignore-_n_76656.html?view=print).

140. The argument that the president's intent should be given equal weight with congressional intent when interpreting the law is undermined by the first words of Article I of the Constitution, "All legislative Powers herein granted shall be vested in a Congress of the United States. . . ." For an analysis of signing statements, see Phillip J. Cooper, "George W. Bush, Edgar Allan Poe, and the Use and Abuse of Presidential Signing Statements," *Presidential Studies Quarterly* 35, no. 3 (September 2005): 515–32.

141. The White House, "President's Statement on Signing of H.R. 2863, the 'Department of Defense, Emergency Supplemental Appropriations to Address Hurricanes in the Gulf of Mexico, and Pandemic Influenza Act, 2006,'" December 30, 2005 (www.whitehouse.gov).

142. For analysis of these constitutional issues see James P. Pfiffner, "Torture and Public Policy," *Public Integrity* 7, no. 4 (Fall 2005): 313–30.

143. Memorandum for the Vice President, et al., Subject: Humane Treatment of al Qaeda and Taliban Detainees (February 7, 2002), signed by President Bush. The memorandum is reproduced in Greenberg and Dratel, *Torture Papers,* pp. 134–35.

144. Even though Iraq was officially covered by the Geneva Conventions, the Schlesinger Report concluded that the techniques used at Guantánamo migrated to Abu Ghraib.

145. Peter Baker, "GOP Infighting on Detainees Intensifies," *Washington Post,* September 16, 2006, p. 1. See the transcript of President Bush's press conference

of September 15, 2006, at www.whitehouse.gov/news/releases/2006/09/2006
0915-2.html.

146. R. Jeffrey Smith, "Behind the Debate, CIA Techniques of Extreme Discomfort," *Washington Post,* September 16, 2006, p. A3; R. Jeffrey Smith, "Detainee Measure to Have Fewer Restrictions," *Washington Post,* September 26, 2006, p. 1; Charles Babington and Jonathan Weisman, "Senate Approves Detainee Bill Backed by Bush," *Washington Post,* September 29, 2006, p. 1.

147. According to Judge Evan Wallach, "To be effective, waterboarding is usually *real* drowning that simulates death. That is, the victim experiences the sensations of drowning; struggle, panic, breath-holding, swallowing, vomiting, taking water into the lungs. . . ." Evan Wallach, "Waterboarding Used to Be a Crime," *Washington Post,* November 4, 2007, p. B1. According to Malcom Nance, former master instructor and chief of training at the U.S. Navy Survival, Evasion, Resistance and Escape School in San Diego: "Waterboarding is not simulation. . . . Waterboarding is a controlled drowning . . . as the lungs are actually filling with water . . . the victim is drowning." Malcom Nance, blog (no title) in *Small Wars Journal* (www.smallwarsjournal.com/blog/2007/10/waterboarding-is-torture-perio/). A Japanese officer, Yukio Asano, was sentenced to fifteen years at hard labor for waterboarding an American in World War II. Walter Pincus, "Waterboarding Historically Controversial," *Washington Post,* October 5, 2006, p. 17.

148. See Shane and Liptak, "Shifting Power to a President," p. 1.

149. "Candidates on Use of Torture to Interrogate Detainees" (no author), *New York Times,* November 3, 2007, p. A13.

150. Tim Golden, "Detainee Memo Created Divide in White House," *New York Times,* October 1, 2006, p. 1.

151. The letter was posted on TimesOnLine on September 15, 2006 (www.timesonline.co.uk).

152. The letter is dated September 12, 2006, and is available at www.humanrightsfirst.info/pdf/06920-etn-krulak-ltr-mccain-ca3.pdf.

153. The letter is dated September 20, 2006, and is posted at www.humanrightsfirst.info/pdf/06920-etn-krulak-ltr-mccain-ca3.pdf. On the same website see also a letter to John McCain from former chairman of the Joint Chiefs of Staff John Vessey dated September 12, 2006.

154. Elsea, "Lawfulness of Interrogation Techniques," p. 5. Smith, "Behind the Debate, CIA Techniques of Extreme Discomfort," *Washington Post.*

155. Mark Mazzetti and Neil A. Lewis, "Military Lawyers Caught in the Middle on Tribunals," *New York Times,* September 16, 2006, p. 1.

156. "Interview of the Vice President by Scott Hennen, WDAY at Radio Day at the White House," Vice President's Office. White House website, October 24, 2006 (www.whitehouse.gov/news/releases/2006/10/print/20061024-7.html). See also Dan Eggen, "Cheney's Remarks Fuel Torture Debate," *Washington Post,*

October 27, 2006, p. A9; Neil A. Lewis, "Furor over Cheney Remark on Tactics for Terror Suspects," *New York Times,* October 28, 2006, p. A8.

157. "Executive Order: Interpretation of the Geneva Conventions Common Article 3 as Applied to a Program of Detention and Interrogation Operated by the Central Intelligence Agency," July 20, 2007, posted on White House website.

158. Mark Mazzetti, "C.I.A. Allowed to Resume Interrogations," *New York Times,* July 20, 2007.

159. See particularly Marty Lederman, "The CIA Interrogation Executive Order: Well, Did You Really Expect Anything Better?" Balkinization Blog, July 20, 2007 (balkin.blogspot.com/).

160. P. X. Kelley and Robert F. Turner, "War Crimes and the White House," *Washington Post,* July, 26, 2007, p. A21.

161. Quoted by Nat Hentoff, "Gitmo: The Worst of the Worst?" *Village Voice,* March 23, 2006 (villagevoice.com).

162. Excerpted in Pious, *War on Terrorism,* pp. 203–05.

163. Charles C. Krulak and Joseph P. Hoar, "It's Our Cage, Too," *Washington Post,* May 17, 2007, p. A17. John Hutson also commented on the danger of allowing any form of torture: "I know from the military that if you tell someone they can do a little of this for the country's good, some people will do a lot of it for the country's better." Scott, Johnston, and Risen, "Secret US Endorsement of Severe Interrogations," p. 1.

Chapter Seven

Epigraphs:

"President Bush: Information Sharing, Patriot Act Vital to Homeland Security," April 20, 2004 (www.whitehouse.gov/news/releases/2004/04/print/2004 0420-2.html).

Franklin quote from *Historical Review of Pennsylvania,* quoted in John Bartlett, *Bartletts's Familiar Quotations* (Boston, Mass.: Little Brown, 1980), p. 348.

1. In August 2007 President Bush signed a law that provided a framework for the administration to undertake warrantless surveillance that he had previously undertaken under his own authority. This will be treated later in the chapter.

2. See the press briefing by Attorney General Gonzales, on December 19, 2005 (www.whitehouse.gov/news/releases/2005/12/20051219-1.html). Part of the beginning of this chapter is taken from James P. Pfiffner, *The Modern Presidency* (Belmont, Calif.: Thompson Wadsworth, 2008).

3. 389 U.S. 347 (1967).

4. *United States* v. *U.S. District Court,* 407 U.S. 297 (1972). See Robert M. Bloom and William J. Dunn, "The Constitutional Infirmity of Warrantless NSA Surveillance," Boston College Law School, Legal Studies Research Paper Series (August 6, 2006), p. 64.

5. President's Radio Address, December 17, 2005 (www.whitehouse.gov/news/releases/2005/12/print/20051217.html).

6. Press briefing by Attorney General Alberto Gonzales and General Michael Hayden, principal deputy director for National Intelligence, White House Briefing Room (December 19, 2005), on White House website.

7. President's News Conference, *Weekly Compilation of Presidential Documents,* vol. 41 (December 19, 2005), p. 1885.

8. *Katz* v. *United States,* 389 U.S. 347 (1967).

9. For a discussion of these issues, see Louis Fisher, "Constitutional Limitations on Domestic Surveillance," statement before the House Committee on the Judiciary, June 7, 2007, pp. 1–2; and Elizabeth B. Bazan and Jennifer K. Elsea, "Presidential Authority to Conduct Warrantless Electronic Surveillance to Gather Foreign Intelligence Information," Congressional Research Service, January 5, 2006, pp. 12–14.

10. Quoted in Bazan and Elsea, "Presidential Authority," p. 13.

11. See *Amicus Curiae Brief ACLU, et al.,* v. *National Security Agency, et al.,* Sixth Circuit Court of Appeals (November 17, 2006), Nos. 06-2095, 06-2140, pp. 7–8.

12. 82 Stat. 214, 18 U.S. par 2511(3), as cited in Bazan and Elsea, "Presidential Authority," p. 17

13. Public Law 95-511, 92 Stat. 1783. See David Cole and others, "On NSA Spying: A Letter to Congress," *New York Review of Books,* February 9, 2006, p. 42.

14. 18 U.S.C. par. 2511(2)(f), Public Law 95-511, 92 State 1783, as quoted in Bazan and Elsea, "Presidential Authority," p. 15.

15. 50 U.S.C. par. 1801(f), par. 1805(a), quoted in *Amicus Curiae Brief ACLU, et al.,* v. *National Security Agency, et al.,* p. 11.

16. Bazan and Elsea, "Presidential Authority," pp. 25–26.

17. Bloom and Dunn, "The Constitutional Infirmity of Warrantless NSA Surveillance," pp. 20–22.

18. David E. Sanger, "In Address, Bush Says He Ordered Domestic Spying," *New York Times,* December 18, 2005, p. 1.

19. Ibid.

20. See Bloom and Dunn, "The Constitutional Infirmity of Warrantless NSA Surveillance," p. 69.

21. *Amicus Curiae Brief ACLU, et al.,* v. *National Security Agency, et al.,* p. 10.

22. Peter Baker and Charles Babington, "Bush Addresses Uproar over Spying," *Washington Post,* December 20, 2005, p. A8. According to data reported in the *New York Times,* from 1995 to 2004 the applications for warrants totaled 10,617, and the court refused only four. See David Johnston and Neil A. Lewis, "Defending Spy Program, Administration Cites Law," *New York Times,* December 23, 2005, p. A18.

23. ABC News, "Cheney Roars Back," December 18, 2005 (abcnews.com: abcnews.go.com/print?id=1419206).

24. *United States* v. *United States District Court,* 407 U.S. 279 (1972), p. 316.

25. Eric Lichtblau, "Bush Defends Spy Program and Denies Misleading Public," *New York Times,* January 2, 2006, p. 11.

26. Suzanne E. Spaulding, "Power Play," *Washington Post,* December 25, 2005, p. B1.

27. Charles Babington and Dafna Linzer, "Senator Sounded Alarm in '03," *Washington Post,* December 20, 2005, p. A10.

28. Fisher, "Constitutional Limitations on Domestic Surveillance."

29. Authorization for Use of Military Force, Public Law 107-40, 115 Stat. 224 (2001), passed the House and Senate on September 14, 2001, and was signed by the president on September 18, 2001. See Richard F. Brimmett, "Authorization of Use of Military Force in Response to the 9/11 Attacks (P.L. 107-40): Legislative History," Congressional Research Service (Order Code RS22357), January 4, 2006.

30. U.S. Department of Justice, Office of Legislative Affairs (December 22, 2005), letter to the ranking members from each party of each house of the Senate Select Committee on Intelligence and the House Permanent Select Committee on Intelligence, p. 2.

31. See *Morales* v. *Trans World Airlines,* 504 U.S. 374 (1992), quoting *International Paper Co.* v. *Oullette,* 479 U.S. 481 (1987): "Because we do not believe Congress intended to undermine this carefully drawn statute through a general saving clause. . . ."

32. 542 U.S. 507 (2004).

33. Department of Justice, "Legal Authorities Supporting the Activities of the National Security Agency Described by the President," January 19, 2006, p. 2.

34. See Tom Daschle, "Power We Didn't Grant," *Washington Post,* December 23, 2006, p. A21.

35. *Youngstown Sheet & Tube Co.* v. *Sawyer,* 343 U.S. 579, 609 (1952), Justice Frankfurter concurring; as quoted in David Cole and others, "On NSA Spying: A Letter to Congress," p. 42.

36. 126 S.Ct. 2749 (2006).

37. Press briefing by Attorney General Alberto Gonzales and General Michael Hayden, December 19, 2005 (www.whitehouse.gov/news/releases/2005/12/2005 1219-1.html).

38. This argument is made in Cole and others, "On NSA Spying: A Letter to Congress," p. 43.

39. Justice Department spokespersons said that the drafts were not intended to affect the NSA spying and that the proposals were not presented to the attorney general or the White House. Dan Eggen, "2003 Draft Legislation Covered Eavesdropping," *Washington Post,* January 28, 2006, p. A02.

40. Press briefing by Attorney General Alberto Gonzales, January 19, 2006 (www.whitehouse.gov/news/releases/2005/12/20051219-1.html).

41. See Morton Halperin and Jerry Berman, "A Legal Analysis of the NSA Warrantless Surveillance Program," draft of January 17, 2006, p. 6 (www.cdt. org/security/nsa).

42. *Youngstown Sheet and Tube* v. *Sawyer,* 343 U.S. 579 (1952).

43. Ibid., p. 587.

44. Ibid., pp. 637–38.

45. U.S. Department of Justice, "Legal Authorities Supporting the Activities of the National Security Agency Described by the President," p. 2; see also Department of Justice, Office of Legislative Affairs, letter to members of Congress, December 22, 2005, pp. 2–3.

46. Department of Justice, "Legal Authorities Supporting the Activities of the National Security Agency Described by the President," p. 3.

47. See Fisher, "Constitutional Limitations on Domestic Surveillance." See also Fisher, "Invoking Inherent Powers: A Primer," *Presidential Studies Quarterly* 37, no. 1 (March 2007).

48. Senate Report No. 95-604, 95th Congress, 1st session, Part 1 (1977), p. 16.

49. Bazan and Elsea, "Presidential Authority," p. 43.

50. Department of Justice, "Legal Authorities Supporting the Activities of the National Security Agency Described by the President," p. 1.

51. *Hamdi* v. *Rumsfeld,* 542 U.S. 507 (2004), p. 537.

52. See Cole and others, "On NSA Spying: A Letter to Congress," p. 43.

53. Eggen, "2003 Draft Legislation Covered Eavesdropping," p. A2.

54. Most of this account is taken from accounts of Comey's congressional testimony: David Johnston, "Bush Intervened in Dispute over N.S.A. Eavesdropping," *New York Times,* May 16, 2007; Dan Eggen and Paul Kane, "Gonzales Hospital Episode Detailed," *Washington Post,* May 16, 2007, p. A1. See also Eric Lichtblau and James Risen, "Justice Deputy Resisted Parts of Spy Program," *New York Times,* January 1, 2006, p. 1; Lichtblau, "Bush Defends Spy Program and Denies Misleading Public"; Daniel Klaidman, Stuart Taylor Jr., and Evan Thomas, "Palace Revolt," *Newsweek,* February 6, 2006, p. 39.

55. The quote is from FBI Director Mueller's personal diary, reproduced in Dan Eggen, "FBI Director's Notes Contradict Gonzales's Version of Ashcroft Visit," *Washington Post,* August 17, 2007, pp. 1, 5.

56. Johnston, "Bush Intervened in Dispute over N.S.A. Eavesdropping."

57. Dan Eggen, "White House Secrecy on Wiretaps Described," *Washington Post,* October 3, 2007.

58. Johnston, "Bush Intervened in Dispute over N.S.A. Eavesdropping."

59. Eggen, "FBI Director's Notes Contradict Gonzales's Version of Ashcroft Visit," p. 1.

60. Johnston, "Bush Intervened in Dispute over N.S.A. Eavesdropping."

61. Ibid.

62. Ibid.

63. All of the quotes and information in this paragraph come from Jack Goldsmith, *The Terror Presidency* (New York: Norton, 2007), pp. 180–82; Eggen, "White House Secrecy on Wiretaps Described."

64. Scott Shane, "Former Phone Chief Says Spy Agency Sought Surveillance Help before 9/11," *New York Times,* October 14, 2007, p. 27. See also Ellen Nakashima and Dan Eggen, "Former CEO Says U.S. Punished Phone Firm," *Washington Post,* November 13, 2007, p. 1. Most of the analysis in this paragraph is based on these two articles. Nacchio was prosecuted later for insider trading and sentenced to six years in prison, though he appealed his conviction. He maintained that when he refused to cooperate with NSA's request for what his counsel determined to be illegal access to client information, NSA decided not to grant him contracts that he had expected to receive.

65. See the comment by Marty Lederman on October 2, 2007, in the Balkinization Blog (balkin.blogspot.com). He points out the irony of the government giving access to many private individuals but not to Department of Justice officials. He argues that the reason was that Justice Department lawyers would have quickly discovered the flawed legal arguments that the White House used to justify the program.

66. "President Bush: Information Sharing, Patriot Act Vital to Homeland Security," April 20, 2004 (www.whitehouse.gov/news/releases/2004/04/print/20040420-2.html).

67. "President Bush Calls for Renewing the USA Patriot Act," Hershey, Pa., April 19, 2004 (www.whitehouse.gov/news/releases/2004/print/20040419-4.html).

68. "President Discusses Patriot Act," Columbus, Ohio, June 9, 2005 (www.whitehouse.gov/news/2005/06/print/20050609-2.html). Note that FISA only required a warrant when a communication involved a person in the United States. The president could legally conduct surveillance on foreigners outside the United States without obtaining a warrant.

69. Lichtblau, "Bush Defends Spy Program and Denies Misleading Public."

70. The administration may have also broken the law in not informing Congress of its warrantless surveillance as required by the National Security Act of 1947 as amended. See Alfred Cumming, "Statutory Procedures under Which Congress Is to Be Informed of U.S. Intelligence Activities, Including Covert Action," Congressional Research Service (January 18, 2006).

71. ABC News, "Cheney Roars Back," interview by Terry Moran, December 18, 2005 (abcnews.gocom/print?id=1419206).

72. President's Radio Address, December 17, 2005 (www.whitehouse.gov/news/releases/2005/12/print/20051217.html).

73. Jim VandeHei and Dan Eggen, "Cheney Cites Justifications for Domestic Eavesdropping," *Washington Post,* January 5, 2006, p. A2. For another statement to this effect by Cheney, see ABC News, "Cheney Roars Back."

74. On the regular forty-five-day review of the program, see U.S. Department of Justice, Office of Legislative Affairs, December 22, 2005, letter to the ranking members from each party of each house of the Senate Select Committee on Intelligence and the House Permanent Select Committee on Intelligence, p. 5.

75. Adam Liptak, "White House Shifting Tactics in Surveillance Cases," *New York Times,* January 19, 2007; Dan Eggen, "Court Will Oversee Wiretap Program," *Washington Post,* January 18, 2007, p. A1.

76. Charles Babington and Dan Eggen, "Gonzales Seeks to Clarify Testimony on Spying," *Washington Post,* March 1, 2006, p. 8.

77. James Risen, "Bush Administration Pulls Back on Surveillance Agreement," *International Herald Tribune,* May 2, 2007.

78. See Murray Waas, "Aborted DOJ Probe Probably Would Have Targeted Gonzales," *National Journal,* March 15, 2007 (www.truthout.org).

79. Scott Shane, "Waterboarding Focus of Inquiry by Justice Department," *New York Times,* February 23, 2008, p. 1.

80. James Risen, "Bush Signs Law to Widen Reach for Wiretapping," *New York Times,* August 6, 2007.

81. Justice Brandeis dissenting, *Olmstead* v. *United States,* 277 U.S. 438 (1928), p. 479.

82. American Bar Association, Resolution and Report, adopted by the House of Delegates, February 13, 2006.

Chapter Eight

Epigraph:
George W. Bush, Law Day 2007 Proclamation, White House, April 28, 2007 (www.whitehouse.gov/news/releases/2007/04/20070428-1.html).

1. "H.R. 2863, Department of Defense Appropriations Act, 2006 (Enrolled as Agreed to or Passed by Both House and Senate)" (thomas.loc.gov/cgi-bin/query/F?c109:7./temp/~c109yVTxt7:e189414:).

2. The White House, "President's Statement on Signing of H.R. 2863, the 'Department of Defense, Emergency Supplemental Appropriations to Address Hurricanes in the Gulf of Mexico, and Pandemic Influenza Act, 2006,'" December 30, 2005 (www.whitehouse.gov).

3. See Charlie Savage, *Takeover: The Return of the Imperial Presidency and the Subversion of American Democracy* (Boston: Little Brown, 2007), pp. 228–29. The signing statement can be found at www.whitehouse.gov/news/releases/2006/03/20060309-8.html.

4. White House, "President Bush Signs H.R. 4986, the National Defense Authorization Act for Fiscal Year 2008 into Law, January 28, 2008" (www.whitehouse.gov/news/releases/2008/01/20080128-10.html).

5. Max Farrand, ed., *The Records of the Federal Convention of 1787,* vol. 1 (Yale University Press, 1966), pp. 103–04.

6. See Christopher N. May, "Presidential Defiance of 'Unconstitutional' Laws: Reviving the Royal Prerogative," *Hastings Constitutional Law Quarterly* 21 (Summer 1994): 869–72, upon which this discussion is based.

7. Trial of the Seven Bishops, 12 State Trials 1831, 427 (K.B. 1688), cited in May, "Presidential Defiance of 'Unconstitutional' Laws," p. 871.

8. The English Bill of Rights of 1689 can be found at www.constitution. org/eng/eng_bor.htm.

9. William Blackstone, *Commentaries on the Laws of England,* vol. 2 (1765), p. 185; quoted in May, "Presidential Defiance of 'Unconstitutional' Laws," p. 872.

10. Philip J. Cooper, "George W. Bush, Edgar Allan Poe and the Use and Abuse of Presidential Signing Statements," *Presidential Studies Quarterly* 35, no. 3 (2005), p. 517.

11. Curtis A. Bradley and Eric A. Posner, "Presidential Signing Statements and Executive Power," *Public Law and Legal Theory Working Paper Series,* University of Chicago Law School (August 18, 2006).

12. T. J. Halstead, "Presidential Signing Statements: Constitutional and Institutional Implications," Congressional Research Service Report (R33667) (April 13, 2007), p. 3.

13. See Samuel A. Alito Jr., "Using Presidential Signing Statement to Make Fuller Use of the President's Constitutionally Assigned Role in the Process of Enacting Law," memorandum to the Litigation Strategy Working Group, February 5, 1986 (www.archives.gov/news/samuel-alito/accession-060-89-269/Acc 060-89-269-box6-SG-LSWG-AlitotoLSWG-Feb1986.pdf). Also Christopher Kelley, "A Matter of Direction: The Reagan Administration, the Signing Statement, and Legislative History," *William and Mary Bill of Rights Journal,* forthcoming (papers.ssrn.com/sol3/papers.cfm?abstract_id=992333).

14. Ralph Tarr to T. Kenneth Cribb, memorandum re: "Presidential Signing Statements," October 28, 1985, Records Group 60, Department of Justice Files of Stephen Galebach, 1985–1987, 060-89-269, box 3, folder: SG/Chronological File. Quoted in Savage, *Takeover,* pp. 232–33.

15. See Alito, "Using Presidential Signing Statements," p. 4.

16. Steven G. Calabresi and Daniel Lev, "The Legal Significance of Presidential Signing Statements," *Forum* 4, no. 2 (2006), Berkeley Electronic Press, p. 1.

17. Calabresi and Lev, "Legal Significance of Presidential Signing Statements," p. 1.

18. Address by Attorney General Edwin Meese III, National Press Club, Washington, D.C. (February 25, 1986).

19. Alito, "Using Presidential Signing Statements," quoted in Halstead, "Presidential Signing Statements," p. 3.

20. Christopher S. Kelley, "'Faithfully Executing' and 'Taking Care'—The Unitary Executive and the Presidential Signing Statement," paper presented at the American Political Science Association annual convention, 2002, p. 32.

21. Halstead, "Presidential Signing Statements," p. 5.

22. Walter Dellinger, Department of Justice, Office of Legal Counsel, "Presidential Authority to Decline to Execute Unconstitutional Statutes," 18 U.S. Op. Office of Legal Counsel (1994), cited in Halstead, "Presidential Signing Statements," p. 6.

23. Halstead, "Presidential Signing Statements," p. 8.

24. Statement of Michelle E. Boardman, Deputy Assistant Attorney General, Office of Legal Counsel, Department of Justice, before the Committee on the Judiciary of the Senate, June 27, 2006, p. 2.

25. Christopher Kelley keeps a running total of signing statements by President Bush on his website. As of February 13, 2008, President Bush had issued challenges to 1,167 provisions in laws. See www.users.muohio.edu/kelleyCS.

26. Savage, *Takeover*, p. 230.

27. Halstead, "Presidential Signing Statements," p. 10.

28. Ibid., p. 8.

29. See ibid., pp. 10–11.

30. Government Accountability Office, "Presidential Signing Statements Accompanying the Fiscal Year 2006 Appropriations Acts," letter to Senator Robert Byrd and Congressman John Conyers, June 18, 2007, pp. 9–10.

31. Bradley and Posner, "Presidential Signing Statements and Executive Power," p. 42.

32. Walter Dellinger, "The Legal Significance of Presidential Signing Statements," memorandum for Bernard N. Nussbaum, Counsel to the President, November 3, 1993 (www.usdoj.gov/ofc/signing.htm).

33. Calabresi and Lev, "Legal Significance of Presidential Signing Statements," p. 9.

34. Ibid., p. 5.

35. All quotations in this paragraph are from Calabresi and Lev, "The Legal Significance of Presidential Signing Statements," pp. 5–9.

36. *Chevron USA v. Natural Resources Defense Council*, 467 U.S. 837 (1984). See Calabresi and Lev, "Legal Significance of Presidential Signing Statements," p. 7.

37. Regional Rail Reorganization Act Cases 419 U.S. 102, at 132 (1974), quoted in Delliger, "Legal Significance of Presidential Signing Statements," p. 7 of 15.

38. Marc N. Garber and Kurt A. Wimmer, "Presidential Signing Statements as Interpretations of Legislative Intent: An Executive Aggrandizement of Power," *Harvard Journal on Legislation* 24 (1987): 363, at p. 367.

39. Ibid., p. 363, at p. 377.

40. Letter Opinion for the General Counsel, Department of Health and Human Services, "Authority of Agency Officials to Prohibit Employees from Providing information to Congress," OLC Opinion, May 21, 2004; quoted in Government Accountability Office, "Presidential Signing Statements Accompanying the Fiscal Year 2006 Appropriations Acts," p. 5.

41. Dellinger, "Legal Significance of Presidential Signing Statements."

42. Calabresi and Lev, "Legal Significance of Presidential Signing Statements," p. 8.

43. May, "Presidential Defiance of 'Unconstitutional' Laws: Reviving the Royal Prerogative," pp. 876–81.

44. Ibid.

45. Farrand, vol. 1, pp. 98–103.

46. May, "Presidential Defiance of 'Unconstitutional' Laws: Reviving the Royal Prerogative," pp. 877–78.

47. Farrand, vol. 2, p. 586.

48. May, "Presidential Defiance of 'Unconstitutional' Laws, p. 879.

49. Quoted in May, "Presidential Defiance of 'Unconstitutional' Laws," p. 884.

50. Statement of Michelle E. Boardman, p. 5.

51. Louis Fisher, "Signing Statements: Constitutional and Practical Limits," *William and Mary Bill of Rights Journal,* forthcoming.

52. See May, "Presidential Defiance of 'Unconstitutional' Laws," pp. 897–98.

53. 272 U.S. 52 (1926).

54. 295 U.S. 602 (1935).

55. For instance, in the Vision 100—Century of Aviation Reauthorization Act of 2003, President Bush said that the act "purports to limit the qualifications of the pool of persons from whom the President may select. . . . The executive branch shall construe [these provisions] . . . as advisory, as is consistent with the Appointments Clause." *Weekly Compilation of Presidential Documents,* vol. 39, p. 1796. Quoted in Cooper, "George W. Bush, Edgar Allan Poe, and the Use and Abuse of Presidential Signing Statements," p. 529.

56. See Fisher, "Signing Statements: Constitutional and Practical Limits," p. 19 of manuscript, citing the Brandeis dissent in *Myers.*

57. Quoted in Halstead, "Presidential Signing Statements," p. 5.

58. 462 U.S. 919 (1983).

59. In objecting to the legislative veto provisions of laws, President Bush used the *Chadha* case to make the point that Congress, in including a legislative veto in a law, was not complying with the presentment clause that requires any law to be presented to the president to provide the opportunity for a veto. But, as Phillip Cooper has pointed out, President Bush was using signing statements to nullify parts of laws without having to issue a veto. Phillip J. Cooper, "George W. Bush, Edgar Allan Poe, and the Use and Abuse of Presidential Signing Statements," p. 525. For instance, in a signing statement for the Department of

Defense, "Emergency Supplemental Appropriations Act, 2006," President Bush stated that "reprogramming of funds, shall be construed as calling solely for notification." See White House, "President's Statement on Signing of H.R. 2863," December 30, 2006, press release (White House website).

60. Fisher, "Signing Statements: Constitutional and Practical Limits."

61. See Louis Fisher, "Congress as Co-Manager of the Executive Branch," in James P. Pfiffner, *The Managerial Presidency* (Texas A&M University Press, 1999), p. 300.

62. President Bush rejected reporting requirements in an appropriation act for the reconstruction of Iraq and Afghanistan (H.R. 3289): "Provisions of the Act that require disclosure of information . . . shall be construed in a manner consistent with the President's constitutional authority to withhold information." See White House, "Statement by the President on H.R. 3289" (www.whitehouse.gov/news/releases/2003/11/print/20031106-12). For further examples of signing statements, see "Examples of the President's Signing Statements," *Boston Globe*, April, 30, 2006. See also Charlie Savage, "Bush Challenges Hundreds of Laws," *Boston Globe*, April 30, 2006. See also Savage, *Takeover*, pp. 237–39, and Cooper, "Presidential Signing Statements," pp. 527–29.

63. Quoted in Cooper, "George W. Bush, Edgar Allan Poe, and the Use and Abuse of Presidential Signing Statements," p. 523.

64. 492 F. 2nd 587 (D.C. Circuit 1974). See Fisher, "Signing Statements: Constitutional and Practical Limits," p. 15 of manuscript.

65. Dellinger, Presidential Authority to Decline to Execute Unconstitutional Statutes: Memorandum for the Honorable Abner J. Mikva, Counsel to the President, November 2, 1994, p. 4.

66. Robert Spitzer, *Saving the Constitution from Lawyers* (Cambridge University Press, 2008), pp. 94–96.

67. Calabresi and Lev, "Legal Significance of Presidential Signing Statements," p. 8. See also Christopher S. Yoo and others, "The Unitary Executive in the Modern Era," *Iowa Law Review* (2005): 601–10.

68. Statute Limiting the President's Authority to Supervise the Director of the Centers for Disease Control in the Distribution of an AIDS Pamphlet, 12 Op. Off. Legal Counsel, 46, 48 (1988); quoted in Government Accountability Office, "Presidential Signing Statements Accompanying the Fiscal Year 2006 Appropriations Acts," p. 5.

69. Spitzer, *Saving the Constitution from Lawyers*, p. 128.

70. Calabresi and Lev, "Legal Significance of Presidential Signing Statements," p. 3, quoting Garber and Wimmer, cited in n. 38 above.

71. Calabresi and Lev, "The Legal Significance of Presidential Signing Statements," p. 1.

72. Ibid., p. 4.

73. Ibid., p. 8, quoting *Youngstown*, 343 U.S. 579 at 610 (1952).

74. 395 U.S. 486, 547 (1969).

75. Mario M. Cuomo, "How Congress Forgot Its Own Strength," *New York Times,* October 7, 2007.

76. *INS* v. *Chadha,* 462 U.S. 919 (1983), p. 942 n. 13.

77. See James P. Pfiffner, *The President, the Budget, and Congress: Impoundment and the 1974 Budget Act* (Bolder, Colo.: Praeger, 1979). See also Fisher, *Presidential Spending Power.*

78. Pfiffner, *The President, the Budget and Congress,* pp. 102–04.

79. Halstead, "Presidential Signing Statements: Constitutional and Institutional Implications," p. 23.

80. Governmental Accountability Office, "Presidential Signing Statements Accompanying the Fiscal Year 2006 Appropriations Acts," p. 43.

Chapter Nine

Epigraphs:

John Locke, *Second Treatise of Government* (originally published in 1690), edited by C. B. Macpherson (Indianapolis, Ind.: Hackett, 1980), p. 103.

Justice Brandeis, *Olmstead* v. *U.S.,* 277 U.S. 438 (1928).

1. See Benjamin Wittes, "Terrorism, the Military and the Courts," *Policy Review* (June & July 2007): 25. Wittes characterized the administration's compliance with the Court: "But the administration's acceptance of a role for the judicial branch is more of a grudging concession to political and jurisprudential reality than an effort to imagine what the most effective judicial involvement would look like" (p. 36).

2. For an analysis of President Clinton's actions in asserting executive authority, see Nancy Kassop, "Clinton, the Constitution and Presidential Power: His Legacy for the Office of the President," paper presented at the Presidential Conference on William Jefferson Clinton at Hofstra University, Hempstead, N.Y., November 10–12, 2005.

3. Bo Li, "What Is Rule of Law?" *Perspectives,* vol. 1, no. 5; available at www.oycf.org/perspectives/5. The following discussion follows part of Li's argument.

4. Thomas Paine, *Collected Writings,* edited by Eric Foner (Washington: Library of America, 1995), p. 34.

5. J. C. Holt, *Magna Carta* (Cambridge University Press, 1992), p. 118–19.

6. *Marbury* v. *Madison,* 5 U.S. 137.

7. A.V. [Albert Venn] Dicey, *The Law of the Constitution* (Indianapolis: Liberty Fund, 1982). Dicey published his first edition in 1885 and his eighth edition in 1915. This volume is a printing of the eighth edition. The two quotes are taken from pages 110 and 114, respectively.

8. George W. Bush, "Address to a Joint Session of Congress and the American People," U.S. Capitol, Washington, D.C., September 20, 2001 (www.whitehouse.gov/news/releases2001/09/20010920-8.html).

9. Excerpt of the Frost interview televised on May 19, 1977, in "*United States v. Nixon* (1974)," published at www.landmark cases.org/Nixon/nixonview.html.

10. Quote from Jim VandeHei and Michael A. Fletcher, "Bush Says Election Ratified Iraq Policy," *Washington Post*, January 16, 2005, p. A1. The Plebiscitary Presidency idea was articulated by Arthur Schlesinger Jr. in *The Imperial Presidency* (Boston: Houghton Mifflin, 1973), p. 376: "The President, instead of being accountable every day to Congress and public opinion, would be accountable every four years to the electorate. Between elections, the President would be accountable only through impeachment and would govern, as much as he could, by decree." See also Theodore Lowi, *The Personal President* (Cornell University Press, 1985).

11. John Yoo, *War by Other Means* (New York: Atlantic Monthly Press, 2006), p. 180.

12. Hearing of the Senate Judiciary Committee on "*Hamdan v. Rumsfeld*: Establishing a Constitutional Process" (July 11, 2006). Found on Lexis-Nexis, August 31, 2007.

13. *Report of the Congressional Committees Investigating the Iran-Contra Affair*, Minority Report of Representative Dick Cheney and four members of the House and two Senators, 110th Congress, 1st Session (November 1987), p. 665. Vice President Cheney said that the Minority Report was a reflection of his view of the constitutional powers of the president: "If you want reference to an obscure text, go look at the minority views that were filed with the Iran-Contra Committee. . . . They were actually authored by a guy working for me, for my staff, that I think are very good in laying out a robust view of the President's prerogative with respect to the conduct of especially foreign policy and national security matters." White House press release, December 20, 2005 (www.white house.gov/news/releases/2005/12/20051220-9.html).

14. Bob Woodward, "Cheney Upholds Power of the Presidency," *Washington Post*, January 20, 2005, p. A7. See also Cheney's statement in Susan Page, "Congress Pushing Back against Bush's Expansion of Presidential Authority," *USA Today*, July 6, 2006, p. 1A: "The president of the United States needs to have his constitutional powers unimpaired. I do think that, to some extent now, we've been able to restore the legitimate authority of the presidency."

15. For an analysis of presidential lies, see James P. Pfiffner, *The Character Factor* (Texas A&M University Press, 2004), chapters 2 and 3. For an analysis of Iran-Contra, see pp. 124–30.

16. See Louis Fisher, *Congressional Abdication on War and Spending* (Texas A&M University Press, 2000).

17. *McCulloch* v. *Maryland*, 17 U.S. 316 (1819).

18. *Korematsu* v. *U.S.*, 323 U.S. 214 (1944). I would like to thank Bob Dudley for calling this statement to my attention.

19. Both quotes from John Locke, *Second Treatise of Government* (originally published in 1690), edited by C. B. Macpherson (Indianapolis: Hackett, 1980), pp. 86–87, chapter 14.

20. Colin Campbell, Bert A. Rockman, and Andrew Rudalevige, eds., *The George W. Bush Legacy* (Washington: CQ Press, forthcoming), p. 130, chapter 6.

21. *Report of the Congressional Committees Investigating the Iran-Contra Affair*, p. 449.

22. "National Defense Strategy of the United States of America," available at: www.globalsecurity.org/military/library/policy/dod/nds-usa_mar2005_ib.htm.

23. Aharon Barak, "The Supreme Court and the Problem of Terrorism," from *Judgments of the Israel Supreme Court: Fighting Terrorism within the Law* (January 2, 2005), available at www.jewishvirtuallibrary.org/jsource/Politics/scterror.html.

INDEX

Aberbach, Joel, 243
Abraham, Stephen E., 110–11, 112
Abu Ghraib, 1, 115, 130–32, 135, 136, 140, 141, 142, 143–45, 151
Act of Succession, 52
Act of Supremacy, 45
Act of Union, 51
Acton, Lord, 1
Adams (J.) administration, 80
Addington, David, 184
Adler, David, 72–73, 79
Afghanistan, 4, 85, 115, 116
Alito, Samuel, 200, 201
Al Qaeda, 114, 115; Bush claims of executive authority over, 157; conditions of detention and interrogation for members of, 99, 100, 102, 106, 117, 144, 164, 166, 213; domestic surveillance and, 169, 170; Geneva Convention protections, 129, 146, 147–49, 153, 155, 160; habeas corpus rights for members of, 93, 99, 106–08; Padilla and, 121, 123. *See also* Detainees in war on terror
Anne, Queen of England, 51–52
Appointment power, 216–17
Arar, Maher, 117–18
Army Field Manual, U.S., 129, 137, 141–42, 153, 159, 230
Articles of Confederation, 54, 58–59, 60, 76

Ashcroft, John, 99, 121, 182–84, 185
Authorization to Use Military Force, 3, 171, 176–78, 180

Baccus, Rick, 141
Barak, Aharon, 245
Bill of Rights, English, 39–41, 51, 197
Bill of Rights, United States, 67–68, 89–90, 92, 168
Black, Hugo, 81, 101
Blackstone, William, 58, 62–63, 70–71, 73, 87, 89, 90–91, 197
Boardman, Michelle, 203, 215
Bo Li, 232
Bollman, Ex parte, 95
Boumedienne v. *Bush,* 109
Bowsher v. *Syner,* 223
Boykin, William, 143
Bradbury, Steven G., 157, 236
Bradley, Curtis, 199, 205–06
Brandeis, Louis, 83, 192, 229
Burghley, Lord, 52
Bush (G. H. W.) administration, 202, 207, 217, 225
Bush (G. W.) administration: authority to order domestic surveillance, 170–71, 176–82; challenges to constitutional principles from, 4–5, 8–10, 11–12, 38, 40–41, 54, 55, 149, 188–89, 191–93, 205, 229–31, 239–45; challenges to

executive authority claims of, 10–11, 229–31; claims regarding warrants in domestic surveillance, 185–89; disclosure of wiretapping program, 169–70, 174; habeas corpus policies of, 4, 11, 54, 85, 86–87, 93, 95, 112–13, 126, 127; implications for future of presidential power, 86–87, 127, 242–43, 244–45; interpretation of national security and war powers, 71–74, 82–83, 85; Justice Department opposition to domestic surveillance policies of, 182–85; justification for domestic surveillance program, 174–76; justification for robust interrogation of detainees in war on terror, 5, 8, 129, 154–55, 160–61, 165–67; orders on detention and trial of suspected terrorists, 99–100; public statements on guilt and treatment of detainees, 129, 139–40; rationale for expanded presidential authority, 3, 5–6, 84, 236; rule of law and, 234–36, 239; scope of claims of presidential authority, 1–3, 9–10, 157–58, 159–60; secrecy of operations, 206, 237–39; state secrets privilege claims, 117, 118–19; Supreme Court cases involving detainees in war on terror, 100–04; threats to individual rights from, 67–68; use of military commissions, 104–13; veto use, 205. *See also* Detainees in war on terror; Rule of law, Bush administration and; Signing statements; Surveillance of American citizens; Torture and severe interrogation

Bybee, Jay, 72, 128, 147, 154–55, 166–67

Calabresi, Steven, 200–01, 207, 208–09, 210, 211, 212, 220

Cambone, Stephen, 143

Card, Andrew, 182–83

Carroll, Lewis, 128

Carter administration, 198, 200

Central Intelligence Agency, 112, 159, 172; allegations of torture against, 120, 131; authorization for enhanced interrogation techniques, 10, 12, 129, 164, 230; el-Masri abduction, 118

Charles I, King of England, 38–39, 48–49, 54, 87–88

Charles II, King of England, 39, 49–50, 88–89

Charter of Liberties, 34–35

Chase, Salmon P., 106–07

Cheney, Dick, 99, 139, 159, 161–63, 166, 175, 176, 187, 188, 236

Chertoff, Michael, 134

Clinton administration: excessive uses of executive authority, 231; signing statements, 202–03, 205–06, 207, 212

Cochran, Bob, 134

Coke, Edward, 37, 38

Coleman, Dan, 138

Collins, Andrew, 165

Combatant Status Review Tribunals, 54, 86, 105–06, 109–11. *See also* Military commissions

Comey, James, 157, 182–83, 185

Commander-in-chief authority: Bush administration claims, 72, 82, 85, 157–58, 160, 171; Congress and, 157–58, 181–82, 228; constitutional limits, 72, 82, 158, 171–72, 181–82, 228; domestic surveillance and, 179, 181; torture of detainees and, 158

Common law: habeas corpus rights, 87; origins, 33

Congress: authority to command executive branch subordinates, 220–21; authorization for military commissions in war on terror, 104; authorization for warrantless surveillance of American citizens, 176–77, 178–79, 181; Bush administration claims of presidential authority and, 2, 3–4, 10–11, 11–12, 228, 230–31, 240; commander-in-chief authority and, 157–58, 181–82, 228; constitutional authority, 57, 66; impoundment of funds by president, 223–24; legislative veto, 217–18; national security authority, 75–83; right to suspend habeas corpus, 91, 94–95, 96; war power authority, 71, 76–77. *See also* Separation of powers

Consent of the governed, 24–25

Constitution: appointment power of executive, 216–17; Article I, 55, 66, 78, 91, 94, 158, 208, 220, 221, 228; Article II, 55, 66, 72, 78, 85, 158, 190, 210–11, 220, 228; Bush administration challenges to, 4–5, 8–10, 11–12, 54, 55, 171–72, 175–76, 188–89, 205, 214, 226–28, 229–31, 239–45; Bush administration use of signing statements and, 195–96; Bush (G. H. W.) signing statement challenges to, 202; Clinton administration signing statement challenges to, 202–03; colonial experience in development of, 59–62; habeas corpus provisions, 89–93; historical and conceptual origins, 6–7, 13–15, 25, 29–32, 33–34, 54, 55, 56, 58–59; legal significance of signing statements, 209–11; limits to commander-in-chief authority, 72, 82, 158, 171–72, 181–82, 228; national security provisions, 75–79; president's authority to command executive branch subordinates, 211–12; protections against government surveillance, 9, 169; purpose, 239; Reagan administration challenges to, 199–202; significance of framers' intent, 15; sovereign power of citizens under, 57–58; on treaty adherence, 149; unitary executive theory, 220; war powers, 7–8, 68–75, 181–82. *See also* Separation of powers; Supreme Court

Continental Congress, 60–61, 75–76

Convention Against Torture and Other Cruel, Inhuman or Degrading Treatment or Punishment, United Nations, 152–53, 154

Court of Star Chamber, 54

Cromwell, Oliver, 39, 49

Cuomo, Mario, 223

Darnel Case, 88

Davis, David, 96–97

Davis, Morris D., 111–12

Declaration of Independence, 24–25, 54, 60

Defense Intelligence Agency, 137–38

Dellinger, Walter, 202, 207, 209–10, 212, 219

De Montfort, Simon, 42–43

Detainees in war on terror: applicability of Geneva Conventions, 147, 150–51; Bush administration rationale for expanded executive authority over, 5; choice of Guantánamo as place of detention for, 99–100; circumstances of capture, 114, 115; deaths among, 1; definition of enemy combatant, 108–09; denial of habeas corpus rights to,

85–86, 93; innocent persons as, 85–86, 113–24; jurisdiction of military commissions over, 104–13; public statements by political leaders on guilt of, 139–40; rights of American citizens, 119–24, 125; Supreme Court cases involving, 100–04; testimony of military officers regarding legal treatment of, 110–12; violations of U.S. law in treatment of, 234. *See also* Torture and severe interrogation

Detainee Treatment Act: habeas corpus rights and, 10, 105–06, 109, 126; interrogation procedures and, 157, 159–60; passage, 159, 225; signing statement, 194, 213, 225

Dicey, A. V., 233

Due process: conceptual origins, 7, 33; evolution of individual rights, 36, 38; habeas corpus rights and, 89, 93; threats to Constitution from Bush administration, 54. *See also* Habeas corpus rights

Dunlavey, Michael B., 142, 166

Edward II, King of England, 43
Edward VI, King of England, 46
Elizabeth I, Queen of England, 46
Elsea, Jennifer, 154
England, Gordon, 161
Executive branch authority: to act contrary to law, 25–27, 231–36; appointment power, 216–17; Bush administration claims regarding scope of, 1–3, 57, 157–58; Bush administration rationale for expanding, 3, 5–6; command over executive branch subordinates, 211–14, 220–21; constitutional provisions and intent, 2, 4, 15, 58–59, 61–62, 64–66; expansive uses of, prior to Bush administra-

tion, 231; foreign affairs authority, 80; implied powers, 181; Locke's political philosophy and, 25–28; oath of office, 233–34; to order surveillance, 170–71, 179–82; prerogative powers, 25–28, 76, 79; principled argument for expanding, 240–41; requirements to report to Congress, 218–19; selection of president, 64, 65; vesting clause of Constitution, 78–79. *See also* Commander-in-chief authority; Separation of powers; Signing statements; Unitary executive

Fay, George, 131–32
Federal Bureau of Investigation, 132, 172
Federative powers, 27
Fifth Amendment, 90
Finnegan, Patrick, 134
Fisher, Louis, 98, 176, 177, 218
Ford administration, 198
Foreign affairs authority, 80
Foreign Intelligence Surveillance Act, 3, 187; amendments, 10–11; Bush administration's legal justification for violating, 177, 178–79, 180–81, 188, 189–90, 237; Bush administration violations of, 55, 170, 171, 189, 234; origins and purpose, 172–73, 191; protections against unlawful surveillance, 9; revisions of warrant process for Bush administration, 189, 190–91, 230; warrant requirements, 173–74, 186
Fourth Amendment, 9, 169, 171, 175
Fracasso, Lee Ann, 120
Frankfurter, Felix, 98, 178
Franklin, Benjamin, 56, 64, 69, 168
Frost, David, 235–36

Garber, Marc, 210

Geneva Convention: Bush administration claims of executive branch authority, 1, 11, 149, 160, 234; Bush administration rationale for non-adherence, 8, 129, 147–49; jurisdiction of military tribunals in war on terror and, 109; Military Commissions Act and, 161–64, 238; rights of detainees in war on terror and, 106, 107; scope of protections, 149–50; on treatment of captured persons, 133, 136, 142, 146–47, 150–51, 154

George I, King of England, 52

George II, King of England, 52, 53

George III, King of England, 53, 54, 59–60

Gerry, Elbridge, 76–77, 77, 214

Goldman, Robert K., 153

Goldsmith, Jack, 156, 183, 184, 185

Gonzales, Alberto, 33, 113, 147, 151, 152, 155–56, 166, 170, 179, 182–83, 184, 189

Goss, Porter, 118, 137

Government Accountability Office (GAO), 204–05

Guantánamo: decision to detain suspected terrorists at, 99–100; habeas corpus rights of detainees at, 85, 93, 105, 109; innocent persons detained in, 85, 86, 93, 113–17; interrogation techniques used at, 132, 138, 140–43, 148–49; release of prisoners from, 124–25; Supreme Court cases involving detainees at, 85, 100–02

Habeas corpus rights: Bush administration rationale for denials of, 85, 99, 110, 242; Bush administration suspensions of, 85, 86, 93, 95, 126; conceptual and legal evolution, 8, 38, 84–85, 87–89; constitutional implications of Bush administration policies, 86–87, 112–13, 127; historic suspensions in United States, 27, 94–98, 242; jurisdiction of military commissions and, 105–06, 109; Padilla case, 1, 121–24; prerogative power of executive and, 27, 28; purpose, 84, 86; relevance to Guantánamo detainees, 85, 93, 105, 109; rights of American citizens detained in war on terror, 119–25; rights of foreign citizens, 100–01, 105, 110; right to suspend, 90–92; significance of, among human rights, 87, 89, 90, 103, 104, 126–27; Supreme Court cases involving detainees in war on terror, 10, 85, 100–04, 106–08, 229–30; threats to Constitution from Bush administration policies and actions, 4, 11, 54; writing of constitutional provisions, 89–93

Halstead, J. J., 203–04

Hamdan v. Rumsfeld, 106–08, 126, 153–54, 160, 178, 230

Hamdi, Yaser Esam, 102

Hamdi v. Rumsfeld, 94, 102–04, 177, 182

Hamilton, Alexander, 64–65, 69, 72, 74, 76, 78, 84, 126–27, 214–15, 221

Haynes, William J., II, 112, 142, 161–63

Henry, King of England, 34–35

Henry III, King of England, 42–43

Henry IV, King of England, 44

Henry VII, King of England, 45

Henry VIII, King of England, 45–47

Hicks, David, 125

Hobbes, Thomas, 6, 18–20, 31–32

Holdsworth, William, 87

Humphrey's Executor v. *U.S.,* 217
Hutson, John D., 166–67

Impeachment authority of English
Parliament, 43–44
Imprisonment without trial: Bush
administration claims of authority,
1, 85; Bush administration rationale for expanded executive
authority, 5; Bush administration
violations of Constitution, 6;
conceptual and legal evolution of
individual rights, 8, 36; rights of
enemy combatants, 102. *See also*
Detainees in war on terror; Habeas
corpus rights
Individual rights: Bush administration
threats to, 67–68; conceptual and
legal evolution, 7, 32, 34–42; U.S.
Bill of Rights, 67–68. *See also*
Habeas corpus rights
Innocent III, Pope, 37
INS v. *Chadha,* 217–18
Intelligence Authorization Act (2002),
219
International Committee of the Red
Cross, 115, 133
International law prohibitions on tor-
ture, 152–54
Interrogation of detainees in war on
terror. *See* Torture and severe
interrogation
Iran-Contra affair, 236, 237, 244
Iraq war, 4, 137–38

Jackson, Robert, 81–82, 101, 180,
242
James I, King of England, 47–48
James II, King of England, 39–40,
50, 197
Jarrett, H. Marshall, 190
Jay, John, 74
Jefferson, Thomas, 61

John, King of England, 35–37
Johnson administration, 231
Johnson v. *Eisentrager,* 100, 101
Jones, Anthony R., 132
Jordan, Steven, 140

Karpinski, Janis, 130, 143
Katsas, Gregory, 119
Katz v. *United States,* 169, 171
Keller, Bill, 187
Kelley, Christopher, 199, 220
Kelley, P. X., 165
Keynes, John Maynard, 13
Klienman, Steven M., 139
Korean War, 81
Krulak, Charles, 167

Law of War Handbook, 153–54
Legislative veto, 217–18
Lev, Daniel, 200, 207, 208–09, 210,
211, 212, 220
Leviathan (Hobbes), 18
Levin, Daniel, 156, 157
Libi, Ibn al-Shaykh al-, 137–38
Lincoln, Abraham, 27, 94–95, 96,
242
Locke, John, 6–7, 13, 16, 20–28,
29–30, 31, 32, 58, 229, 242
Long Parliament, 39, 48

Machiavelli, Niccolò, 6, 15–18
Madison, James, 61–62, 66, 69,
74–75, 76–77, 78, 127, 192,
221, 243
Magna Carta, 7, 33, 35–38, 42,
87–88
Marshall, John, 80, 95, 233, 241
Martial law: habeas corpus rights
and, 96; in peacetime, evolution
of prohibitions against, 38
Mason, George, 64, 69
Masri, Khaled el-, 118–19
McCain, John, 10, 137, 159, 194

McConnell, Michael, 190
McDonald, Forrest, 78–79
Meese, Edwin, 200, 201
Merryman, Ex parte, 95
Merryman, John, 95
Mikolashek, Paul T., 131
Military commissions: Bush administration justification, 243; Bush administration policy, 104–05, 234; constitutional implications of Bush administration policies, 112–13, 244; historical applications, 105; Roosevelt administration use of, 97–98, 243; Supreme Court cases involving detainees in war on terror, 106–08; testimony of military officers regarding procedures of, 110–12. *See also* Military Commissions Act
Military Commissions Act: Bush administration authority under, 3, 10, 126, 160, 162, 163–64, 230; enemy combatant classification under, 125; interrogation provisions, 10, 129, 160–65, 230, 238; major provisions, 108–09; purpose, 108
Miller, Geoffrey, 130, 141, 143–44
Milligan, Ex parte, 96–97, 106
Milligan, Lambden, 96
Montesquieu, Charles-Louis de Secondat, baron de La Brède et de, 6, 7, 13, 16, 29–32, 58, 62, 66
Morris, Gouverneur, 57, 65
Mueller, Robert, 182
Mukasey, Michael, 190
Myers v. U.S., 216–17

Nacchio, Joseph, 184–85, 188
National Defense Authorization Act, 195
National security: as justification for not reporting to Congress, 218–19; prerogative power and, 28, 236; separation of powers, 75–82, 83; war power provisions of Constitution, 68–75, 82–83. *See also* Commander-in-chief authority; War powers
National Security Agency: Bush administration policy, 1, 9, 168, 234; justification for warrantless surveillance of American citizens, 174; Terrorist Surveillance Program, 169–72, 175, 182–85, 186–87
National Treasury Employee Union v. Nixon, 219
Niemöller, Martin, 84
Nixon administration, 172–73, 192, 223–25, 231, 235–36

Oath of office, 233–34
O'Conner, Sandra Day, 102, 103, 181–82
O'Connor, Dennis R., 118
Olson, Theodore, 102, 183
Omnibus Crime Control and Safe Streets Act, 173

Padilla, Jose, 1, 121–24, 125
Paine, Thomas, 60, 233
Pappas, Thomas, 143, 144
Parliament of England: development of responsible government, 51–54; English Civil War and, 47–51, 49; Habeas Corpus Act, 88–89; historical significance of, 41–42, 54, 55, 58; impeachment powers, 43–44; origins and early development, 42–43; suspending of laws by monarch, 196–97; in Tudor period, 44–47; war power authority, 69–71
Paterson, William, 215
Peel, Robert, 54

Petition of Right, 38–39, 88
Petraeus, David, 139
Phifer, Jerald, 141
Pinckney, Charles, 76, 90
Pitt, William, 53
Posner, Eric, 199, 205–06
Powell, Colin, 99–100, 147–48, 161, 166
Powell v. McCormack, 223
Prerogative power, 25–28, 76, 79, 236
The Prince (Machiavelli), 16
Public perception and understanding: Bush administration claims of presidential authority and, 3; legitimate use of government power, 15

Qahtani, Mohammed al, 138
Quirin, Ex parte, 97–98

Rakove, Jack, 79
Randolf, Edmund, 64
Randolph, Edmund, 64
Rasul v. Bush, 100–01
Reagan administration: excessive uses of executive authority, 231; Iran-Contra affair, 236, 237; signing statements, 198, 199–202, 207, 222–23, 225
Republican form of government, 18, 20, 57–58
Rice, Condoleezza, 99
Richard II, King of England, 44
Rockefeller, Jay, 176
Romig, Thomas J., 148–49
Roosevelt (Franklin) administration, 80, 97–98, 217, 231, 243
Rowell, Willie J., 137
Rule of law: Bush administration and, 4, 7, 9, 10, 11, 55, 68, 170, 185, 189, 191, 194, 195, 213, 227, 234–36, 239; conceptual and legal development, 24, 28, 35; definition and purpose, 23, 229, 231–34;

limits of executive power, 24, 108, 158
Rumsfeld, Donald, 114, 115, 139–40, 142, 149, 166

Sanchez, General, 144–45
Scalia, Antonin, 85, 94, 98, 103–04, 127
Schlesinger Report, 140–41, 142, 145
Second Treatise (Locke), 25, 27
Secret policies and legal interpretations, 206, 237–39
Seldon, John, 88
Separation of powers: Bush administration challenges to, 2–3, 157–58, 195–96, 243–45; establishment of English Parliament, 41–51; national security authority, 75–82; origins and development of constitutional premises, 6–7, 13–15, 29–32, 55, 56, 60–62; prerogative power, 25–28; principled argument for expanded executive power, 240–41; provisions and intent of Constitution, 2, 56–57, 62–67, 157, 158, 241; role of judicial branch, 61, 66; signing statements and, 195–96; Supreme Court decisions on national security matters, 79–82, 179–80; surveillance of American citizens and, 175–76; system of checks and balances, 215–16; unitary executive theory and, 221–22; war power, 68–75, 181–82
Shelton, Hugh, 161
Shultz, George, 237
Signing statements: Bush administration conceptualization of executive power and, 206–07, 222–23, 225, 226; Bush administration rationale, 203–04, 205–06, 216–19, 243; Bush (G. H. W.) administration,

202, 207, 225; challenges to constitution in Bush administration use
of, 4, 9, 11, 41, 55, 194, 195–96,
197, 205, 214, 226–28, 244;
Clinton administration, 202–03,
205–06, 207, 212; to command
subordinate branches of executive
branch, 211–14; definition, 198;
Detainee Treatment Act, 159–60,
194, 213, 225; to evade reporting
to Congress, 218–19; extent of
Bush administration use of, 2,
9–10, 204–05; historical uses,
198–99, 222–23; intended purpose,
159, 200–02, 206, 207–08; legal
status, 208–11; National Defense
Authorization Act, 195; Nixon
administration impoundment of
funds, 223–24; to nullify law,
214–16; PATRIOT Act, 194–95;
presidential appointment power
and, 216–17; Reagan administration, 198, 199–202, 207, 222–23,
225; significant features of Bush administration use of, 203, 206, 226
Sixth Amendment, 90
The Spirit of the Laws (Montesquieu),
30, 31
Spitzer, Robert, 220, 222
State secrets privilege, 117, 118–19
Steel seizure case. *See Youngstown
Sheet and Tube* v. *Sawyer*
Stevens, John Paul, 104, 106–07,
153–54
Sulzberger, Arthur, 187
Supreme Court: Bush administration
claims of presidential authority
and, 10, 11–12; cases involving
detainees in war on terror, 85,
100–04, 106–08, 121–22, 126,
229–30; cases involving jurisdiction of military commissions,
109–10; decisions on separation of

powers in national security matters, 79–82, 179–80; historical
habeas corpus cases, 95–98; on
Nixon administration impoundment of funds, 224; surveillance
cases, 169. *See also* Constitution
Surveillance of American citizens:
abuses of law before Bush administration, 172–73; Bush administration actions before *9/11* terrorist attacks, 184–85, 188; Bush
administration assertions about
warrant rules and compliance,
168, 185–89; Bush administration
claims of authority for, 1, 9, 171,
176–82, 190–91; Bush administration justification for, 5, 8–9,
174–76, 187–88; challenges to
Constitution from Bush administration actions, 4, 6, 11, 40–41,
191–93, 244; constitutional protections, 9, 169, 191; denial of
security clearances for Justice
Department investigation of, 190;
disclosure of Bush administration
program, 169–70, 174; implied
powers of executive branch, 181;
Justice Department opposition to
Bush administration policies,
182–85; legal procedures for, 171,
173–74; significance of National
Security Agency program, 170–71;
warrant requirements, 169
Sutherland, Justice, 80

Taft-Hartley Act, 81
Taguba, Antonio, 131, 144
Taliban, 116; bounties for capture of,
115; Geneva Convention protections, 146, 147–49, 152; habeas
corpus rights, 85; interrogation
policies, 164. *See also* Detainees in
war on terror; Terrorism, war on

Taney, Roger, 95
Taxes: American colonial experience, 59–60, 61; authority of English monarch and Parliament, 33, 35, 36, 38, 39, 42, 43, 47–48, 50, 70, 73, 196; signing statements to avoid congressional control over, 196
Terrorism, war on: Bush administration rationale for expanded executive authority, 3, 5–6; Bush administration rationale for suspension of Geneva Conventions, 147–49; justifications for torture of suspects in, 133–37; prerogative power and, 28. *See also* Detainees in war on terror; National security
Thatch, Charles, 78–79
Titmore, Brian D., 153
Torture and severe interrogation: Bush administration claims of authority over, 1, 5, 8, 145–46, 157–58, 165–66, 230; Bush administration executive orders regarding, 129, 132, 162–65; Bush administration rationale for denial of habeas corpus rights of detainees, 110, 123–24; congressional action, 10; deaths of persons in U.S. custody, 1, 131, 133; definitions of torture, 128, 152, 154–55; Detainee Treatment Act and, 159–60; geopolitical implications of U.S. policy, 148, 166, 167; government-sanctioned, 128–29; Guantánamo detainees and, 93; laws and conventions governing, 145–57, 159–60; leadership and command responsibility, 139–45; Military Commissions Act and, 160–65, 238; reliability of information obtained by, 137–39; scope of U.S. actions during Bush administration, 1, 129, 130–33, 141–42, 243–44; signing statements authorizing, 213; "ticking time bomb" justification, 134–37; of U.S. citizens detained in war on terror, 119, 120, 122–23; violations of U.S. law and Constitution in Bush administration policies, 4, 6, 11, 149, 234
Townsend, Fran, 140
Truman administration, 80–81, 179–80, 198, 231
Turner, Robert F., 165
"Twenty Four" (tv show), 134

Unitary executive, 66, 75, 201; conceptual basis, 220; justification for warrantless surveillance of American citizens, 175; separation of powers and, 221–22; as theoretical basis of signing statements, 203–04
Universal Declaration of Human Rights, 37
U.S. v. Curtiss-Wright Export Corporation, 80
USA PATRIOT Act, 3, 179, 186–87, 218; signing statement, 194–95

Vance, Donald, 119–21
Vesting clause of Constitution, 78–79, 220
Veto: Bush use of, 159; executive authority, 66, 81, 196, 202, 203; historical meaning and use, 29, 31, 47, 49, 59, 60, 64, 196; signing statements and, 201
Veto power, 205, 214; legislative veto, 217–18
Vician, Todd, 123
Vile, M. J. C., 30

Walpole, Robert, 52–53
War Crimes Act, 151–52, 154

War of American Independence, 13, 24–25, 53, 54

War powers: authority to declare war, 76–77; commander in chief status and, 72–73, 82–83, 181; prerogative power theory, 25, 28; provisions and intent of Constitution, 7–8, 68–75, 76–77, 82–83; separation of powers and, 181–82; vesting clause, 78–79

Washington, George, 65–66, 69, 72

Waterboarding, 161, 162–63

Wellington, Duke of, 72

West Point Combating Terrorism Center, 115

William and Mary, 29, 40, 45, 47, 50–51

William the Conqueror, 34

Wilson, James, 64, 65, 76, 90

Wilson administration, 216–17

Wimmer, Kurt A., 210

Wittes, Benjamin, 86

Yoo, John, 56, 71–72, 73–74, 75, 99, 146, 156–57, 158, 166–67, 184, 236

Youngstown Sheet and Tube v. *Sawyer*, 80–81, 178, 179–80

Zelikow, Philip, 161